Oracle GoldenGate 11*g*
Implementer's guide

Design, install, and configure high-performance data replication solutions using Oracle GoldenGate

John P. Jeffries

[PACKT] enterprise
PUBLISHING
professional expertise distilled

BIRMINGHAM - MUMBAI

Oracle GoldenGate 11*g* Implementer's guide

First published: February 2011

Production Reference: 1150211

Published by Packt Publishing Ltd.
32 Lincoln Road
Olton
Birmingham, B27 6PA, UK.

ISBN 978-1-849682-00-8

www.packtpub.com

Cover Image by David Guettirrez (bilbaorocker@yahoo.co.uk)

Credits

Author
John P. Jeffries

Reviewers
ShuXuan Nie

Anirudh Pucha

Gavin Soorma

Development Editor
Maitreya Bhakal

Technical Editor
Neha Damle

Indexer
Rekha Nair

Editorial Team Leader
Vinodhan Nair

Project Team Leader
Lata Basantani

Project Coordinator
Vishal Bodwani

Proofreader
Aaron Nash

Graphics
Geetanjali Sawant

Production Coordinator
Alwin Roy

Cover Work
Alwin Roy

Foreword

Oracle GoldenGate is a product that covers many use cases in the business of data replication. It is not only useful for classical distributed databases, it is also useful for High Availability Architectures and especially for Data Warehouse and Decision Support Systems. Thus, the variety of techniques and methods spreads from unidirectional environments for query offloading/reporting to bidirectional or Peer-to-Peer architectures in an active-active fashion. Besides this, Oracle GoldenGate is not only available for heterogeneous Oracle-to-Oracle databases, but it also scales in heterogeneous non Oracle database environments which is also one topic in the Data Warehouse business. The flexibility of the product is amazing and the functionality manages a wide spectrum such as filtering, performing transformations, event handling, and many other options.

I am happy that John Jeffries summarized the main topics of Oracle Golden Gate in this book. Both parts, configuration & implementation as well as monitoring and performance tuning/troubleshooting, is described for developers and administrators. The book does start from a common architectural overview, shows up standard implementation steps, and explains how to manage the distributed environment.

John Jeffries has been an expert of Oracle databases for years. Besides the knowledge of distributed databases, his skills cover a wide area of the Oracle core technology. So, he is not only able to discuss the topics individually, but he also puts the individual pieces together that rounds up the overall common architecture. This work is very valuable as it is raised from a fundamental practical experience.

Volker Kuhr
Oracle Advanced Customer Support (ACS)
Team Leader for Distributed Databases

About the Author

John P. Jeffries has lived in the southeast of England for most of his life. Although predominantly based in London, he has worked in many countries around the world. He enjoys travel and is the Director of his own consultancy business: www. spirotek.co.uk.

Originally from a development background, he has worked for a number of global software companies including Oracle Corporation and Siebel Systems. His time at Siebel was spent designing and developing ETL solutions for Data Warehouses, ultimately enhancing the eBilling and Billing Analytics products with an Oracle Warehouse Builder based API. He spent six years working in Oracle Consulting in EMEA and Oracle Advanced Customer Services in the UK as a Senior Principal Consultant, earning the internal title of "The UK's Data Replication Expert". Now a freelance consultant, the author can be found onsite in many of the world's most respected financial institutions in London, consulting on Oracle GoldenGate, Streams, and Active Data Guard. With over 15 years of Oracle experience, and an OCP since Oracle 8*i*, the author has extensive knowledge of Oracle databases, including Enterprise Linux and RAC, coupled with the ability to design and build high performance distributed database systems. He has trained internal and external clients in Data Warehousing and Data Replication techniques, and continues to share his knowledge and experience through his own website: www.oracle11ggotchas.com.

Thank you for purchasing my book, which would not have been possible without the help and support from a number of key individuals and organizations.

Firstly I wish to thank my wife, Wendy, for both her drive and encouragement. Also the sacrifice that she has endured, putting aside other commitments to support me in my accomplishment.

Secondly, I wish to thank my friend and colleague, Paul Vale for his depth of knowledge of Oracle Streams. I worked closely with Paul for two years on an extensive data replication project where our shared knowledge and experience inspired me to write a book on Oracle GoldenGate.

Finally, I wish to thank Packt Publishing for agreeing to work with me and publish this book. Even now, I am astounded by the lack of available technical material on GoldenGate; this being another reason for writing. I trust you will find this book both interesting and informative, helping you to successfully implement an Oracle 11g GoldenGate environment.

About the Reviewers

ShuXuan Nie is a software engineer specializing in SOA and Java technologies.

ShuXuan has more than nine years of experience in IT industry that includes SOA technologies such as BPEL, ESB, SOAP, XML, and Enterprise Java technologies, Eclipse plug-ins, and other areas such as C++ cross-platform development.

Since July 2010, Shuxuan has been working in Rubiconred and focusing on helping customers solve their middleware problems.

Before joining Rubiconred, ShuXuan had been working in the Oracle Global Customer Support team and focused on helping customers solve their SOA integration problems.

Before joining Oracle, ShuXuan had been working in IBM China Software Development Lab for four years as a staff software engineer, participating in several complex products on IBM Lotus Workplace, Webshpere, and Eclipse platform; and then joined the Australia Bureau of Meteorology Research Center, responsible for implementation of Automated Thunderstorm Interactive Forecast System for Aviation and Defence.

ShuXuan holds a MS in Computer Science from Beijing University of Aeronautics and Astronautics.

Anirudh Pucha is a SOA and Cloud Computing Strategist working on Fusion Middleware Integration products in Oracle Corporation. He has been working in the SOA Integration space for over five years focusing on .NET, J2EE, Oracle SOA Suite, BPEL, ESB, Adapters, BAM, Business Rules, BPM. He is one of the top contributors in the Oracle SOA and BPEL Technology Forums. He is a certified webMethods Developer and Oracle Certified Professional. He is an Ex-Microsoft Student Ambassador and Platform Evangelist appointed by Microsoft Corporation. He is the Asst.Manager of DNUGHS (DotNet Users Group of Hyd, supported by Microsoft Corp). He is a INETA (International .NET Association) – APAC Volunteer, The SPOKE member, Culminis member and a member of several renowned NGOs. He is a speaker at various conferences, bar-camps, and a guest lecturer for several universities and colleges. He is a native of Hyderabad (India), certified Latin American Dancer, professional singer, dubbing artist, cricketer, cartoonist, sculpturist, and a fashion model. He can be contacted on LinkedIn at http://in.linkedin.com/in/anirudhpucha and his website at http://www.anirudhpucha.tk/.

I am thankful to GOD, my mother – Smt. Pucha Annapurna, father – Shri. Pucha Hanumanth Rao, cute nephew – Karthik Achintya and niece – Pallavi Shriya.

Gavin Soorma is an Oracle Certified Master with over 17 years of experience. He also is an Oracle Certified Professional (versions 7.3, 8i, 9i, 10g, and 11g) as well as an Oracle Certified Expert in 10g RAC.

Gavin is a regular presenter at various Oracle conferences and seminars having presented several papers at the IOUG, South African Oracle User's Group, Oracle Open World, and the Australian Oracle User Group. Recently, at this year's AUSOUG held in Melbourne and Perth he presented a paper on Oracle GoldenGate titled 'Real Time Access to Real Time Information'.

He is currently employed as a Senior Principal Consultant for an Oracle solution provider, OnCall DBA based in Perth, Western Australia. Prior to this, he held the position of Senior Oracle DBA and Team Lead with Bank West in Perth. Before migrating to Australia, Gavin worked for Emirates Airline Group IT in Dubai for over 15 years where he held the position of Technical Team Manager, Databases.

He has also written a number of tutorials and notes on Oracle GoldenGate which can be accessed via his personal blog website http://gavinsoorma.com.

www.PacktPub.com

Support files, eBooks, discount offers and more

You might want to visit www.PacktPub.com for support files and downloads related to your book.

Did you know that Packt offers eBook versions of every book published, with PDF and ePub files available? You can upgrade to the eBook version at www.PacktPub.com and as a print book customer, you are entitled to a discount on the eBook copy. Get in touch with us at service@packtpub.com for more details.

At www.PacktPub.com, you can also read a collection of free technical articles, sign up for a range of free newsletters and receive exclusive discounts and offers on Packt books and eBooks.

http://PacktLib.PacktPub.com

Do you need instant solutions to your IT questions? PacktLib is Packt's online digital book library. Here, you can access, read and search across Packt's entire library of books.

Why Subscribe?

- Fully searchable across every book published by Packt
- Copy & paste, print and bookmark content
- On demand and accessible via web browser

Free Access for Packt account holders

If you have an account with Packt at www.PacktPub.com, you can use this to access PacktLib today and view nine entirely free books. Simply use your login credentials for immediate access.

Instant Updates on New Packt Books

Get notified! Find out when new books are published by following @PacktEnterprise on Twitter, or the Packt Enterprise Facebook page.

Table of Contents

Preface

Data replication is an important part of any database system that is growing due to today's demand for real-time reporting and regulatory requirements. GoldenGate has recently become Oracle's strategic real-time data replication solution. Until now, very little has been written about how to implement GoldenGate in a production enterprise environment where performance, scalability, and data integrity are paramount.

Your days of dismay over the lack of documentation over Oracle GoldenGate are over.

Welcome to Oracle GoldenGate 11g Implementer's guide— a comprehensive, practical book that will deliver answers to your questions in a clear, concise style, allowing you to progress effectively in a timeline-driven environment. Based on the author's own experience, this long awaited GoldenGate administration book has all that is required to install, design, configure, and tune data replication solutions suited to every environment. Be the first to master GoldenGate's power and flexibility by reading this unique hands-on implementation companion.

Computers need to send data from one system to another in a timely manner to satisfy the ever-increasing need for speed. Regardless of whether you are a novice or an expert – or someone in between – this book will guide you through all the steps necessary to build a high-performance GoldenGate solution on Oracle11gR1. Expert users can dive into key topic areas such as performance tuning or troubleshooting, while novice users can step through the early installation and configuration chapters, later progressing to the advanced chapters.

This book is more than an implementation guide. It offers detailed real-life examples, encouraging additional thought and discussion by going beyond the manual.

With Oracle GoldenGate 11g Implementer's guide in hand, you'll be designing, installing, and configuring high-performance solutions using GoldenGate within minutes.

What this book covers

Chapter 1, Getting Started, provides an introduction to Oracle GoldenGate, inspiring thought by describing the key components, processes, and considerations required to build and implement a GoldenGate solution.

The topics covered the evolution of GoldenGate Software, including the architecture behind the technology followed by the solutions GoldenGate can provide, coupled with effective design.

Chapter 2, Installing and Preparing GoldenGate, walks you through the individual tasks needed to complete an end-to-end GoldenGate installation, including the download of the software through to creating a simple data replication environment.

Chapter 3, Design Considerations, addresses some of the issues that influence the decision making process when designing a GoldenGate solution. These include design considerations for both performance and high availability. Here you can choose the appropriate hardware and topology to deliver a fast, robust and scalable solution.

Chapter 4, Configuring Oracle GoldenGate, initially discusses the main GoldenGate parameters, and provides a methodical approach to the configuration process, stepping through each task to give the depth of information necessary to successfully implement GoldenGate on Oracle 11*g*. By providing the building blocks, this chapter forms the basis for more complex configurations.

Chapter 5, Configuration Options, looks at the available options that allow your configuration to extend in functionality and performance. We start with performance enhancements, later exploring the security features, including data compression and encryption, and finally discussing the options available to implement DDL replication.

Chapter 6, Configuring GoldenGate for HA teaches you how to configure Oracle GoldenGate in a RAC environment and explores the various components that effectively enable HA for data replication and integration.

Chapter 7, Advanced Configuration, gives you a deeper understanding of GoldenGate configuration. By the time you are done with this chapter, you will be able to explore and realize each parameter specification and further develop your GoldenGate configuration.

Chapter 8, Managing Oracle GoldenGate, focuses on the management features already built in to the GoldenGate Command Interpreter (GGSCI). We discuss and implement a number of utilities, including tips and tricks that allow you to manage your GoldenGate environment effectively at no extra cost. This includes a Perl script that will format the text output from the GGSCI "INFO ALL" command so that the data can be loaded into MS Excel for graphing and trend analysis.

Chapter 9, Performance Tuning, focuses on the main areas that lend themselves to tuning, especially parallel processing and load balancing, enabling high data throughput and very low latency. Performance enhancing new features that are available in the next version of GoldenGate are also discussed and evaluated.

Chapter 10, Troubleshooting GoldenGate, provides a troubleshooting guide for Oracle GoldenGate. We address some of the common issues faced by the implementer, followed by a discussion of the tools and utilities available to help resolve them. This includes the creation of an Exception Handler that automatically logs the details of a failed transaction for further analysis and resolution.

This book has three appendices; their purpose is to provide a "quick reference" as well as address any subjects and terminology not addressed in the previous chapters.

Appendix A, GGSCI Commands, provides a quick reference guide to all the available GoldenGate Software Command Interface (GGSCI) commands.

Appendix B, GoldenGate Installed Components, lists the GoldenGate installed components and their description.

Appendix C, The Future of Oracle GoldenGate, discusses Oracle's strategic approach to data replication and integration. The latest release of GoldenGate including its sister products are described along with links to official documentation and forums on the Oracle website.

What you need for this book

As a minimum you will require the following elements to run the code featured in this book. Starting with the hardware, you can configure a simple GoldenGate solution on just one personal computer acting as a database server, running Oracle or Redhat Enterprise Linux x86 version 5.2. This can be native Linux or Linux virtual machine hosted on MS Windows XP.

Ideally, another PC is required as a client that supports terminal emulation software for logging onto the database server, plus MS Excel for graphing and analysis of statistics.

The following list provides the minimum hardware specification for each PC:

- 1 x 2.5 GHz Dual Core Intel based 32 bit architecture CPU
- 2 GB of physical memory
- 250 GB hard disk drive for the database server
- 150 GB hard disk drive for the MS Windows client
- 1 x 100Mb/s Ethernet adapter

To implement a simple point to point data replication solution, you will need two Oracle 11*g* Release 1 databases. Both source and target databases can reside on the same machine. Please refer to the pre-installation requirements found on the Oracle Website at the following link: `http://download.oracle.com/docs/cd/B28359_01/install.111/b32002/pre_install.htm`

The following list provides the software requirements:

- Oracle or Redhat Enterprise Linux Server release 5.2 - 32-bit
- Oracle Server 11.1.0.6 on Oracle Enterprise Linux 5.0 32-bit, patched to 11.1.0.7 (this is required for the two Oracle databases, source & target)
- Oracle GoldenGate V10.4.0.x for Oracle 11g on Oracle Enterprise Linux 5.0 32-bit
- MS Windows XP 32-bit Professional Edition, Service Pack 3 with MS Excel 2007 installed
- Perl v5.8.8 (included with OEL/RHEL 5.2)
- PuTTY 0.56 for MS Windows XP (terminal emulation software that supports SSH protocol)
- WinSCP Version 3.8.2 for MS Windows XP (file transfer software that supports SFTP protocol)

Who this book is for

This book is for Solution Architects and Database Architects who wish to learn about the functionality and efforts required in implementing a data replication, migration or integration solution using GoldenGate. It is also designed for System Administrators and Database Administrators who want to implement, or those who have already implemented, GoldenGate and who want to explore its advanced features. An intermediate understanding of Oracle database technology is assumed.

Conventions

In this book, you will find a number of styles of text that distinguish between different kinds of information. Here are some examples of these styles, and an explanation of their meaning.

Code words in text are shown as follows: "We can include other contexts through the use of the `include` directive."

A block of code is set as follows:

```
EXTRACT EPMP01
PASSTHRU
RMTHOST dbserver2, MGRPORT 7809
RMTTRAIL ./dirdat/ta
TABLE SRC.DEPT;
TABLE SRC.EMP;
```

When we wish to draw your attention to a particular part of a code block, the relevant lines or items are set in bold:

```
EXTRACT EPMP01
PASSTHRU
RMTHOST dbserver2, MGRPORT 7809
RMTTRAIL ./dirdat/ta
TABLE SRC.DEPT;
TABLE SRC.EMP;
```

Any command-line input or output is written as follows:

```
cd /home/oracle/ggs
```

New terms and **important words** are shown in bold. Words that you see on the screen, in menus or dialog boxes for example, appear in the text like this: "clicking the **Next** button moves you to the next screen".

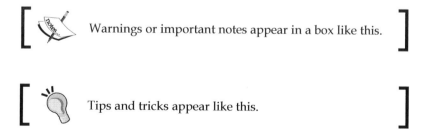

Warnings or important notes appear in a box like this.

Tips and tricks appear like this.

Reader feedback

Feedback from our readers is always welcome. Let us know what you think about this book—what you liked or may have disliked. Reader feedback is important for us to develop titles that you really get the most out of.

To send us general feedback, simply send an e-mail to feedback@packtpub.com, and mention the book title via the subject of your message.

If there is a book that you need and would like to see us publish, please send us a note in the **SUGGEST A TITLE** form on www.packtpub.com or e-mail suggest@packtpub.com.

If there is a topic that you have expertise in and you are interested in either writing or contributing to a book, see our author guide on www.packtpub.com/authors.

Customer support

Now that you are the proud owner of a Packt book, we have a number of things to help you to get the most from your purchase.

Downloading the example code for this book

You can download the example code files for all Packt books you have purchased from your account at http://www.PacktPub.com. If you purchased this book elsewhere, you can visit http://www.PacktPub.com/support and register to have the files e-mailed directly to you.

Errata

Although we have taken every care to ensure the accuracy of our content, mistakes do happen. If you find a mistake in one of our books—maybe a mistake in the text or the code—we would be grateful if you would report this to us. By doing so, you can save other readers from frustration and help us improve subsequent versions of this book. If you find any errata, please report them by visiting http://www.packtpub.com/support, selecting your book, clicking on the errata submission form link, and entering the details of your errata. Once your errata are verified, your submission will be accepted and the errata will be uploaded on our website, or added to any list of existing errata, under the Errata section of that title. Any existing errata can be viewed by selecting your title from http://www.packtpub.com/support.

Piracy

Piracy of copyright material on the Internet is an ongoing problem across all media. At Packt, we take the protection of our copyright and licenses very seriously. If you come across any illegal copies of our works, in any form, on the Internet, please provide us with the location address or website name immediately so that we can pursue a remedy.

Please contact us at copyright@packtpub.com with a link to the suspected pirated material.

We appreciate your help in protecting our authors, and our ability to bring you valuable content.

Questions

You can contact us at questions@packtpub.com if you are having a problem with any aspect of the book, and we will do our best to address it.

1
Getting Started

The objective of this chapter is to get you started using Oracle GoldenGate 10.4. We will discuss the history and evolution of GoldenGate Software, its success in the market and ultimate Oracle acquisition. You will become accustomed with the concepts of data replication and how GoldenGate provides enterprise-wide solutions to address the business requirements.

Although an introduction, this chapter is designed to inspire thought by drilling into the key components, processes, and considerations required to build and implement a GoldenGate solution.

In this chapter, we will discuss the following points surrounding GoldenGate:

- The evolution of GoldenGate software
- The technology and architecture
- The solutions offered by GoldenGate
- The architecture and topology of GoldenGate, plus design considerations
- The supported platform and database versions

Let's begin by learning what GoldenGate is and what you can expect from this book.

What is GoldenGate?

Oracle GoldenGate is Oracle's strategic solution for real time data integration. GoldenGate software enables mission critical systems to have continuous availability and access to real-time data. It offers a fast and robust solution for replicating transactional data between operational and analytical systems.

Oracle GoldenGate captures, filters, routes, verifies, transforms, and delivers transactional data in real-time, across Oracle and heterogeneous environments with very low impact and preserved transaction integrity. The transaction data management provides read consistency, maintaining referential integrity between source and target systems.

This book aims to illustrate through example, providing the reader with solid information and tips for implementing GoldenGate software in a production environment.

In this book, we will not be making direct comparisons between Oracle GoldenGate and Oracle Streams. At the time of writing, Oracle is leveraging the advantages of GoldenGate by enhancing the product whilst continuing to fully support Streams.

As a competitor to Oracle GoldenGate, data replication products and solutions exist from other software companies and vendors. These are mainly storage replication solutions that provide fast point in time data restoration. The following is a list of the most common solutions available today:

- EMC SRDF and EMC RecoverPoint
- IBM PPRC and Global Mirror (known together as IBM Copy Services)
- Hitachi TrueCopy
- Hewlett-Packard Continuous Access (HP CA)
- Symantec Veritas Volume Replicator (VVR)
- DataCore SANsymphony and SANmelody
- FalconStor Replication and Mirroring
- Compellent Remote Instant Replay

Data replication techniques have improved enormously over the past 10 years and have always been a requirement in nearly every IT project in every industry. Whether for Disaster Recovery (DR), High Availability (HA), Business Intelligence (BI), or even regulatory reasons, the requirements and expected performance have also increased, making the implementation of efficient and scalable data replication solutions a welcome challenge.

Oracle GoldenGate evolution

GoldenGate Software Inc was founded in 1995. Originating in San Francisco, the company was named after the famous Golden Gate Bridge by its founders, Eric Fish and Todd Davidson. The tried and tested product that emerged quickly became very popular within the financial industry. Originally designed for the fault tolerant Tandem computers, the resilient and fast data replication solution was in demand. The banks initially used GoldenGate software in their ATM networks for sending transactional data from high street machines to mainframe central computers. The data integrity and guaranteed zero data loss is obviously paramount and plays a key factor. The key architectural properties of the product are as follows:

- Data is sent in "real time" with sub-second speed.
- Supports heterogeneous environments across different database and hardware types. "Transaction aware" — maintaining its read-consistent and referential integrity between source and target systems.
- High performance with low impact; able to move large volumes of data very efficiently while maintaining very low lag times and latency.
- Flexible modular architecture.
- Reliable and extremely resilient to failure and data loss. No single point of failure or dependencies, and easy to recover.

Oracle Corporation acquired GoldenGate Software in September 2009. Today there are more than 500 customers around the world using GoldenGate technology for over 4000 solutions, realizing over $100 million in revenue for Oracle.

Oracle GoldenGate solutions

Oracle GoldenGate provides five data replication solutions:

1. High Availability
    - Live Standby for an immediate fail-over solution that can later re-synchronize with your primary source.
    - Active-Active solutions for continuous availability and transaction load distribution between two or more active systems.

2. Zero-Downtime Upgrades and Migrations
    - Eliminates downtime for upgrades and migrations.

3. Live Reporting
   - Feeding a reporting database so as not to burden the source production systems with BI users or tools.

4. Operational Business Intelligence (BI)
   - Real-time data feeds to operational data stores or data warehouses, directly or via **Extract Transform and Load** (ETL) tools.

5. Transactional Data Integration
   - Real-time data feeds to messaging systems for business activity monitoring, business process monitoring, and complex event processing.
   - Uses event-driven architecture and service-oriented architecture (SOA).

The following diagram shows the basic architecture for the various solutions available from GoldenGate software:

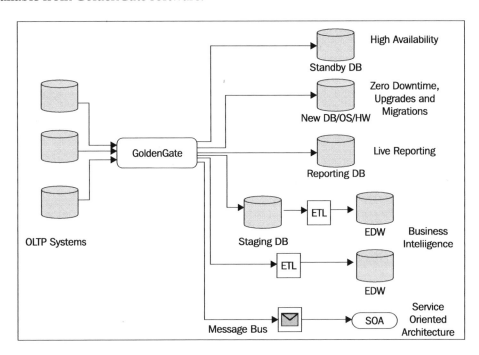

We have discovered there are many solutions where GoldenGate can be applied. Now we can dive into how GoldenGate works, the individual processes, and the data flow that is adopted for all.

Oracle GoldenGate technology overview

Let's take a look at GoldenGate's fundamental building blocks; the Capture process, Trail files, Data pump, Server collector, and Apply processes. In fact, the order in which the processes are listed depicts the sequence of events for GoldenGate data replication across distributed systems. A Manager process runs on both the source and the target systems that "oversee" the processing and transmission of data.

All the individual processes are modular and can be easily decoupled or combined to provide the best solution to meet the business requirements. It is normal practice to configure multiple Capture and Apply processes to balance the load and enhance performance. You can read more about this in *Chapter 9, Performance Tuning*.

Filtering and transformation of the data can be done at either the source by the Capture or at the target by the Apply processes. This is achieved through parameter files, and is explained in detail in *Chapter 3, Configuring Oracle GoldenGate*.

The capture process (Extract)

Oracle GoldenGate's capture process, known as Extract, obtains the necessary data from the databases' transaction logs. For Oracle, these are the online redo logs that contain all the data changes made in the database. GoldenGate does not require access to the source database and only extracts the committed transactions from the online redo logs. It can however, read archived redo logs to extract the data from long running transactions, but more about that later in the book.

The Extract process will regularly checkpoint its read and write position, typically to a file. The checkpoint data insures GoldenGate can recover its processes without data loss in the case of failure.

The Extract process can have one the following statuses:

- STOPPED
- STARTING
- RUNNING
- ABENDED

The ABENDED status stems back to the Tandem computer, where processes either stop (end normally) or abend (end abnormally). Abend is short for abnormal end.

Trail files

To replicate transactional data efficiently from one database to another, Oracle GoldenGate converts the captured data into a Canonical Format which is written to trail files, both on the source and the target system. The provision of source and target trail files in the GoldenGates architecture eliminates any single point of failure and ensures data integrity is maintained. A dedicated checkpoint process keeps track of the data being written to the trails on both the source and target for fault tolerance.

It is possible to configure GoldenGate not to use trail files on the source system and write data directly from the database's redo logs to the target server data collector. In this case, the Extract process sends data in large blocks across a TCP/IP network to the target system. However, this configuration is not recommended due to the possibility of data loss occurring during unplanned system or network outages. Best practice states, the use of local trail files would provide a history of transactions and support the recovery of data for retransmission via a Data Pump.

Data Pump

When using trail files on the source system, known as a local trail, GoldenGate requires an additional Extract process called Data Pump that sends data in large blocks across a TCP/IP network to the target system. As previously sated, this is best practice and should be adopted for all Extract configurations.

Server Collector

The Server Collector process runs on the target system and accepts data from the source (Extract/Data Pump). Its job is to reassemble the data and write it to a GoldenGate trail file, known as a remote trail.

The Apply process (Replicat)

The Apply process, known in GoldenGate as Replicat, is the final step in the data delivery. It reads the trail file and applies it to the target database in the form of DML (deletes, updates and inserts) or DDL*. (database structural changes). This can be concurrent with the data capture or performed later.

The Replicat process will regularly checkpoint its read and write position, typically to a file. The checkpoint data ensures that GoldenGate can recover its processes without data loss in the case of failure.

The Replicat process can have one of the following statuses:

- STOPPED
- STARTING
- RUNNING
- ABENDED

* DDL is only supported in unidirectional configurations and non-heterogeneous (Oracle to Oracle) environments.

The Manager process

The Manager process runs on both source and target systems. Its job is to control activities such as starting, monitoring, and restarting processes; allocating data storage; and reporting errors and events. The Manager process must exist in any GoldenGate implementation. However, there can be only one Manager process per Changed Data Capture configuration on the source and target.

The Manager process can have either of the following statuses:

- STOPPED
- RUNNING

GGSCI

In addition to the processes previously described, Oracle GoldenGate 10.4 ships with its own command line interface known as **GoldenGate Software Command Interface (GGSCI)**. This tool provides the administrator with a comprehensive set of commands to create, configure, and monitor all GoldenGate processes. You will become very familiar with GGSCI as you continue through this book.

Oracle GoldenGate 10.4 is command-line driven. However, there is a product called Oracle GoldenGate Director that provides a GUI for configuration and management of your GoldenGate environment.

Process data flow

The following diagram illustrates the GoldenGate processes and their dependencies. The arrows largely depict replicated data flow (committed transactions), apart from checkpoint data and configuration data. The Extract and Replicat processes periodically checkpoint to a file for persistence. The parameter file provides the configuration data. As described in the previous paragraphs, two options exist for sending data from source to target; these are shown as broken arrows:

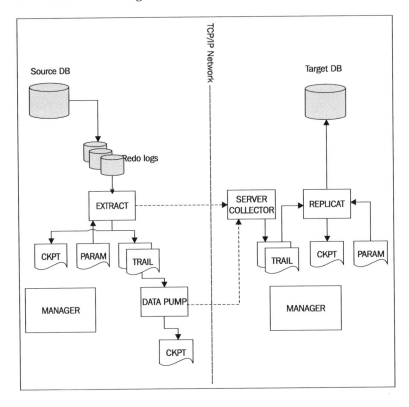

Having discovered all the processes required for GoldenGate to replicate data, let's now dive a little deeper into the architecture and configurations.

Oracle GoldenGate architecture

So what makes GoldenGate different from other data replication products? The quick answer is the architecture. GoldenGate can achieve heterogeneous and homogeneous-real-time transactional Change Data Capture and integration by decoupling itself from the database architecture. This in itself provides a performance boost as well as flexibility through its modular components.

A number of system architecture solutions are offered for data replication and synchronization:

- One-to-one (source to target)
- One-to-many (one source to many targets)
- Many to one (hub and spoke)
- Cascading
- Bi-directional (active active)
- Bi-directional (active passive)

No one configuration is better than another. The one you choose is largely dependent on your business requirements.

One-to-One

By far the simplest and most common configuration is the "source to target". Here we are performing real-time or batch change data replication between two sites in a unidirectional fashion. This could be, for example, between a primary and standby site for **Disaster Recovery (DR)** or an OLTP to data warehouse for **Business Intelligence (BI)** and OLAP.

One-to-One architecture provides a data replication solution that offers the following key benefits:

- Live reporting
- Fastest possible recovery and switchover (when the target is synchronized with the source)
- Backup site that can be used for reporting
- Supports DDL replication

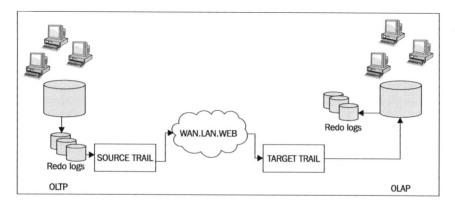

Due to its simplicity, the One-to-One architecture is referred to many times in this book to effectively demonstrate:

- Process configuration
- Data transformation
- Troubleshooting techniques
- Performance tuning tips and tricks

One-to-Many

Another popular GoldenGate configuration is the One-to-Many architecture. This architecture lends itself perfectly to provide two solutions. One data replication feed for reporting and one for backup and DR. The following example helps to illustrate the method.

One-to-Many architecture provides a data replication solution that offers the following key benefits:

- Dedicated site for Live reporting.
- Dedicated site for backup data from source database.
- Fastest possible recovery and switchover, when using a dedicated backup site. It minimizes logical data corruption as the backup database is separate from the read-write OLAP database.

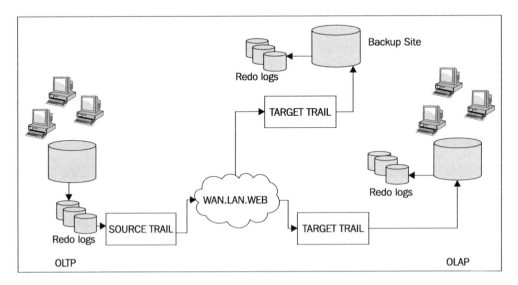

The One-to-Many architecture is very flexible, given that it provides two solutions in one—a reporting and a standby database, both of which can have different table structures.

Many-to-One

The Many-to-One configuration comes into play for peripheral sites updating a central computer system representing a hub and spokes on a wheel. This scenario is common in all industries, from retail outlets taking customer orders to high street bank branches processing customer transactions. Ultimately, the data needs to make it to the central database ASAP and cannot become lost or corrupted. GoldenGate's architecture lends itself perfectly to this scenario, as seen in the next example. Here we have three spoke sites sending data to the central hub site.

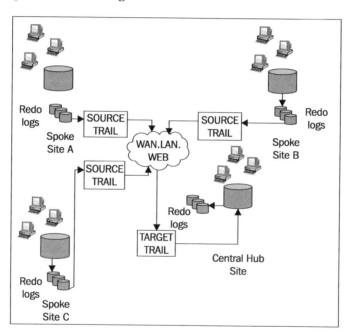

One important point to mention here is Conflict Handling. In a "hub and spoke" configuration, with concurrent updates taking place, data conflicts are highly likely to occur. Should the same database table row or field be updated by more than one source, on the target the conflict must be handled by GoldenGate to allow either one of the transactions to succeed or to fail all.

Another "hub and spoke" solution includes the One-to-Many configuration. A typical example being the company head office sending data to its branches. Here, conflict handling is less of an issue.

Cascading

The cascading architecture offers data replication at n sites, originating from a single source. As the data flows from the originating source database, parts or all of it are "dropped off" at each site in a cascading fashion until the final target is populated. In the following example, we have one source (Site A) and three targets (Sites B, C and D). Intermediate Sites B and C have both source and target trails, whereas Site A has only a source and Site D only a target trail.

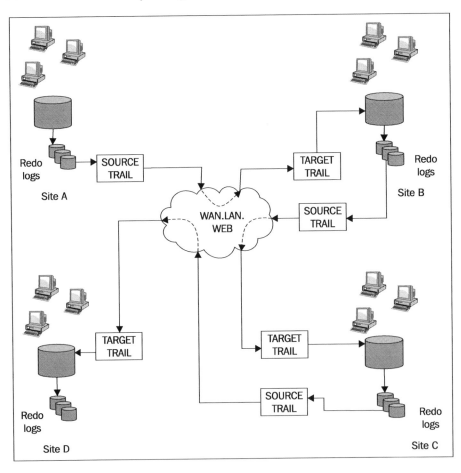

What data to replicate is configured by using Filters in the GoldenGate parameter files at each target site, making the Cascade architecture one of the most powerful, yet complex configurations. Users at each site input data that can also be replicated to the next site.

Bi-directional (Active-Active)

The following is an example of an active-active configuration, where Site A sends changed data to Site B and vice versa. Again, Conflict Handling is an important consideration. A conflict is likely to occur in a bi-directional environment, where the same row or field is being updated at both sites. When the change is replicated, a conflict occurs. This needs to be resolved by GoldenGate based on the business rules, that is, should data from Site B overwrite Site A, or should both transactions fail?

Bi-directional (active-active) architecture provides a data replication solution that offers the following key benefits:

- High availability
- Transaction load distribution
- Performance scalability

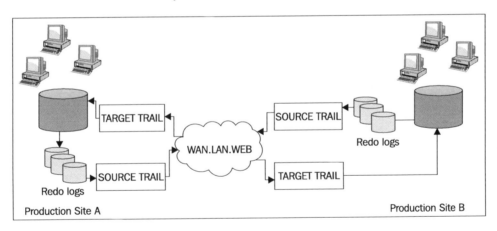

Another key element to include in your configuration is Loop Detection. We do not want data changes going round in a loop, where Site A updates Site B, then Site B updates Site A, and so on.

Do not be put off by the Bi-directional architecture. When configured correctly, this architecture offers the most appropriate solution for global companies and organizations, allowing users in two centers, both sides of the globe to share the same system and data.

The active-active configuration is very different from the active-passive, which we discuss in the following section.

Bi-directional (Active-Passive)

The following is an example of an active-passive configuration, sometimes called "Live Standby", where Site A sends changed data to Site B only. You'll notice that the path from Site B to Site A is "grayed-out", suggesting that the data replication path can be re-enabled at short notice. This means that the GoldenGate processes exist and are configured, but have not been started.

Bi-directional (active-passive) architecture provides a data replication solution that offers the following key benefits:

- Both sites have database open read-write
- Fastest possible recovery and switchover
- Reverse direction data replication ready

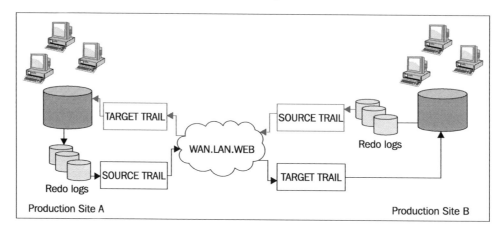

The active-passive configuration lends itself to being a DR solution, supporting a backup site should processes fail on the production site.

Supported platforms and databases

As this book is Oracle centric, below is a list of certified platforms and Oracle databases that officially support GoldenGate 10.4. The full comprehensive list for all certified platforms and databases is available at the My Oracle Support Website: `https://support.oracle.com`. (formerly, Metalink).

Follow the steps below to obtain the official Oracle Certification Matrix:

1. Log on to your My Oracle Support account and click on the **Knowledge** tab.

2. In the **Search Product** box near the top left of the page, type **Oracle GoldenGate** and click on the magnifying glass icon.

3. In the next search box type "Certification Matrix" and click on the magnifying glass icon to display the document ID 9762871.

Although GoldenGate supports earlier versions of Oracle, the following table lists the platforms supported by GoldenGate for Oracle 11*g*:

Supported platforms for Oracle Database 11*g*

DB	Version	Architecture	OS	Version	Platform
Oracle	11.1	64	AIX	5.3	IBM PowerPC
Oracle	11.1	32	AIX	5.3	IBM PowerPC
Oracle	11.1	64	AIX	6.1	IBM PowerPC
Oracle	11.1 / 11.2	64	HP-UX	11.23	HP Intel IA64
Oracle	11.1 / 11.2	64	HP-UX	11.31	HP Intel IA64
Oracle	11.1 / 11.2	64	RedHat AS	4	AMD/Intel x64
Oracle	11.1 / 11.2	32	RedHat AS	4	Intel x86
Oracle	11.1 / 11.2	64	RedHat AS	5	AMD/Intel x64
Oracle	11.1 / 11.2	64	Solaris	10	Sun SPARC
Oracle	11.1 / 11.2	64	Windows	2003	AMD/Intel x64

When downloading the GoldenGate software from Oracle Websites, ensure you choose the correct GoldenGate version, supported platform, architecture (32 or 64 bit) and database type and version.

For example, once unzipped and extracted, the following tar file installs GoldenGate 10.4.0.19 for Oracle 11*g* on Redhat or Oracle Enterprise Linux 32bit:

```
ggs_redhatAS50_x86_ora11g_32bit_v10.4.0.19_002.tar
```

The following is a list of certified non-Oracle databases that support Oracle GoldenGate 10.4:

Supported non-Oracle databases	
Database	**DB Version**
IBM DB2 UDB	8.1
IBM DB2 UDB	8.2
IBM DB2 UDB	9.1 / 9.5
Microsoft SQL Server	2000
Microsoft SQL Server	2005
Microsoft SQL Server	2008 Delivery
MySQL	4.1
MySQL	5
Sybase ASE	12.5.4
Sybase ASE	15
Teradata	V2R5
Teradata	V2R6
SQL/MX	2.3
SQL/MP	N/A
TimesTen	7.0.5
Enscribe	N/A

Oracle GoldenGate is ideal for heterogeneous environments by replicating and integrating data across differing vendor systems. Log-based **Change Data Capture (CDC)** is supported for nearly all major database vendors. GoldenGate can also integrate with JMS-based messaging systems to enable event driven architecture (EDA) and to support service oriented architecture (SOA). Further, integration support includes Extract Transformation and Load (ETL) products for OLAP and Data Warehouse implementations.

Oracle Goldengate topology

The Oracle GoldenGate topology is a representation of the databases in a GoldenGate environment, the GoldenGate components configured on each server, and the flow of data between these components.

The flow of data in separate trails is read, written, validated and check-pointed at each stage. GoldenGate is written in C and because it is native to the operating system, can run extremely fast. The sending, receiving, and validation have very little impact on the overall machine performance. Should performance become an issue due to the sheer volumes of data being replicated, you may consider configuring parallel Extract and/or Replicat processes.

Process topology

The following sections describe the process topology. Firstly discussing the rules that you must adhere to when implementing GoldenGate, followed by the order in which the processes must execute for end to end data replication.

The rules

When using parallel Extract and/or Replicat processes, ensure you keep related DDL and DML together in the same process group to ensure data integrity. The topology rules for configuring the processes are as follows:

- All objects that are relational to an object are processed by the same group as the parent object
- All DDL and DML for any given database object are processed by the same Extract group and by the same Replicat group

Should a referential constraint exist between tables, the child table with the foreign key must be included in the same Extract and Replicat group as the parent table having the primary key.

If an Extract group writes to multiple trails that are read by different Replicat groups, the Extract process sends all of the DDL to all of the trails. It is therefore necessary to configure each Replicat group to filter the DDL accordingly.

Position

The following tables show the position of each link in the process topology for the two fundamental configuration types:

Change Data Capture and Delivery using a Data Pump		
Start Component	**End Component**	**Position**
Extract Process	Local Trail File	1
Local Trail File	Data Pump	2
Data Pump	Server Collector	3
Server Collector	Remote Trail File	4
Remote Trail File	Replicat Process	5

Change Data Capture and Delivery without using a Data Pump		
Start Component	**End Component**	**Position**
Extract Process	Server Collector	1
Server Collector	Remote Trail File	2
Remote Trail File	Replicat Process	3

Statistics

In terms of performance monitoring, the GGSCI tool provides real-time statistics as well as comprehensive reports for each process configured in the GoldenGate topology. In addition to reporting on demand, it is also possible to schedule reports to be run. This can be particularly useful when performance tuning a process for a given load and period.

The INFO ALL command provides a comprehensive overview of process status and lag, whereas the STATS option gives more detail on the number of operations. Both commands offer real-time reporting. This is demonstrated in the following screen shots:

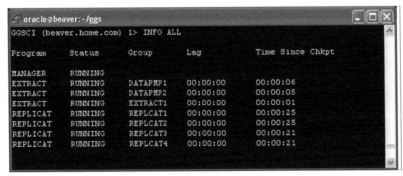

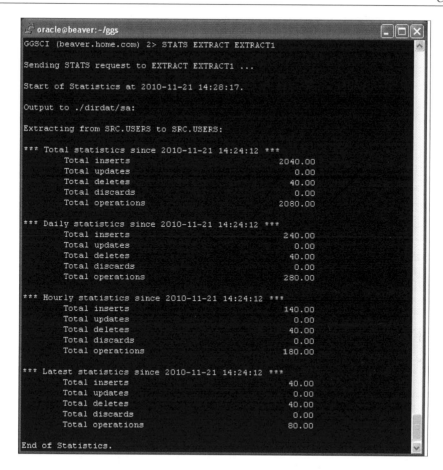

From the screenshot you can see that the STATS command provides daily and hourly cumulative statistics for a given process, including the overall total and the latest real-time figures.

Design considerations

The first thing to consider and probably one of the most important steps in any IT project is the design. If you get this wrong, your system will neither perform nor be scalable, and ultimately the project will fail. The next project may be to address all the design issues and start again from scratch! Not ideal.

So how do you design our GoldenGate implementation? Where do you start? What is important in the design? There are obviously lots of questions, so let's try and answer them.

Choosing a solution

You have already seen the different solutions GoldenGate has to offer at the beginning of this chapter. You need to choose the most appropriate architecture based on the business requirements. To do this it is necessary to first understand the requirements of the system and what the system has to achieve. These requirements' are both functional and non-functional. Examples of non-functional requirements are performance and scalability.

To address the functional requirements you need to know:

- The overall system architecture and all of its components and interfaces. Ask yourself the question "what data do we need to replicate and to where?"

For the non-functional requirements, you need to know:

- The maximum latency that is acceptable. Again, ask yourself the question "how far behind the source can the target system(s) be?"

These are all important factors when considering a design. In the earlier section "Oracle GoldenGate Topology" in this chapter, we mentioned the use of parallel Extract and Replicate processes to increase data throughput. The number of parallel trails is largely dependent on the hardware footprint. How many CPU cores do I have? How much memory is available? Etc.

Network

Other areas to consider are the Network and Database Schema design. Starting with the Network, this is fundamental to a data replication solution. If you have a slow network, you will not be able to replicate high volumes of data in real-time. Furthermore, should your network be unreliable, you need to consider the cost of retransmission or transmitting a backlog of trail files. Redundant networks are very important too and can help to alleviate this problem. If you can avoid the network outage altogether by routing data over a backup network, it will save a number of problems.

Database schema

Database Schema design is another important consideration. Imagine a schema where every table is related to nearly every other table, and the cascading referential constraints are so complex, that it would be impossible to logically separate groups of related tables for data extract. GoldenGate does provide a solution to this problem by using the @RANGE function. However, this is not ideal. Apart from the complex configuration, GoldenGate has to spend more CPU processing the configuration filters and artificially "splitting" the data into a pre-defined number of trails. A good schema design would be to ensure that logical separation exists between table groups, allowing a simple, effective configuration that performs well. The number of table groups being directly proportional to the number of Extract processes configured.

What to Replicate?

Another key decision in any GoldenGate implementation is what data to replicate. There is little point replicating data that doesn't need to be, as this will cause unnecessary additional overhead. Furthermore, if you decide that you need to replicate everything, GoldenGate may not necessarily provide the best solution. Other products such as Oracle 11*g* Active Data Guard may be more appropriate. The forthcoming paragraphs talk not only about what to replicate but also how to replicate, plus important functional and design considerations.

Object mapping and data selection

The power of GoldenGate comes into its own when you select what data you wish to replicate, by using its inbuilt tools and functions. You may even wish to transform the data before it hits the target. There are numerous options at your disposal, but choosing the right combination is paramount.

The configuration of GoldenGate includes mapping of source objects to target objects. Given the enormity of parameters and functions available, it is easy to over complicate your GoldenGate Extract or Replicat process configuration through redundant operations. Try to keep your configuration as simple as possible, choosing the right parameter, option, or function for the job. Although it is possible to string these together to achieve a powerful solution, this may cause significant additional processing and performance will suffer as a result.

GoldenGate provides the ability to select or filter out data based on a variety of levels and conditions. Typical data mapping and selection parameters are as follows:

- TABLE/MAP
  - Specifies the source and target objects to replicate. TABLE is used in Extract and MAP in Replicat parameter files.

- WHERE
  - Similar to the SQL WHERE clause, the WHERE option included with a TABLE or MAP parameter enables basic data filtering.

- FILTER
  - Provides complex data filtering. The FILTER option can be used with a TABLE or MAP parameter.

- COLS/COLSEXCEPT
  - The COLS and COLSEXCEPT option allows columns to be mapped or excluded when included with a TABLE or MAP parameter.

Before GoldenGate can extract data from the databases' online redo logs, the relevant data needs to be written to its log files. A number of pre-requisites exist to ensure the changed data can be replicated:

- Enable supplemental logging.
- Setting at database level overrides any NOLOGGING operations and ensures all changed data is written to the redo logs.
- Forces the logging of the full before and after image for updates.
- Ensure each source table has a primary key.
- GoldenGate requires a primary key to uniquely identify a row.
- If the primary key does not exist on the source table, GoldenGate will create its own unique identifier by concatenating all the table columns together. This can be grossly inefficient given the volume of data that needs to be extracted from the redo logs. Ideally, only the primary key plus the changed data (before and after images in the case of an update statement) are required.

It is also advisable to have a primary key defined on your target table(s) to ensure fast lookup when the Replicat recreates and applies the DML statements against the target database. This is particularly important for UPDATE and DELETE operations.

Initial Load

Initial Load is the process of instantiating the objects on the source database, synchronizing the target database objects with the source and providing the starting point for data replication. The process enables "change synchronization" which keeps track of ongoing transactional changes while the load is being applied. This allows users to continue to change data on the source during the Initial Load process.

The Initial Load can be successfully conducted using the following:

- A database load utility such as import / export or data pump.
- An Extract process to write data to files in ASCII format. Replicat then applies the files to the target tables.
- An Extract process to write data to files in ASCII format. SQL*Loader (direct load) can be used to load the data into the target tables.
- An Extract process that communicates directly with the Replicat process across TCP/IP without using a Collector process or files.

CSN co-ordination

An Oracle database uses the System Change Number (SCN) to keep track of transactions. For every commit, a new SCN is assigned. The data changes including primary key and SCN are written to the databases' online redo logs. Oracle requires these logs for crash recovery, which allows the committed transactions to be recovered (uncommitted transactions are rolled back). GoldenGate leverages this mechanism by reading the online redo logs, extracting the data and storing the SCN as a series of bytes. The Replicat process replays the data in SCN order when applying data changes on the target database. The GoldenGate manuals refer to the SCN as a CSN (Commit Sequence Number).

Trail file format

GoldenGate's Trail files are in Canonical Format. Backed by checkpoint files for persistence, they store the changed data in a hierarchical form including metadata definitions. The GoldenGate software includes a comprehensive utility named Logdump that has a number of commands to search and view the internal file format.

Summary

This chapter has provided the foundation for the rest of the book. It covers the key components of GoldenGate including processes, data flow, architecture, topology, configuration, plus performance and design considerations.

We learn that good design reaches far beyond GoldenGate's architecture into the database schema, allowing us to create an efficient and scalable data replication model. We also discussed the importance of Conflict Handling in certain configurations, plus network speed and resilience.

We have now gained a good understanding of what GoldenGate has to offer and are keen to learn more. Some of the available solutions have been discussed inspiring thought for real life implementations. This chapter has also touched upon inter-process dependencies, trail file format and reporting statistics. The subsequent chapters dive a little deeper, giving tangible examples for building enterprise-wide production like environments.

The next chapter starts at the beginning of the GoldenGate implementation, the installation. This includes preparing the environment as well as downloading and unpacking the software.

2
Installing and Preparing GoldenGate

Nowadays the DBA has Sys Admin skills and vice versa. For a successful GoldenGate installation, you will need both, but don't let this put you off! This chapter describes the process of downloading, installing, and configuring the GoldenGate software, plus the pre-installation steps from the Operating System and database preparation to confirming the software and hardware requirements. Consideration has been made to the GoldenGate environment and the Oracle database setup, including a configuration overview that allows you to swiftly get up and running. The final section guides you through the de-installation of the GoldenGate software.

This chapter will step you through the tasks needed to complete an end to end GoldenGate installation in the order specified as follows:

1. Downloading the software from the Oracle Website.
2. Unpacking the installation zip file.
3. Preparing the source and target systems.
4. Installing the software on source and target systems.
5. Preparing the source database.
6. Configuring the Manager process on the source and target systems.
7. Configuring the Extract process on the source system.
8. Configuring the Data Pump process on the source system.
9. Configuring the Replicat process on the target system.
10. Starting the Extract process.
11. Starting the Data Pump process.
12. Starting the Replicat process.

Prerequisites

Although the installation process may vary between platforms, for the purpose of this book, the discussion topics and demonstrations will be based on Oracle GoldenGate V10.4.0.x for Oracle 11*g* on Oracle Enterprise Linux 5.0 32-bit.

There are a number of prerequisites we need to be aware of before installing Oracle GoldenGate 10.4. Let's take a look at these.

Downloading the software

At the time of writing, to obtain an evaluation copy of GoldenGate 10.4, we need to log on to the Oracle eDelivery website:

`http://edelivery.oracle.com`

 You will need to register and accept the license agreement before you can download any software.

Oracle has placed GoldenGate in the Oracle Fusion Middleware family section, under Business Intelligence. Here you will find Oracle GoldenGate for Oracle and non-Oracle environments on a number of supported platforms.

For example, choose Linux x86 from the drop-down and select **Oracle Media Pack v2 for Linux x86**. Then click the **Continue** button.

On the next screen download **Oracle GoldenGate V10.4.0.x for Oracle 11g on RedHat 5.0** by clicking on the **Download** button.

Select	Name	Part Number	Size (Bytes)
Download	Oracle GoldenGate V10.4.0.x for Oracle 9i on RedHat 3 / SuSE 9	V20453-01	48M
Download	Oracle GoldenGate V10.4.0.x for Oracle 10g on RedHat 3.0	V18153-01	48M
Download	Oracle GoldenGate V10.4.0.x for Oracle 9i on RedHat 4.0 and SUSE 10	V20452-01	26M
Download	Oracle GoldenGate V10.4.0.x for Oracle 10g on RedHat 4.0	V18156-01	48M
Download	Oracle GoldenGate V10.4.0.x for Oracle 11g on RedHat 4.0	V18427-01	48M
Download	Oracle GoldenGate V10.4.0.x for Oracle 10g on RedHat 5.0	V18428-01	26M
Download	Oracle GoldenGate V10.4.0.x for Oracle 11g on RedHat 5.0	V18429-01	26M
Download	Oracle GoldenGate Documentation on Oracle	V20521-01	7.0M
Total: 8			

A dialog box will appear allowing you to choose where to save the file on your local file-system. The download time is small as the zipped installation file is just a few megabytes.

It is also possible to download the Oracle GoldenGate documentation from the same screen. The part number is **V20521-01**.

Software requirements

Starting with the operating system, Oracle Enterprise Linux (OEL) is the same as Redhat Enterprise Linux (RHEL), essentially rebadged. OEL 5 and RHEL 5 both use kernel version 2.6.18. Oracle and Redhat Support and Development teams collaborate to produce bug fixes for future releases.

To view the version of Linux, execute the following command as the Oracle user:

```
$ cat /etc/redhat-release
Enterprise Linux Enterprise Linux Server release 5.2 (Carthage)
```

The installation is a breeze. In fact it should only take a couple of minutes, by unpacking the UNIX tar file found in `V18429-01.zip` that you downloaded earlier from the Oracle Website. Configuring GoldenGate will take a bit longer, but we will discuss that later in this chapter.

When installing GoldenGate on a clustered environment such as Oracle Real Application Clusters (RAC), ensure the GoldenGate home or at least its subdirectories are mounted on a shared filesystem. This allows the GoldenGate processes to be started from any of the nodes and processing checkpoints to be preserved across the cluster.

For Linux installations, there are no specific requirements for kernel parameter settings or RPMs. Typically, GoldenGate is installed on a database server which has the necessary kernel parameter settings and OS RPMs for Oracle. That said, you may wish to adjust the network related kernel parameters to enhance performance. This topic is discussed in detail in *Chapter 9, Performance Tuning*, section *Tuning the Network*.

Hardware requirements

The hardware requirements for GoldenGate include the size of the physical and virtual memory, the number of CPUs and the available disk space.

Memory

The GoldenGate binaries only consume around 50MB of disk space; however, each GoldenGate instance can support up to 300 concurrent Extract and Replicat processes (inclusive). Each process consumes around 50MB of memory. So, if you plan on using the maximum number of processes, you will need at least 16GB of physical memory to support not only GoldenGate, but have enough system resources available for the OS. If you have an Oracle Instance running on the same machine (which is highly likely), additional memory will be required. Most modern day enterprise specification database servers have at least 32GB of physical RAM.

CPU

Let's consider the CPU requirements. GoldenGate will use 1 CPU core per Extract or Replicat process. However, having a large number of CPUs available is both very expensive and not necessary, as GoldenGate will typically use only 5% of a systems CPU resource. Modern Operating Systems can share available resources very efficiently; the machine will not necessarily become CPU bound. It is important however to size your requirements effectively, obtaining a balance between the maximum possible number of concurrent processes and number of CPUs.

Network

In your GoldenGate environment, you may find that CPU and memory are not the performance bottlenecks. After all, modern CPUs can process data very quickly and GoldenGate may actually be waiting to send data across the network. Therefore, ensure you have a fast network between your source and target systems. If the network between sites is a WAN, the bandwidth may not be available for high performance data transfer. In this case, you could reduce the CPU requirement to alleviate the network bottleneck.

GoldenGate requires a number of TCP/IP ports in which to operate. It is important that your network firewall is allowed to pass traffic on these ports. One port is used solely for communication between the Manager process and other GoldenGate processes. This is normally set to port 7809 but can be changed. A range of other ports are for local GoldenGate communications. These can be the default range starting at port 7840 or a predefined range of up to 256 other ports.

Disk

The final hardware requirement is disk space. Firstly, the GoldenGate cache manager uses the OS memory management functions, paging least-used information to disk and allocating virtual memory (VM) on demand. This operation uses disk space, swapping data out to temporary files in the `dirtmp` subdirectory. To calculate the required swap space, obtain the value of **PROCESS VM AVAIL FROM OS** (min) from the Extract or Replicat report files and multiply by the number of concurrent processes.

Secondly, an additional 40 MB of disk space is required for the working directories of each GoldenGate instance, plus at least 1GB for the trail files.

Software installation

Having satisfied all the necessary prerequisities, you are now ready to install the GoldenGate software. The next paragraphs offer a step-by-step guide to the installation process.

Installing GoldenGate

To use GoldenGate software you must install it on both source and target systems. When installing GoldenGate on Linux or UNIX, it is highly recommended that the software is installed by the Oracle user. To install, follow these simple steps:

1. Extract the Oracle GoldenGate Mediapack zipped file on a Windows system by using **WinZip** or an equivalent file compression product. This produces a **UNIX tar** file.

2. FTP the tar file in binary mode to the UNIX system (database server) and directory where you want GoldenGate to be installed.

3. Log on using telnet or ssh client to the database server as the Oracle user.

Ensure you have your Oracle environment variables set correctly, including LD_LIBRARY_PATH defined.

For example, if using bash or korn shell set the variable as follows:

```
export LD_LIBRARY_PATH=$ORACLE_HOME/lib
```

To make the environment variable setting persistent, define them in the .bashrc (bash shell) **or** .profile **(korn shell)** files. An example .bashrc file is shown next:

```
# .bashrc

# Source global definitions
if [ -f /etc/bashrc ]; then
        . /etc/bashrc
fi

# User specific aliases and functions
ORACLE_SID=oltp
ORACLE_BASE=/opt/oracle
ORACLE_HOME=$ORACLE_BASE/app/product/11.1.0/db_1
LD_LIBRARY_PATH=$ORACLE_HOME/lib

PATH=$PATH:$ORACLE_HOME/bin:.

export ORACLE_SID ORACLE_BASE ORACLE_HOME PATH LD_
LIBRARY_PATH
```

4. Extract the tar file. The GoldenGate files are extracted into the current working directory.

```
tar -xvof <filename>.tar
```

5. Change directories to the new GoldenGate directory.

```
cd ggs
```

6. From the GoldenGate directory, run the **GoldenGate Software Command line Interpreter (GGSCI)** program.

    ```
    ggsci
    ```

7. In GGSCI, issue the **CREATE SUBDIRS** command to create the GoldenGate working directories.

    ```
    GGSCI (dbserver1) 1> CREATE SUBDIRS
    ```

8. Issue the following command to exit GGSCI:

    ```
    GGSCI (dbserver1) 2> EXIT
    ```

    Example:

    ```
    [oracle@dbserver1 ~]$ cd ggs

    [oracle@dbserver1 ggs]$ tar -xvof ggs_redhatAS50_x86_ora11g_32bit_
    v10.4.0.19_002.tar

    [oracle@dbserver1 ~]$ ggsci

    Oracle GoldenGate Command Interpreter for Oracle

    Version 10.4.0.19 Build 002

    Linux, x86, 32bit (optimized), Oracle 11 on Sep 29 2009 08:50:50

    Copyright (C) 1995, 2009, Oracle and/or its affiliates.  All
    rights reserved.

    [oracle@dbserver1 ggs]$ ggsci

    Oracle GoldenGate Command Interpreter for Oracle

    Version 10.4.0.19 Build 002

    Linux, x86, 32bit (optimized), Oracle 11 on Sep 29 2009 08:50:50

    Copyright (C) 1995, 2009, Oracle and/or its affiliates.  All
    rights reserved.

    GGSCI (dbserver1.mydomain.com) 1> create subdirs

    Creating subdirectories under current directory /home/oracle/ggs

    Parameter files              /home/oracle/ggs/dirprm: created
    Report files                 /home/oracle/ggs/dirrpt: created
    Checkpoint files             /home/oracle/ggs/dirchk: created
    Process status files         /home/oracle/ggs/dirpcs: created
    SQL script files             /home/oracle/ggs/dirsql: created
    ```

```
Database definitions files        /home/oracle/ggs/dirdef: created
Extract data files                /home/oracle/ggs/dirdat: created
Temporary files                   /home/oracle/ggs/dirtmp: created
Veridata files                    /home/oracle/ggs/dirver: created
Veridata Lock files               /home/oracle/ggs/dirver/lock:
created
Veridata Out-Of-Sync files        /home/oracle/ggs/dirver/oos:
created
Veridata Out-Of-Sync XML files /home/oracle/ggs/dirver/oosxml:
created
Veridata Parameter files          /home/oracle/ggs/dirver/params:
created
Veridata Report files             /home/oracle/ggs/dirver/report:
created
Veridata Status files             /home/oracle/ggs/dirver/status:
created
Veridata Trace files              /home/oracle/ggs/dirver/trace:
created
Stdout files                      /home/oracle/ggs/dirout: created
GGSCI (dbserver1.mydomain.com) 2> exit
```

The GGSCI commands are not case sensitive, but do support wildcards (*) where appropriate.

9. When using Oracle Automatic Storage Manager (ASM) as the storage solution for your database, ensure you have a TNS entry configured for the ASM instance in the tnsnames.ora file on the source database server.

The database server's tnsnames.ora file can be found in the following directory:

$ORACLE_HOME/network/admin

An example tnsnames.ora entry is shown next:

```
ASM =
  (DESCRIPTION =
    (ADDRESS = (PROTOCOL = TCP)(HOST = dbserver1)(PORT = 1521))
    (CONNECT_DATA =
      (SERVER = DEDICATED)
      (SID = +ASM)
    )
  )
```

The subdirectories

In step 7 of the installation, we create subdirectories beneath the GoldenGate home. These are the default locations that can be moved, for example, to a Storage Area Network (SAN). The subdirectory names and what specific files they contain are described below.

dirchk

The `dirchk` subdirectory is the default location for checkpoint files created by the Extract and Replicat processes that provide data persistence of read and write operations. The file name format is `<group name><sequence number>.<file extension>`.

A group is a processing group consisting of either an Extract or Replicat, its parameter file, its checkpoint file, and any other files associated with the process. The group name can be up to eight characters including non-alphanumeric.

The file extension is `cpe` for Extract checkpoint files or `cpr` for Replicat checkpoint files.

dirdat

The `dirdat` subdirectory is the default location for GoldenGate trail files and extract files created by the Extract processes. These files are subsequently processed by either a Replicat process or another application or utility.

The file name format for trail files is `< prefix> <sequence number>`

The prefix must be two alphanumeric characters specified during Extract or Replicat creation. Typical prefix names are as follows:

- **sa, sb, sc** etc for the 1st, 2nd and 3rd trail files on the source
- **ta, tb, tc** etc for the 1st, 2nd and 3rd trail files on the target

A 6-digit sequential number is automatically appended to each file prefix for each new trail file created.

The filename for extract files is user-defined name and has no sequence number.

 This subdirectory can fill up very quickly during Extract processing. The default size of trail files is 10M. Ensure that adequate space is available in the filesystem to prevent the Extract process(es) from abending. Processed trail files can be purged periodically as part of the GoldenGate manager configuration.

dirdef

The `dirdef` subdirectory is the default location for data definition files created by the DEFGEN utility. These ASCII files contain source or target data definitions used in a heterogeneous synchronization environment.

The file name format is user-defined and specified explicitly in the DEFGEN parameter file. Typically the DEFGEN data file is called `defs.dat`.

dirpcs

The `dirpcs` subdirectory is the default location for process status files. These files are only created while a process is running. The file shows the program and process name, the port, and process ID.

The file name format is `<group name>.<file extension>`.

The file extension is `pce` for Extract, `pcr` for Replicat, or `pcm` for Manager processes.

dirprm

The `dirprm` subdirectory is the default location for GoldenGate parameter files created by administrators configuring run-time parameters for GoldenGate process groups or utilities. These ASCII files are generally edited through the GGSCI utility but can be edited directly.

The file name format is `<group name/user-defined name>.prm` or `mgr.prm`.

dirrpt

The `dirrpt` subdirectory is the default location for report files created by Extract, Replicat, and Manager processes. These ASCII files report statistical information relating to a processing run. When a process abends the file is updated automatically. However, to obtain process statistics "on the fly", the REPORT command must be invoked from within the GGSCI tool.

The file name format is `<group name><sequence number>.rpt`.

dirsql

The `dirsql` subdirectory is the default location for SQL scripts.

dirtmp

The `dirtmp` subdirectory is the default location for GoldenGate process temporary files that "swap out" data related to large transactions that exceed the allocated memory size. It is recommended that this subdirectory be created on its own disk to reduce I/O contention.

Preparing the environment

Preparation is the key to just about any task. Get the preparation right and you will be rewarded with the best results. This is also true for GoldenGate, where a number of fundamental areas need to be prepared before the installation can take place.

Preparing the database for data replication

To successfully create, configure and start our Extract, Data Pump, and Replicat processes, it's important to configure the source database. As described in *Chapter 1, Getting Started*, GoldenGate relies on the database's changed data to accomplish data replication.

Enabling supplemental logging

In order to extract the committed transactions from the source Oracle database's online redo logs, as a minimum the database must be configured for supplemental logging on Primary Key columns. This can be enabled at database level using the following DDL executed as SYSDBA:

```
[oracle@dbserver1 ggs]$ sqlplus '/as sysdba'
SQL> alter database add supplemental log data (primary key) columns;

Database altered
```

Initiate a log file switch to start supplemental logging:

```
SQL> alter system switch logfile;

System altered.
```

The following SQL shows the result of enabling the supplemental logging:

```
SQL> select SUPPLEMENTAL_LOG_DATA_MIN, SUPPLEMENTAL_LOG_DATA_PK,
SUPPLEMENTAL_LOG_DATA_UI from v$database;

SUPPLEME SUP SUP
-------- --- ---
IMPLICIT YES NO
```

We now need to configure GoldenGate to add supplemental log data to the source tables using GGSCI's **ADD TRANDATA** command. This is shown in the following example for the SCOTT.DEPT and SCOTT.EMP tables:

```
[oracle@dbserver1 ggs]$ ggsci

GGSCI (dbserver1) 1> DBLOGIN USERID ggs_admin, PASSWORD ggs_admin

Successfully logged into database.

GGSCI (dbserver1) 2> ADD TRANDATA scott.DEPT

Logging of supplemental redo data enabled for table SCOTT.DEPT.

GGSCI (dbserver1) 3> ADD TRANDATA scott.EMP

Logging of supplemental redo data enabled for table SCOTT.EMP.
```

> Every source table must have a Primary Key enabled else GoldenGate will define all viable columns to represent uniqueness. This will increase the volume of supplemental log data being written to the redologs and subsequent trail files.

The source database is now ready for data replication!

If you have a lot of tables in your source schema that you wish to replicate, then you could use SQL to generate the **ADD TRANDATA** statements. Log on to the source database schema using SQL*Plus and execute the following commands:

```
SQL> set pages 0
SQL> select 'ADD TRANDATA SRC.'||tname from tab;
```

Preparing the operating system

GoldenGate relies heavily on TCP/IP networking and therefore must be configured correctly. In the earlier sections of this chapter, we configured a Data Pump process that sends data across a TCP/IP network from the source to the target system. In the Data Pump parameter file we specified a remote hostname, which must be resolved to an IP address.

On Linux, the hosts file provides the mapping between host and IP address. For example:

```
[oracle@dbserver1 ~]$ cat /etc/hosts
127.0.0.1      localhost.localdomain      localhost
192.168.1.65  dbserver1
192.168.1.66  dbserver2
```

 To edit the hosts file you must be the root (super) user.

In the case of a clustered environment, such as Oracle RAC, the hosts file must contain the Virtual IP (VIP) address of the remote nodes.

Creating the initial configuration

This section describes the concept behind the configuration of GoldenGate and how to set up data replication. The configuration examples are of a basic level and are based on the Oracle Scott/Tiger schema. They do not necessarily represent a production environment. Chapter 7, Advanced Configuration provides greater detail.

You may also wish to refer to the Oracle GoldenGate Reference Guide 10.4 to support your understanding of commands and parameters.

The following steps create a simple GoldenGate unidirectional source-to-target configuration, where data is replicated from the SRC schema in the OLTP database on dbserver1, to the TGT schema in the OLAP database on dbserver2.

Creating the GoldenGate administrator

Before any configuration can take place, we need to create a GoldenGate Administrator user account on both source and target databases. This account provides access to the database tables for GoldenGate configuration and runtime operations.

Log on to each database as SYSDBA and issue the following commands:

```
[oracle@dbserver1 ggs]$ sqlplus '/as sysdba'
SQL> create user ggs_admin identified by ggs_admin;

User created.

SQL> grant dba to ggs_admin;

Grant succeeded.
```

You will notice that the DBA Role has been granted to the GGS_ADMIN database user. This is deliberate because of the high level of database access required. However, the GoldenGate installation and setup guide lists the minimum individual roles and privileges required against each process, which also command a high privilege.

 For security reasons, it is important the GGS_ADMIN account is not compromised and only used for GoldenGate administration and operations.

The Manager process

GoldenGate configuration starts with the Manager process. The first parameter file to create is the `mgr.prm` file. This file is implicitly created in the `dirprms` subdirectory by typing the following command on the GGSCI command line:

```
GGSCI (dbserver1) 1> EDIT PARAM MGR
```

The EDIT command invokes your default editor. In the case of Linux, that will be the vi editor. The following is a typical GoldenGate Manager configuration for the source system, stored in the mgr.prm file. We will learn more about the Manager process parameter file contents in the Chapter 4 , *Configuring Oracle GoldenGate*.

```
-- GoldenGate Manager parameter file
PORT 7809
PURGEOLDEXTRACTS ./dirdat/sa*, USECHECKPOINTS, MINKEEPHOURS 2
```

A double hyphen (--) prefix allows comments to be placed in the GoldenGate parameter files.

A period (.) depicts the GoldenGate home directory.

The Manager process must be configured on both source and target systems and must be started before any other configuration tasks are performed in GGSCI.

```
GGSCI (dbserver1) 2> START MGR
Manager started.
```

You will also notice that the GGSCI tool (Linux) includes the following useful information at the command prompt:

GGSCI (<hostname>) <command sequence number> >

The Extract process

The next parameter file to create is the Extract parameter file. Again, the file `<group name>.prm` is implicitly created in the `dirprm` subdirectory by typing the following command on the GGSCI command line. For example:

```
GGSCI (dbserver1) 3> EDIT PARAMS EOLTP01
```

The Extract process scans the database online or archived redo logs for committed transactions. Should your source Oracle database be using Automatic Storage Management (ASM) to store all its database files, GoldenGate will require access to the ASM disk groups to scan the logs in the Flash Recovery Area (FRA). In this case, the ASM SYS username and password will be required in the parameter file.

> GoldenGate does not support OS authentication, which is the reason for the password to be hardcoded in its Extract process parameter files. However, this can be encrypted and is discussed in *Chapter 5, Configuration Options*. ASM itself necessitates a SYS password file.

The basic configuration consists of:

- The Extract group name
- The Oracle Database System ID (`ORACLE_SID`)
- The source database GoldenGate username and password
- The source trail file path and prefix
- The ASM SYS username and password (if the database is using ASM)
- The source table names

The following code demonstrates the basic configuration required for the Extract process. Our source system's Oracle System ID is OLTP, set by the SETENV parameter. We also need to include the database user login information for the GoldenGate administrator user; ggs_admin.

```
-- Change Data Capture parameter file to extract
-- OLTP table changes
--
EXTRACT EOLTP01
SETENV (ORACLE_SID=OLTP)
USERID ggs_admin, PASSWORD ggs_admin
EXTTRAIL ./dirdat/sa
TRANLOGOPTIONS ASMUSER SYS@ASM, ASMPASSWORD Password1
TABLE SRC.DEPT;
TABLE SRC.EMP;
```

Creating and starting an Extract process

Now that we have created an Extract parameter file, the next step is to add the Extract to GoldenGate using GGSCI. The following example uses the Extract parameter file (EOLTP01.prm) shown in paragraph titled "The Extract Process":

```
[oracle@dbserver1 ggs]$ ggsci

GGSCI (dbserver1) 1> add extract EOLTP01, tranlog, begin now, threads 1

EXTRACT added.
```

The previous GGSCI command string includes the TRANLOG keyword that tells GoldenGate to extract data from the source database's online redologs. The BEGIN NOW statement tells GoldenGate to start data replication immediately.

 In a RAC environment, the THREADS parameter must be set to the number of database instances. The default is 1 for a single instance database.

The next step is to define the local trail for the Extract process. The GGSCI command string below specifies a local trail having the prefix **sa**. Also, each trail file associated with the EOLTP01 Extract process will be a maximum of 50MB in size:

```
GGSCI (dbserver1) 2> add exttrail ./dirdat/sa, extract EOLTP01,
megabytes 50

EXTTRAIL added.
```

Before starting the Extract process, let's define its associated Data Pump process, ensuring that the **sa** trail prefix is specified. The example below uses the Extract parameter file `EPMP01.prm` shown in paragraph titled "The Data Pump Process":

```
GGSCI (dbserver1) 3> add extract EPMP01, exttrailsource ./dirdat/sa,
begin now

EXTRACT added.
```

Now that we have an Extract and Data Pump process defined and configured, we can start them:

```
GGSCI (dbserver1) 4> start extract EOLTP01

Sending START request to MANAGER ...

EXTRACT EOLTP01 starting

GGSCI (dbserver1) 5> start EXTRACT EPMP01

Sending START request to MANAGER ...
EXTRACT EPMP01 starting
```

To view the status of the Extract process, use the following command:

```
GGSCI (dbserver1) 6> info all
```

Program	Status	Group	Lag	Time Since Chkpt
MANAGER	RUNNING			
EXTRACT	RUNNING	EOLTP01	00:00:00	00:00:02
EXTRACT	RUNNING	EPMP01	00:00:00	00:00:00

The Data Pump process

If you plan to use a Data Pump process, which is highly recommended, you need to create a Data Pump parameter file on the source system. Create the file `<group name>.prm` by typing the following command on the GGSCI command line. For example:

```
GGSCI (dbserver1) 4> EDIT PARAMS EPMP01
```

The Data Pump process is in essence an Extract process that sends changed data to the target system. The basic configuration consists of:

- The Data Pump name
- The data processing option (PASSTHRU or NOPASSTHRU)
- The target hostname
- The target trail file path and prefix
- The Manager port TCP/IP port number
- The source table names

The following code demonstrates the basic configuration required for the Data Pump process. We have chosen to use the PASSTHRU parameter ensuring that the data is propagated to the target host without any manipulation.

```
-- Data Pump parameter file to read the local
-- trail of table changes
--
EXTRACT EPMP01
PASSTHRU
RMTHOST dbserver2, MGRPORT 7809
RMTTRAIL ./dirdat/ta
TABLE SRC.DEPT;
TABLE SRC.EMP;
```

The Replicat process

To use a Replicat process, you need to create a Replicat parameter file on the target system. Create the file <group name>.prm by typing the following command on the GGSCI command line. For example:

```
GGSCI (dbserver2) 1> EDIT PARAMS ROLAP01
```

The Replicat process reads the target trail files and converts the GoldenGate messages to DML or DDL and applies the changes to the target database. The basic configuration consists of:

- The Replicat group name
- The Oracle Database System ID (ORACLE_SID)
- The target database GoldenGate username and password
- The target trail file path and prefix
- The discarded data file (data records that suffer an error during apply)
- The mapping information between source table and target table

The following code demonstrates the basic configuration required for the Replicat process. Similar in structure to the Extract process, we have defined a process name, the target database's Oracle System ID, which is OLAP, the GoldenGate user login credentials and a discard file. We have also defined the mapping between source and target tables.

```
-- Replicator parameter file to apply changes
-- to tables
--
REPLICAT ROLAP01
SETENV (ORACLE_SID=OLAP)
USERID ggs_admin, PASSWORD ggs_admin
DISCARDFILE ./dirrpt/rolap01.dsc, PURGE
MAP SRC.DEPT, TARGET TGT.DEPT;
MAP SRC.EMP, TARGET TGT.EMP;
```

Creating and starting a Replicat process

Perform the Replicat process creation on the target system. The example below uses the Replicat parameter file `ROLAP01.prm` shown in paragraph titled "The Replicat Process":

```
[oracle@dbserver2 ggs]$ ggsci
GGSCI (dbserver2) 1> add replicat ROLAP01, exttrail ./dirdat/ta

REPLICAT added.
```

Note that the above GGSCI command string includes the Replicat group name ROLAP01 and the **ta** remote trail prefix as specified in the Data Pump parameter file `EPMP01.prm`.

Now start the newly created Replicat process:

```
GGSCI (dbserver2) 2> start replicat ROLAP01

Sending START request to MANAGER ...
REPLICAT ROLAP01 starting

GGSCI (dbserver2) 3> info all
```

Program	Status	Group	Lag	Time Since Chkpt
MANAGER	RUNNING			
REPLICAT	RUNNING	ROLAP01	00:00:00	00:00:02

Configuration summary

To summarize the configuration overview, the tables below describe the naming convention and mapping between roles, file names, processes, hostnames, databases, and schemas used in the configuration examples.

Role	Process	Process Group Name	Parameter Filename	Trail Filename Prefix
Source / Target	MGR	MGR	mgr.prm	N/A
Source	EXTRACT	EOLTP01	eoltp01.prm	sa
Source	EXTRACT (Data Pump)	EPMP01	epmp01.prm	sa (local) ta (remote)
Target	REPLICAT	ROLAP01	rolap01.prm	ta

Role	Database Server Hostname	Database Name	Schema Name
Source	dbserver1	OLTP	SRC
Target	dbserver2	OLAP	TGT

Uninstalling GoldenGate from Linux/UNIX

Uninstalling the GoldenGate software is, as one would expect, the reverse of installing it. The de-installation is as simple as the installation and can be done by following the example below:

1. Log on to the database server (as oracle) where the GoldenGate software is installed.

2. Change directory to the GoldenGate home:

   ```
   cd /home/oracle/ggs
   ```

3. Start GGSCI:

   ```
   ggsci
   ```

4. Stop all GoldenGate processes:

   ```
   GGSCI (dbserver1) 1> stop EXTRACT *
   ```

   Or:

   ```
   GGSCI (dbserver1) 1> stop REPLICAT *
   ```

Then:

```
GGSCI (dbserver1) 2> stop MGR

Manager process is required by other GGS processes.

Are you sure you want to stop it (y/n)? y

Sending STOP request to MANAGER ...

Request processed.

Manager stopped.


GGSCI (dbserver1) 3> exit
```

5. Change directory to the installation directory:

```
cd /home/oracle
```

6. Remove the GoldenGate files:

```
rm -rf ggs
```

7. Logon to the Oracle database as SYSDBA and drop the GoldenGate Admin user. Include the CASCADE keyword:

```
sqlplus / as sysdba
SQL> drop user ggs_admin cascade;

User dropped.
```

Summary

This chapter has provided us with an introduction to the end to end process of preparing the environment and installing the GoldenGate software. Although the initial configuration is relatively simple compared to a production environment, it has delivered the foundation, allowing us to build a working GoldenGate data replication solution.

In the next chapter, we look at design considerations, which is probably the most important step when implementing a GoldenGate solution..

3
Design Considerations

The most important step in any IT development project is the design. This must be the first step as changes to the design at a later stage will cost time and money. Get the design right and your system will continue to perform well as the user base increases.

At a high level, the design must include the following generic requirements:

- Hardware
- Software
- Network
- Storage
- Performance

All the above must be factored into the overall system architecture. So let's take a look at some of the options and the key design issues.

In this chapter, we will discuss the following areas to help answer some of the questions that influence the decision making process.

- Methods for replicating data: What do we want to achieve?
- Networking: How do we make our solution resilient to network outages?
- Performance and scalability: Will our solution support future non functional requirements?
- Backup and recovery: Can we restore service quickly with no data loss?
- Hardware: What is the size of our budget? Do we need powerful servers? Can we cluster lower spec machines?

Replication methods

So you have a fast reliable network between your source and target sites. You also have a schema design that is scalable and logically split. You now need to choose the replication architecture; One to One, One to Many, active-active, active-passive, and so on. This consideration may already be answered for you by the sheer fact of what the system has to achieve. Let's take a look at some configuration options.

Active-active

Let's assume a multi-national computer hardware company has an office in London and New York. Data entry clerks are employed at both sites inputting orders into an Order Management System. There is also a procurement department that updates the system inventory with volumes of stock and new products related to a US or European market. European countries are managed by London, and the US States are managed by New York. A requirement exists where the underlying database systems must be kept in synchronisation. Should one of the systems fail, London users can connect to New York and vice-versa allowing business to continue and orders to be taken. Oracle GoldenGate's active-active architecture provides the best solution to this requirement, ensuring that the database systems on both sides of the pond are kept synchronised in case of failure.

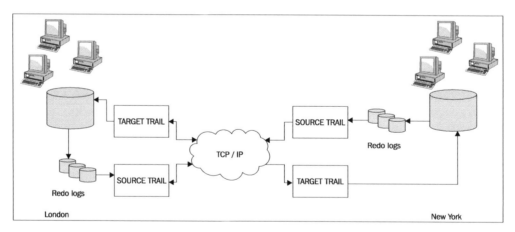

Another feature the active-active configuration has to offer is the ability to load balance operations. Rather than have effectively a DR site in both locations, the European users could be allowed access to New York and London systems and vice-versa. Should a site fail, then the DR solution could be quickly implemented.

Active-passive

The active-passive bi-directional configuration replicates data from an active primary database to a full replica database. Sticking with the earlier example, the business would need to decide which site is the primary where all users connect. For example, in the event of a failure in London, the application could be configured to failover to New York.

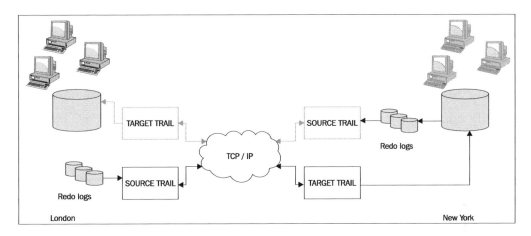

Depending on the failure scenario, another option is to start up the passive configuration, effectively turning the active-passive configuration into active-active.

Cascading

The Cascading GoldenGate topology offers a number of "drop-off" points that are intermediate targets being populated from a single source. The question here is "what data do I drop at which site?" Once this question has been answered by the business, it is then a case of configuring filters in Replicat parameter files allowing just the selected data to be replicated. All of the data is passed on to the next target where it is filtered and applied again.

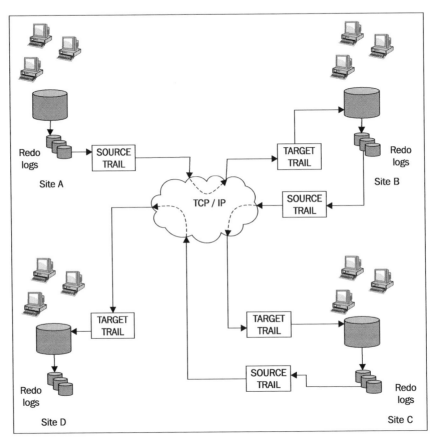

This type of configuration lends itself to a head office system updating its satellite office systems in a round robin fashion. In this case, only the relevant data is replicated at each target site. Another design, already discussed in Chapter 1, is the Hub and Spoke solution, where all target sites are updated simultaneously. This is a typical head office topology, but additional configuration and resources would be required at the source site to ship the data in a timely manner. The CPU, network, and file storage requirements must be sufficient to accommodate and send the data to multiple targets.

Physical Standby

A Physical Standby database is a robust Oracle DR solution managed by the Oracle Data Guard product. The Physical Standby database is essentially a mirror copy of its Primary, which lends itself perfectly for failover scenarios. However , it is not easy to replicate data from the Physical Standby database, because it does not generate any of its own redo. That said, it is possible to configure GoldenGate to read the archived standby logs in **Archive Log Only (ALO)** mode. Despite being potentially slower, it may be prudent to feed a downstream system on the DR site using this mechanism, rather than having two data streams configured from the Primary database. This reduces network bandwidth utilization, as shown in the following diagram:

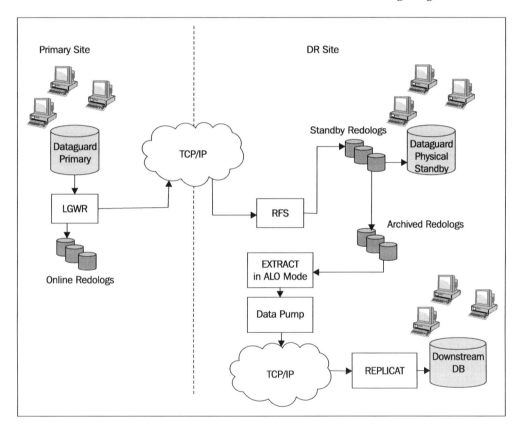

Reducing network traffic is particularly important when there is considerable distance between the primary and the DR site.

Networking

The network should not be taken for granted. It is a fundamental component in data replication and must be considered in the design process. Not only must it be fast, it must be reliable. In the following paragraphs, we look at ways to make our network resilient to faults and subsequent outages, in an effort to maintain zero downtime.

Surviving network outages

Probably one of your biggest fears in a replication environment is network failure. Should the network fail, the source trail will fill as the transactions continue on the source database, ultimately filling the filesystem to 100% utilization, causing the Extract process to abend. Depending on the length of the outage, data in the database's redologs may be overwritten causing you the additional task of configuring GoldenGate to extract data from the database's archived logs. This is not ideal as you already have the backlog of data in the trail files to ship to the target site once the network is restored. Therefore, ensure there is sufficient disk space available to accommodate data for the longest network outage during the busiest period.

Disks are relatively cheap nowadays. Providing ample space for your trail files will help to reduce the recovery time from the network outage.

Redundant networks

One of the key components in your GoldenGate implementation is the network. Without the ability to transfer data from the source to the target, it is rendered useless. So, you not only need a fast network but one that will always be available. This is where redundant networks come into play, offering speed and reliability.

NIC teaming

One method of achieving redundancy is **Network Interface Card (NIC)** teaming or bonding. Here two or more Ethernet ports can be "coupled" to form a bonded network supporting one IP address. The main goal of NIC teaming is to use two or more Ethernet ports connected to two or more different access network switches thus avoiding a single point of failure. The following diagram illustrates the redundant features of NIC teaming:

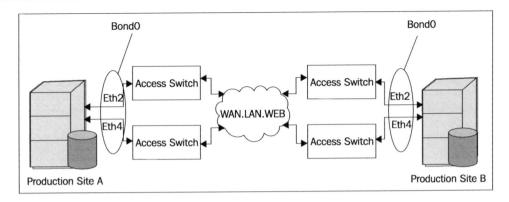

Linux (OEL/RHEL 4 and above) supports NIC teaming with no additional software requirements. It is purely a matter of network configuration stored in text files in the `/etc/sysconfig/network-scripts` directory. The following steps show how to configure a server for NIC teaming:

1. First, you need to log on as root user and create a `bond0` config file using the vi text editor.

   ```
   # vi /etc/sysconfig/network-scripts/ifcfg-bond0
   ```

2. Append the following lines to it, replacing the IP address with your actual IP address, then save file and exit to shell prompt:

   ```
   DEVICE=bond0
   IPADDR=192.168.1.20
   NETWORK=192.168.1.0
   NETMASK=255.255.255.0
   USERCTL=no
   BOOTPROTO=none
   ONBOOT=yes
   ```

3. Choose the Ethernet ports you wish to bond, and then open both configurations in turn using the vi text editor, replacing `ethn` with the respective port number.

   ```
   # vi /etc/sysconfig/network-scripts/ifcfg-eth2
   # vi /etc/sysconfig/network-scripts/ifcfg-eth4
   ```

4. Modify the configuration as follows:

   ```
   DEVICE=ethn
   USERCTL=no
   ONBOOT=yes
   MASTER=bond0
   SLAVE=yes
   BOOTPROTO=none
   ```

5. Save the files and exit to shell prompt.

6. To make sure the bonding module is loaded when the bonding interface (bond0) is brought up, you need to modify the kernel modules configuration file:

    ```
    # vi /etc/modprobe.conf
    ```

7. Append the following two lines to the file:

    ```
    alias bond0 bonding
    options bond0 mode=balance-alb miimon=100
    ```

8. Finally, load the bonding module and restart the network services:

    ```
    # modprobe bonding
    # service network restart
    ```

You now have a bonded network that will load balance when both physical networks are available, providing additional bandwidth and enhanced performance. Should one network fail, the available bandwidth will be halved, but the network will still be available.

Non-functional requirements (NFRs)

Irrespective of the functional requirements, the design must also include the non-functional requirements (NFR) in order to achieve the overall goal of delivering a robust, high performance, and stable system.

Latency

One of the main NFRs is performance. How long does it take to replicate a transaction from the source database to the target? This is known as end-to-end latency that typically has a threshold that must not be breeched in order to satisfy the specified NFR.

GoldenGate refers to latency as lag, which can be measured at different intervals in the replication process. These are:

*   **Source to Extract**: The time taken for a record to be processed by the Extract compared to the commit timestamp on the database
*   **Replicat to Target**: The time taken for the last record to be processed by the Replicat compared to the record creation time in the trail file

A well designed system may encounter spikes in latency but it should never be continuous or growing. Trying to tune GoldenGate when the design is poor is a difficult situation to be in. For the system to perform well you may need to revisit the design.

Availability

Another important NFR is availability. Normally quoted as a percentage, the system must be available for the specified length of time. An example NFR of 99.9% availability equates to a downtime of 8.76 hours a year, which sounds quite a lot, especially if it were to occur all at once.

Oracle's maximum availability architecture (MAA) offers enhanced availability through products such as RAC and Dataguard. However, as we have previously discussed, the network plays a major role in data replication. The NFR probably relates to the whole system, so you need to be sure your design covers all components.

We look at configuring GoldenGate on Real Application Clusters (RAC) as a MAA solution in the Chapter 6, Configuring GoldenGate for High Availability.

Backup and recovery

Equally important as the other NFRs is the recovery time. If you cannot recover from a disaster your system will be unavailable or worse still, data will be lost. GoldenGate prides itself on robustness, having proven to the industry that zero downtime data migrations are possible whilst users are still online!

Of course, you need to backup your source and target databases regularly using a product such as Oracle Recovery Manager (RMAN)—typically performing a full backup once a week on a Sunday with incremental backups running each night over a 7 day window, but this is not the full story. We need to consider backing up the GoldenGate home and sub-directories that contain the trail files, checkpoint files, and so on. Without these, GoldenGate could not recover from the last checkpoint and a new initial load would be required. RMAN (11*g*R1) will not back up OS or non-database files so either use UNIX shell commands or a third party product such as Veritas NetBackup.

You may decide to place your GoldenGate sub-directories on shared storage such as a **Storage Area Network (SAN)** where data resilience is automatically maintained. This may be the best design solution given that the disks are shared and the available speed of recovery. For example, restoring data from EMC SnapView.

The best recovery solution is the **Disaster Recovery (DR)** site, where you can quickly switchover or failover to a backup system. GoldenGate may already be part of this strategy, so ensure your DR solution is robust by scheduling regular backups as previously discussed.

The following example architecture diagram helps to illustrate the design:

Although a key area in the overall design B & R is sometimes overlooked. Oracle provides a number of HA solutions that offer fast and reliable mechanisms to ensure your data is not only backed up but always available. In this chapter, we have already discussed Oracle RAC, Dataguard and RMAN, with GoldenGate we have a fourth member of the MAA team.

Hardware considerations

Hardware is one of the most important components in the overall design. Without the appropriate memory footprint, CPU power, network, or storage solution our design will fail before the project even "gets off the ground". Another consideration is how to arrange the hardware to obtain the best performance and scalability. Let's take a look at a few options.

Computing architectures

The configuration and arrangement of hardware components is known as the system architecture. This section concentrates on the common computer architectures available and discusses their advantages and disadvantages for distributed database network supporting a Web-based application.

The following diagram shows the typical hardware components required:

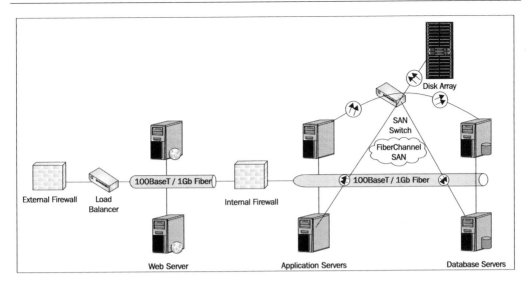

GoldenGate is deemed as middleware and normally runs on the database tier where the software can access the database and it's online redo logs.

Grid computing

Nowadays, highly powerful servers can be procured preconfigured to the customer's specification. One of the most cost effective is the x86 64 bit Linux server, which offers high performance at a budget price. Should your system require more "horse power", you just add more servers. This is known as Grid computing.

Grid computing offers multiple applications to share computing infrastructure, resulting in greater flexibility, low cost, power efficiency, performance, scalability and availability, all at the same time.

What does this mean for GoldenGate? As we know, GoldenGate runs a number of local processes. Should we wish to synchronize data between more than one server we would have to adopt a shared storage solution or maybe in-memory caching such as Oracle Coherence. This all adds to the overall complexity of the design.

Single server

A single database and application server may also be a low cost option. However, it is not scalable and will cost you a lot more having to upgrade the hardware as the number of users increase. On the other hand, the single server option does provide simplicity and can be easily configured and maintained. The choice in architecture is largely dependent on the application, not just the cost!

Clusters

There is nothing new about clustered environments; they have existed for years. DEC VMS is a classic example. Clustered environments have proven their worth over the years; for example, Oracle Real Application Clusters (RAC) has been around since Oracle 9*i* and before that in Oracle 8 it was known as **Oracle Parallel Server (OPS)**. Today, RAC is one of the most common database architectures offering performance, resilience, and scalability at a reasonable cost (depending on the number of nodes and CPU cores). RAC does however demand shared storage, which may add to the cost.

As with Grid computing, GoldenGate requires shared storage in order to replicate data from more than one thread or instance.

Machines

Although GoldenGate is multi-platform and supports heterogeneous databases, this book focuses on Linux and Oracle. In a production environment, the database server is typically a powerful machine costing thousands of dollars. However, the hardware investment can be significantly reduced without compromising performance by using the Linux x86-64 operating system on Intel based machines with 64 bit architecture.

The x86-64 Linux Server

The x86-64 Linux Server is essentially a PC having 64 bit Red Hat or Oracle Enterprise Linux installed. Typically, a standard Linux business server delivered from HP or Dell would have the following minimum hardware specification:

- 4 Quad-Core Intel or AMD processors
- 16 GB Memory
- 2 x 500 GB Hard disks (possibly a mirrored pair)
- 4 x Gigabit Ethernet Ports

Depending on the application, the hardware specification is more than adequate for clustered or grid environments, but may not be sufficient as a single server. We must also consider the different layers involved in a computer system, from the application and middleware layers up to the database tier, which includes the storage.

How many servers are you going to allocate to each layer?

Good question. It is common to have more application servers than database servers supporting the system. The application servers providing the "user experience" offering the functionality and response times through load balancing and caching technologies, ultimately querying, or modifying data in the database before rendering and serving Web pages.

The Database Machine

Since Oracle's acquisition of Sun Microsystems in January 2010, the corporation has marketed the "Database Machine" and Exadata2. At the time of writing, the minimum specification Database Machine (half rack) comprises of two database servers having the following:

- 2 Quad-Core Intel Xeon E5540 Processors
- 72 GB Memory
- Disk Controller HBA with 512MB Battery Backed Write Cache
- 4 x 146 GB SAS 10,000 RPM disks
- Dual-Port QDR InfiniBand Host Channel Adapter
- 4 Embedded Gigabit Ethernet Ports

Plus the shared storage:

- 3 x Sun Oracle Exadata Storage Servers with 12 x 600 GB 15,000 RPM SAS disks or
- 12 x 2 TB 7,200 RPM SATA disks
- Including 1.1 TB Exadata Smart Flash Cache

The Database Machine is purely supporting the database tier, uniquely designed for Oracle databases, offering very high speed transactional processing capabilities with Exadata V2 storage. This is undoubtedly the "Ferrari" of all database servers, which has proved to be a highly successful product for Oracle. However, Ferrari's are not cheap and nor are Oracle Sun Database Machines! Your design therefore needs to balance the costs against acceptable performance and scalability.

Scaling up and out

Probably one of the most difficult decisions to make in your overall design is whether to scale up or scale out. If you choose to scale up and use a single powerful database server with expansion for additional CPU and memory, this may prove to be a short term solution. Eventually, your application's performance will "hit the buffers" where the database server has no more capacity to scale. To resolve this problem by replacing the server with an even more powerful machine would incur significant costs.

So is the answer to scale out? Not necessarily, scaling out is not without its problems. Considering Oracle RAC as a clustered database solution, where multiple instances hosted on multiple nodes all connect to the same database on shared storage, we move into a world of global cache locking and waits.

Consider a user connected to instance 1 on node A executing a query that causes a full table scan against a long table having over 1 million rows. To try to reduce the cost of I/O, Oracle will look at the global cache to see if the blocks reside in memory. However, had a similar query been executed on a remote node, Oracle will transfer the blocks across the interconnect network between the nodes which may be a slower operation than scanning the underlying disk subsystem. For this reason and to reduce the potential performance overhead, it is possible to configure a 2 node Oracle RAC system in active-passive mode. Here, one instance takes the load while the other instance becomes the redundant standby. But we are back to one node again!

The key is to find the right balance. For example, you would not want to overwhelm your database servers with requests from an enormous array of application servers. The application response time would suffer as the database becomes the bottleneck. It is a case of tuning the system to achieve the best performance across the available hardware. By all means leverage the advantages of Oracle RAC on low cost servers, but make sure your application's SQL is optimized for the database. Look at schema design, table partitioning, even instance partitioning where data can be grouped across the nodes. An example of this would be countries. Users from the UK connect to instance 1, French users to instance 2, German users to instance 3, and so on.

What is important for GoldenGate is the database redo logs. These need to be on shared storage on fast disks and accessible to the Extract processes. It is an Oracle best practice to place the database's online redo logs on fast disks that are striped and mirrored (not RAID 5), because the database is constantly writing to them. RAID5 is slower on write operations as it is not recommended for redo logs. Furthermore, if the I/O is slow, the database performance will suffer as a result of the 'logfile sync' wait event.

Changed data management

It's all very well replicating data in real-time between a source and target database, but what if something disastrous happens to the source data; a user drops a table or deletes important records or the data becomes corrupt? The answer maybe to build a delay into the changed data delivery but this seems to defeat the object of fast data replication. What can be done to manage the changed data, ensuring that only the valid transactions succeed?

There are a number of solutions to this problem, none of which prevent user error or data corruption. Let's now take a look at some of these, which are provided by the Oracle database.

Point in Time Recovery (PITR)

Since Oracle 10*g*, the database provides "flashback" technology allowing the database, a table or even a transaction to be flashed back to a SCN or timestamp. The Flashback technology provides a fast reliable recovery mechanism over the traditional method of performing a point in time recovery.

Oracle Recovery Manager (RMAN)

RMAN supports PITR. However, the database would have to be mounted and not open preventing users from connecting. Furthermore, the database would need to be restored from a backup and then recovered to a specified SCN or timestamp. All this takes time and is unacceptable, particularly with the database offline!

Flashback

A far quicker recovery method is the Oracle 11*g* Flashback technology. Here, a dropped table can be recovered instantaneously from the Recycle Bin by one command and with the database open. It is a similar story for individual for transactions too. These can be backed out using the information provided from a Flashback Transaction Query. The result of adopting these methods would also generate redo that the GoldenGate Extract process would then write to the trail files for onward replication. Therefore, no action is required on the target database.

Should you wish to flashback the whole database to a point in time before the error, Flashback would need to have been enabled at database level. This operation causes the database to generate flashback logs in addition to its redo logs, all of which are written to the Flash Recovery Area (FRA). To recover from data loss or corruption in a GoldenGate environment, it is important to perform the flashback on both source and target databases. This is however, an off-line operation. The GoldenGate Veridata product can be used to perform the data comparison following recovery.

To guard against human error, Flashback technology appears to provide the solution, but what does this mean for GoldenGate? Simply alter your Extract process to start replicating data from the specified timestamp.

 For a bit of insurance and peace of mind, it's worth enabling Flashback on your mission critical source and target databases, making sure you factor in the additional storage requirements for the FRA in your design.

SAN Snapshot

SAN Snapshots provide an alternative solution to PITR. Typically, snaps are scheduled every 30 minutes, capturing a "snapshot" of the data that will provide a restore point. The beauty of the SAN Snapshot is its ability to snap all file types as an online operation; database files, raw files, filesystems etc, which lends itself perfectly to a GoldenGate environment. You no longer need to concern yourself with winding back your database and your Extract process to a point in time, just restore the snap and wind forward to just before the error by applying the database archived logs. The GoldenGate trail and checkpoint files will remain in synchronization with the database as if nothing ever happened. The only issue you may face is having to manually replay any legitimate transactions that occurred after the error or corruption.

Summary

In this chapter, we revisited the GoldenGate topology, this time from a design viewpoint. We discussed the different replication methods and architectures and the hardware associated with each one. Functional and non-functional requirements were evaluated against the cost of hardware resources, encouraging a mindful balance in the overall design. Finally, we concentrated on Backup and Recovery options that are often overlooked, but have huge importance in your GoldenGate implementation.

In the next chapter, we delve a little deeper into the configuration detail, discussing the range and scope of available options and functions that make GoldenGate such a powerful and feature-rich product.

4
Configuring Oracle GoldenGate

Having installed Oracle GoldenGate 10.4, it must be configured in order to meet all of your data replication, data migration, or upgrade requirements. Initially discussing the main GoldenGate parameters, this chapter provides a methodical approach to the configuration process, stepping through each task to give the depth of information necessary to successfully implement GoldenGate on Oracle 11g. Helping to provide the building blocks, this chapter forms the basis for more complex configurations

In this chapter, you will learn about the following:

- Choosing the appropriate Initial Load method to synchronize the source database with the target
- Preparing and configuring the Initial Capture on the source system
- Configuring Change Data Capture on the source system
- Configuring Change Delivery on the target system

If you are a "command-line junkie" you will love this chapter, walking you through the basic steps necessary to configure a One-to-One GoldenGate environment, including data synchronization between the source and target databases.

GoldenGate parameters

Parameters play a huge part in the configuration of GoldenGate. Every configurable process is driven from an associated parameter file. We have already used a handful in *Chapter 2, Installing and Preparing GoldenGate*, giving us a basic configuration following a software install. Let's now look at the scope and application of the GoldenGate parameters used in this chapter.

The following table groups the parameters and their descriptions by process type. This is by no means an exhaustive list, just those parameters we will become familiar with as we continue our journey through the book:

Process	Parameter Name	Parameter Description
MGR	PORT	The TCP/IP port number that the Manager process uses for communication with other processes.
MGR	PURGEOLDEXTRACTS	Enables purging of Extract and Replicat trail files from associated trail locations.
MGR	AUTOSTART	Directs the Manager process to automatically start Extract and Replicat processes.
MGR	AUTORESTART	Directs the Manager process to automatically restart Extract and Replicat processes after failure.
EXTRACT	EXTRACT	Defines the name of the Extract process.
EXTRACT	SOURCEISTABLE	Defines the source as database table. Used in Initial Load only.
EXTRACT	RMTTASK	Configures Extract to communicate directly with Replicat over TCP/IP for direct load Initial Load methods.
EXTRACT	RMTFILE	Defines the location and filename on the remote system where the Extract process writes its data. Used in Initial Load and batch processing operations.
EXTRACT	RMTTRAIL	Configures Extract to write data to a remote trail. Used in the Data Pump Extract parameter file.
EXTRACT	RMTHOST	Defines the remote system's hostname. If a hostname is used, it must resolve to an IP address.

Process	Parameter Name	Parameter Description
EXTRACT	EXTFILE	Defines the name and location for a file used to temporarily store the data changes written to by the Extract process. Used in conjunction with SPECIALRUN for Initial Load and batch processing operations.
EXTRACT	MGRPORT	Defines the Manager Port number.
EXTRACT/ REPLICAT	USERID	Oracle database GGS Admin user ID.
EXTRACT/ REPLICAT	PASSWORD	Oracle database GGS Admin user password.
EXTRACT/ REPLICAT	TABLE	Defines the source (Extract) or target (Replicat) table name.
EXTRACT/ REPLICAT	DISCARDFILE	Defines the name and location of the process discarded data file.
EXTRACT/ REPLICAT	SETENV	Specifies the Oracle environment for GoldenGate connection to the Oracle database. For example, sets the ORACLE_SID environment variable.
REPLICAT	REPLICAT	Defines the name of the Replicat process.
REPLICAT	SPECIALRUN	Indicates the Replicat is a "one-off" process, typically an Initial Load. Use with END RUNTIME parameter.
REPLICAT	RUNTIME	All unprocessed records with timestamps up to the current point in time are processed; otherwise the Replicat process is terminated.
REPLICAT	ASSUMETARGETDEFS	Declares the source tables are identical in structure as the target tables.
REPLICAT	HANDLECOLLISIONS	Directs automatic resolution of duplicate and missing-record errors when applying data on the target database. This parameter is generally only used for the Initial Load.
REPLICAT	MAP	Defines the mapping between source and target tables. Can be used for column mapping and transformations.
REPLICAT	BULKLOAD	Directs the Replicat to use the bulk load method of Initial Load, writing data directly to the SQL*Loader interface

We are now armed with the most common GoldenGate configuration parameters. Let's now choose and create our "Initial Load" method.

Configuring the Initial Load

An Initial Load synchronizes the source and target databases, which is an important first step in data replication. It extracts an entire copy of the source data set, transforms it if necessary, and applies it to the target tables. Data replication can now continue from this point.

One really cool feature is the ability for GoldenGate's "change synchronization" to keep track of ongoing transactional changes while the initial load is being applied. If configured, the Change Data Capture and Delivery concurrent process tracks the incremental changes, which are then reconciled with the results of the Initial Load.

So why is the Initial Load so important? To answer this question, consider an UPDATE statement. By its pure nature the row to be updated must exist on the target table else the transaction will fail. This is also true for DELETE operations. To avoid the ORA-01403 no data found error, synchronize your source and target databases unless your target is configured as INSERT only, in which case DELETE and UPDATE statements won't exist in your apply data stream.

Choosing a method

Various methods exist outside GoldenGate that perform data synchronization:

- Oracle Transportable Tablespaces
- Oracle import/export or Datapump
- Oracle Warehouse Builder or thirrd party ETL tool

We are going to configure Oracle GoldenGate's Initial Load to do this. The advantages for using the GoldenGate method are as follows:

- No application downtime required
- No locking required on source tables
- The data is fetched in arrays of 1000 rows to improve performance
- Parallel processing can be configured using WHERE clauses or the @RANGE function
- GoldenGate Change Delivery can handle collisions with initial load
- Heterogeneous environments are supported

Chapter 4

A number of Initial Load options exist, providing flexible load alternatives. These are as follows:

- File to Replicat
  - ○ A simple method that allows the Extract process to write to a file on the target system that Replicat applies using SQL INSERT statements.

- File to database utility
  - ○ Similar to the Direct Bulk Load method, the Extract process writes to a file formatted for a DB bulk load utility, not just SQL*Loader. This method supports Oracle, DB2, and SQL Server databases.

- Direct Load
  - ○ The standard method of Initial Load and probably the most flexible. The Extract process sends data from the source database tables directly to the Replicat, which applies the data using SQL. This method supports heterogeneous environments and data transformations.

- Direct Bulk Load
  - ○ The Replicat process uses Oracle SQL*Loader API, which offers high data load performance, but with some datatype and security limitations.

The following paragraphs and schematic diagrams explain these methods in more detail.

File to Replicat

The Extract process writes to a file in universal format for the Replicat to load. This is similar in essence to the "normal" GoldenGate method of data replication, used by **Change Data Capture (CDC)**.

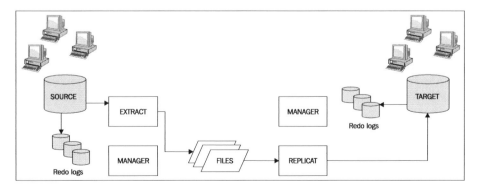

Extract parameters

The *File to Replicat* method uses the parameters SOURCEISTABLE and RMTFILE.

SOURCEISTABLE tells GoldenGate to extract data directly from the source database. RMTFILE defines the name of the extract file on a remote system where the extracted data is written. The PURGE option ensures any previously created extract file is deleted before the operation starts.

```
EXTRACT <name>
SOURCEISTABLE
USERID ggs_admin@<source_database>, PASSWORD <password>
RMTHOST <target_hostname>, MGRPORT <port_number>RMTFILE ./
dirdat/<name>.dat, PURGE
TABLE <source_schema_name>.<table_name>;
```

Once the Initial Load parameter file is saved in the dirprm directory on the source system, the Extract process can be invoked via the Linux command line, calling its necessary configuration from the file. Note the inclusion of a report file in the following command string example, ensuring the task execution results are logged:

```
$ extract paramfile dirprm/initload.prm reportfile dirrpt/initload.rpt
```

Replicat parameters

In addition to the SPECIALRUN parameter, EXTFILE defines the remote filename and location that contains the data needed to synchronize the target database. This method also allows for transformations to be included in the configuration, which are defined in the Replicat parameter file.

```
REPLICAT <name>
SPECIALRUN
USERID ggs_admin@<target_database>, PASSWORD <password>
EXTFILE ./dirdat/<name>.dat
DISCARDFILE ./dirrpt/<name>.dsc, PURGE
ASSUMETARGETDEFS
HANDLECOLLISIONS
MAP <source_schema_name>.*, TARGET <target_schema_name>.*;
END RUNTIME
```

File to database utility

The Extract process writes to ASCII files formatted for database utilities to load, such as SQL*Loader. The SQL*Loader utility has been available since before Oracle 6, when it was the primary method for data loading data. It's no surprise that Oracle 11*g* supports SQL*Loader; it is still used as part of the External table mechanism for reading flat files. It can utilize SQL functions to manipulate the data being read from the input file.

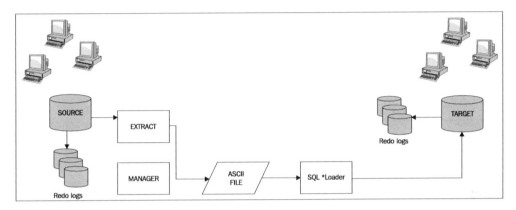

Extract parameters

The File to Database Utility method also uses the parameters SOURCEISTABLE and RMTFILE with the additional parameter FORMATASCII.

FORMATASCII with the SQLLOADER option produces a fixed-length, ASCII-formatted file. SQL*Loader control files are created dynamically on the target database to load the data as part of the process. Other format parameters are FORMATXML and FORMATSQL. The latter is compatible with SQL*Plus for inserting, updating, and deleting data on the target database.

```
EXTRACT <name>
SOURCEISTABLE
USERID ggs_admin@<source_database>, PASSWORD <password>
RMTHOST <target_hostname>, MGRPORT <port_number>
RMTFILE ./dirdat/<name>.dat, PURGE
FORMATASCII, SQLLOADER
TABLE <source_schema>.<table_name>;
```

Ensure that the FORMATASCII parameter is before the RMTFILE parameter, else it will be ignored and a canonical format file will result. If you prefer a comma delimited format file for loading via SQL*Loader manually, this can be achieved using the DELIMITER option shown in the following example, with additional options to suppress header information:

```
SOURCEISTABLE
USERID ggs_admin@oltp, PASSWORD ggs_admin
RMTHOST dbserver2, MGRPORT 7809
FORMATASCII, DELIMITER ',', NONAMES, NOHDRFIELDS, PLACEHOLDERS
RMTFILE ./dirdat/INITLOAD01.DAT, PURGE
TABLE HR.DEPARTMENTS;
```

This produces just the table data as shown in the following output:

```
10,'Administration',200,1700

20,'Marketing',201,1800

30,'Purchasing',114,1700

40,'Human Resources',203,2400
```

In comparison, using FORMATASCII, SQLLOADER produces the following:

IAN10	NAdministration	N200	N1700
IAN20	NMarketing	N201	N1800
IAN30	NPurchasing	N114	N1700
IAN40	NHuman Resources	N203	N2400

Replicat parameters

There are no Replicat parameters required, as the load is handled by SQL*Loader.

Direct Load

The Extract process writes directly to the Replicat which loads the data via SQL. A batch process is started dynamically by the Manager process which does not require the use of a Data Collector or Initial Load file. The Replicat converts the data stream to SQL INSERT statements which are applied directly to the target database.

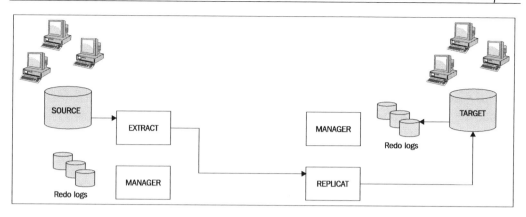

Extract parameters

The Direct Load method uses the parameters SOURCEISTABLE and RMTTASK. RMTTASK instructs the Manager process on the target system to start a Replicat process with the group name specified in the GROUP clause. Ideally, the Extract Group name should be different from the Replicat group name. I prefer to specify an "E" prefix for Extracts and an "R" for Replicats.

```
EXTRACT <name>
SOURCEISTABLE
USERID ggs_admin@<source_database>, PASSWORD <password>
RMTHOST <remote_hostname>, MGRPORT <port_number>
RMTTASK REPLICAT, GROUP <name>
TABLE <source_schema>.*;
```

Replicat parameters

The parameter SPECIALRUN specifies a one-time batch process. Note that checkpoints are not maintained. If the job fails it will need to be restarted. The advantage of using a Replicat process to control the load, is its ability to perform data transformations. These can be configured in the Replicat's parameter file and adopted in the Change Delivery configuration.

```
REPLICAT <name>
SPECIALRUN
USERID ggs_admin@<target_database>, PASSWORD <password>
ASSUMETARGETDEFS
MAP <source_schema_name>.*, TARGET <target_schema_name>.*;END RUNTIME
```

Direct Bulk Load

The Extract process writes directly to the Replicat process, which loads data using the SQL*Loader API. This is the fastest method, sending data to the SQL*Loader utility to load data as a Direct Path Bulk Load. A Direct Path operation bypasses the SQL parser making data loading much quicker. LOB datatypes and data encryption are not supported by SQL*Loader. In these cases, use the File to Replicat method of Initial Load.

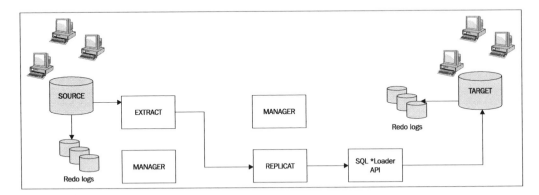

Extract parameters

The Direct Bulk Load method uses the parameters SOURCEISTABLE and RMTFILE. The Initial Load is started by the Extract process on the source system. On the target, the Replicat process will be started dynamically by the Manager process.

```
EXTRACT <name>
SOURCEISTABLE
USERID ggs_admin@<source_database>, PASSWORD <password>
RMTHOST <remote_hostname>, MGRPORT <port_number>
RMTTASK REPLICAT, GROUP <name>
TABLE <source_schema>.*;
```

Replicat parameters

In addition to the SPECIALRUN parameter, BULKLOAD distinguishes this process from the normal Direct Load method.

Like the File to Database Initial Load, this method does not require the manual creation of an SQL*Loader control file, as this is generated automatically as part of the API.

```
REPLICAT <name>
SPECIALRUN
BULKLOAD
USERID ggs_admin@<target_database>, PASSWORD <password>
ASSUMETARGETDEFS
MAP <source_schema_name>.*, TARGET <target_schema_name>.*;
END RUNTIME
```

Having chosen and configured an Initial Load method, it's time to enable the data synchronization process. The next section describes how to perform the Initial Load preparing GoldenGate for *Change Data Capture and Delivery*.

Performing the Initial Load

Let's now step through the necessary tasks required to perform an Initial Load using the *File to Replicat* method. For small and simple data synchronization with no transformations, this is the preferred solution.

Example architecture

This example assumes the target tables are truncated and are identical in structure to the source tables. The configuration includes the following methods:

Initial Load: File to Replicat data synchronization

One-to-One: Change Data Capture and Delivery

The system schematic diagram below illustrates the architecture and naming convention used in this chapter's examples:

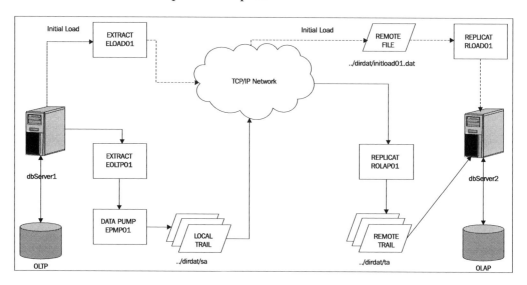

File to Replicat method

We will be using the *File to Replicat* method to perform our Initial Load, starting with the Initial Data Capture configuration.

Configuring Initial Data Capture

The first step is to create the Initial Data Capture Extract parameter file for EMP and DEPT tables that exist in the SRC schema of the OLTP source database. The SRC schema is based on the Oracle example SCOTT/TIGER schema that is included with the database.

1. Log on to the database server (as the oracle user).

2. Change directory to the GoldenGate home.

    ```
    cd /home/oracle/ggs
    ```

3. Run GGSCI.

    ```
    ggsci
    ```

4. Execute the following commands on the source system to create an Extract named ELOAD01:

    ```
    GGSCI (dbserver1) 1> EDIT PARAMS ELOAD01

    SOURCEISTABLE
    ```

```
USERID ggs_admin@oltp, PASSWORD ggs_admin
RMTHOST dbserver2, MGRPORT 7809
RMTFILE ./dirdat/INITLOAD01.DAT, PURGE
TABLE SRC.DEPT;
TABLE SRC.EMP;


GGSCI (dbserver1) 2> EXIT
```

The SOURCEISTABLE parameter is used in the Initial Data Capture telling the Extract process to extract the data directly from the database tables. The data is then written to a single data file on the remote system, in universal format that will later be read by the Replicat process.

 It is important to list your tables in referential order, that is, the parent table before the child. Otherwise, the Replicat process will abend to ORA-02291: integrity constraint violated.

1. You can start the initial load Extract directly from the Linux command line using the following command:

   ```
   extract paramfile dirprm/eload01.prm reportfile dirrpt/ELOAD01.rpt
   ```

2. To confirm the Extract process has started, we can use the following GGSCI command:

   ```
   GGSCI (dbserver1) 1> INFO EXTRACT ELOAD01

   EXTRACT     ENMHMSG    Last Started 2010-06-19 17:10:01    Status
   RUNNING
   ```

3. The report file generated for the Data Capture Extract process and can be viewed using the following GGSCI command:

   ```
   GGSCI (dbserver1) 2> VIEW REPORT ELOAD01

   ./dirrpt/ELOAD01.rpt

   ***************************************************************
                    Oracle GoldenGate Capture for Oracle
                        Version 10.4.0.19 Build 002
       Linux, x86, 32bit (optimized), Oracle 11 on Sep 29 2009
   08:57:20


   Copyright (C) 1995, 2009, Oracle and/or its affiliates.  All
   rights reserved.
   ```

The following is a sample of a report produced by the Extract process which includes the number of inserted records per table:

```
****************************************************************
**              Running with the following parameters         **
****************************************************************
SOURCEISTABLE

2010-06-19 17:10:02  GGS INFO      414  Wildcard resolution set to
IMMEDIATE because SOURCEISTABLE is used.
USERID ggs_admin@oltp, PASSWORD ********
RMTHOST dbserver2, MGRPORT 7809
RMTFILE ./dirdat/INITLOAD01.DAT, PURGE
TABLE SRC.DEPT;

Using the following key columns for source table SRC.DEPT: DEPTNO.
TABLE SRC.EMP;

2010-06-19 17:10:03  GGS INFO      Z0-05M  Output file ./dirdat/
INITLOAD01.DAT is using format RELEASE 10.4.

2010-06-19 17:10:08  GGS INFO      406  Socket buffer size set to 27985
(flush size 27985).

Processing table SRC.DEPT

Processing table SRC.EMP

****************************************************************
*                 ** Run Time Statistics **                    *
****************************************************************

Report at 2010-06-19 17:10:08 (activity since 2010-06-19 17:10:03)

Output to ./dirdat/INITLOAD01.DAT:

From Table SRC.DEPT:
       #                    inserts:        4
       #                    updates:        0
       #                    deletes:        0
       #                    discards:       0
From Table SRC.EMP:
       #                    inserts:        14
```

```
#              updates:        0
#              deletes:        0
#              discards:       0
```

Although not a huge amount of data, the example demonstrates the Initial Data Capture Extract process, combining runtime statistics with environment settings and configuration. All GoldenGate reports generated by the GGSCI tool share this format. You will quickly become familiar with this when monitoring GoldenGate processes.

If the report shows NO errors and the data extract was successful, we can now configure the Initial Data Delivery on the target system.

Configuring Initial Data Delivery

On our target system dbserver2, we now have 1 DAT file containing the Initial Load data. The following steps load the data into the EMP and DEPT tables in the TGT schema of the OLAP target database:

1. Log on to the database server (as Oracle).

2. Change directory to the GoldenGate home.

   ```
   cd /home/oracle/ggs
   ```

3. Run GGSCI.

   ```
   ggsci
   ```

4. Execute the following commands on the target system to create a Replicat parameter file for the associated RLOAD01 process.

   ```
   GGSCI (dbserver2) 1> EDIT PARAMS RLOAD01
   REPLICAT RLOAD01
   SPECIALRUN
   ASSUMETARGETDEFS
   HANDLECOLLISIONS
   USERID ggs_admin@olap, PASSWORD ggs_admin
   EXTFILE ./dirdat/INITLOAD01.DAT
   DISCARDFILE ./dirrpt/RLOAD01.dsc, PURGE
   MAP SRC.*, TARGET TGT.*;
   END RUNTIME
   ```

The ASSUMETARGETDEFS parameter assumes the source and target tables are identical, making column mapping declarations unnecessary. The Data Mapping section in *Chapter 7, Advanced Configuration*, discusses the mapping requirements for non-identical source and target tables using a definitions file.

Another shortcut in the configuration is the use of Wildcards for the target tables. There is little point painstakingly declaring every single table mapping in the parameter file, when GoldenGate knows to load the whole data file.

The HANDLECOLLISIONS parameter tells the Replicat process to resolve duplicate and missing-record errors when applying data on the target database. This parameter is generally only used for the Initial Load.

As we delve deeper into GoldenGate commands, we will see that Wildcards are supported in most cases—a very useful feature!

The DISCARDFILE parameter defines the discard file that contains the records that fail to load. The PURGE option ensures the discard file is deleted each time the load operation is repeated.

1. Staying with the GGSCI command line on the target system, add the special run Replicat process and exit GGSCI:

```
GGSCI (dbserver2) 2> ADD REPLICAT RLOAD01, EXTFILE ./dirdat/
INITLOAD01.DAT

REPLICAT added.

GGSCI (dbserver2) 3> exit
```

2. Now execute the following command to perform the data load:

```
cd /home/oracle/ggs

replicat paramfile dirprm/rload01.prm reportfile dirrpt/RLOAD01.
rpt
```

3. Run GGSCI again and view the Replicat report for the Initial Load ensuring there are no errors.

```
ggsci

GGSCI (dbserver2) 1> VIEW REPORT RLOAD01
```

Now that our Initial Load is complete and both source and target database schemas are synchronized, we can enable data replication, which can be broken into two distinct processes:

- **Change Data Capture (CDC)**

  This includes the Extract and Data Pump process that extracts the data changes from the redo logs and writes the changes to GoldenGate local and remote Trail files.

- **Change Delivery**

   It is the Replicat process that reads the remote Trail and applies the data natively to the target database.

Configuring Change Data Capture

Oracle recommends that Change Data Capture (CDC) is configured and started before the Initial Load. This enables "change synchronization" to keep track of ongoing transactional changes while the load is being applied—a very useful feature when you cannot afford for your source system to be taken offline. In fact GoldenGate can manage and combine the online transactional changes plus the initial data extract with ease, ensuring no data loss or down-time.

So let's take a look at the steps required to configure and start CDC.

As stated in Chapter 1, the Extract process extracts only committed transactions from the database's redologs. The first task, therefore, is to create the Extract process.

1. Log on to the source database server (as oracle).

2. Change directory to the GoldenGate home.

    ```
    cd /home/oracle/ggs
    ```

3. Start GGSCI.

4. Execute the following commands on the source system to create a parameter file for the Extract process named EOLTP01:

    ```
    GGSCI (dbserver1) 1> EDIT PARAMS EOLTP01

    EXTRACT EOLTP01

    SETENV (ORACLE_SID=oltp)

    USERID ggs_admin, PASSWORD ggs_admin

    EXTTRAIL ./dirdat/sa

    TABLE SRC.DEPT;

    TABLE SRC.EMP;
    ```

    The EXTRACT parameter defines the name of the Extract process.

    The EXTTRAIL parameter defines the directory and file prefix for the trail files.

    Explicitly defining the ORACLE_SID using the SETENV parameter is an alternative method of connection to the source database.

5. Add the Extract process EOLTP01 using GGSCI:

```
GGSCI (dbserver1) 2> add extract EOLTP01, tranlog, begin now,
threads 1
EXTRACT added.
```

Specifying TRANLOG tells the Extract process to read the database's online redologs. We have also requested that the CDC should begin now for the single instance source database.

1. Now add the associated trail files for Extract EOLTP01.

```
GGSCI (dbserver1) 3> add exttrail ./dirdat/sa, extract EOLTP01,
megabytes 5
EXTRACT added.
```

The above GGSCI command will create a local trail, each trail file having a maximum size of 5 Megabytes and file prefix "sa".

2. Let's configure a Data Pump Extract process named EPMP01, to send the data to the remote system.

```
GGSCI (dbserver1) 4> EDIT PARAMS EPMP01
EXTRACT EPMP01
PASSTHRU
RMTHOST dbserver2, MGRPORT 7809
RMTTRAIL ./dirdat/ta
TABLE SRC.DEPT;
TABLE SRC.EMP;
```

The PASSTHRU parameter specifies that no transformations are to be made to the extracted data. Therefore, no table definition lookup in the database is necessary and the data is allowed to pass through from source to target.

Data Pump is an Extract process and therefore references source objects. Be sure to include the source schema tables in its parameter file, else Data Pump will not send the extracted data to the Replicat process.

1. Add the Data Pump process EPMP01 using GGSCI, associating it with the newly created local source trail.

```
GGSCI (dbserver1) 5> add extract EPMP01, exttrailsource ./dirdat/
sa
EXTRACT added.
```

2. Then add the remote trail from the source system using GGSCI.

```
GGSCI (dbserver1) 6> add rmttrail ./dirdat/ta, EXTRACT EPMP01,
megabytes 10

RMTTRAIL added.
```

The above GGSCI command will create a remote trail, each trail file having a maximum size of 10 Megabytes and file prefix "ta".

3. Finally, we can now start our Extract processes as follows:

```
GGSCI (dbserver1) 7> start EXTRACT *

Sending START request to MANAGER ...
EXTRACT EOLTP01 starting

Sending START request to MANAGER ...
EXTRACT EPMP01 starting
```

4. Check the processes are running using the GGSCI command INFO ALL.

```
GGSCI (dbserver1) 8> INFO ALL
```

Program	Status	Group	Lag	Time Since Chkpt
MANAGER	RUNNING			
EXTRACT	RUNNING	EOLTP01	00:00:00	00:00:02
EXTRACT	RUNNING	EPMP01	00:00:00	00:00:00

Should a processes abend, a report file will automatically be generated. The following example would display the error report for the EOLTP Extract process:

```
GGSCI (dbserver1) 9> view REPORT EOLTP01
```

With our data extract and propagation working, it's time to configure the delivery. The next section walks through the necessary steps to create, configure, and start the Replicat process.

Configuring Change Delivery

Change Delivery is the process of applying the transactions that contain the data changes from the source database to the target database. As we know, this is the responsibility of the Replicat process. The Replicat extracts the pure DML and DDL from the remote trail files and applies them on the target database. This process can often cause a bottleneck, depending on the volume of data being replicated. Oracle recommends multiple Replicats to enable parallel processing to enhance performance.

For this example, we shall create just one Replicat named ROLAP01.

Before we create and configure our Replicat process, we must first create a Checkpoint table in the target database. The Checkpoint table keeps track of all the GoldenGate checkpoints and sequences that support recovery following a shutdown or failure.

Although a Checkpoint table is optional, Oracle highly recommends it over the Checkpoint file as it enables the checkpoint to be included within Replicat's transaction, ensuring complete recovery from all failure scenarios.

1. Log on to the target database server (as oracle).
2. Change directory to the GoldenGate home.

   ```
   cd /home/oracle/ggs
   ```

3. Start GGSCI.

   ```
   ggsci
   ```

   Define the Checkpoint table in the GoldenGate global parameters file.

   ```
   GGSCI (dbserver2) 1> EDIT PARAMS ./GLOBALS
   CHECKPOINTTABLE ggs_admin.ggschkpt
   ```

   Exit and Start GGSCI for the new configuration to take effect.

   ```
   GGSCI (dbserver2) 2> EXIT
   ggsci

   GGSCI (dbserver2) 1>
   ```

Log on to the target database as the `ggs_admin` user from the GGSCI command line.

```
GGSCI (dbserver2) 2> dblogin userid ggs_admin, password ggs_admin
Successfully logged into database.
```

Create the Checkpoint table in the `GGS_ADMIN` schema.

```
GGSCI (dbserver2) 3>  add checkpointtable
No checkpoint table specified, using GLOBALS specification (ggs_admin.
ggschkpt)...

Successfully created checkpoint table GGS_ADMIN.GGSCHKPT.
```

Now we can create the Replicat parameter file using GGSCI.

```
GGSCI (dbserver2) 4> EDIT PARAMS ROLAP01
   REPLICAT ROLAP01
   SETENV (ORACLE_SID=OLAP)
```

```
USERID ggs_admin, PASSWORD ggs_admin
ASSUMETARGETDEFS
DISCARDFILE ./dirrpt/rolap01.dsc, PURGE
MAP SRC.DEPT, TGT.DEPT;
MAP SRC.EMP, TGT.EMP;
```

1. Add the Replicat using the following GGSCI command:

   ```
   GGSCI (dbserver2) 5> add replicat ROLAP01, exttrail ./dirdat/ta

   REPLICAT added.
   ```

   The above GGSCI command will create a Replicat process named ROLAP01, associating it with the trail file we defined in the Data Pump configuration, having a file prefix "ta".

2. To complete the Change Delivery configuration, we can now start our Replicat process as follows:

   ```
   GGSCI (dbserver2) 6> start REPLICAT *


   Sending START request to MANAGER ...
   REPLICAT ROLAP01 starting
   ```

3. Check the processes are running.

   ```
   GGSCI (dbserver2) 7> INFO ALL

   Program      Status      Group       Lag          Time Since Chkpt

   MANAGER      RUNNING

   REPLICAT     RUNNING     ROLAP01     00:00:00     00:00:02
   ```

   As mentioned previously in the Extract configuration, should a processes abend, a report file will automatically be generated. The following example would display the error report for the ROLAP01 Replicat process:

   ```
   GGSCI (dbserver2) 8> view REPORT ROLAP01
   ```

With all configured processes running on both source and target systems, any data changes made to the defined source tables will be captured and sent to the target. Let's test it and see!

Testing Change Data Capture and Delivery

To test if the CDC is working we must make some data changes on our source database and ensure that they are propagated to and applied on the target. The following simple steps provide a basic test case that will confirm all is well:

1. On the source database server, start a SQL*Plus session and connect to the OLTP database as the SRC user.

    ```
    sqlplus SRC/SRC@OLTP

    SQL>
    ```

2. Insert a new record into the DEPT table and commit the transaction.

    ```
    SQL> INSERT INTO dept VALUES (50, 'TEST', 'LONDON');


    1 row created.


    SQL> COMMIT;

    Commit complete.
    ```

    Issuing a commit forces Oracle to write the transaction details to the database's online redo logs. These are subsequently read by the Extract process (EOLTP01) in real-time and written to the local trail. The transaction in the local trail is read by the Data Pump process (EPMP01) that transfers the data via TCP/IP to the remote trail. The Replicat process (ROLAP01) reads the remote trail, converts the transaction data to DML and applies it to the database.

3. On the target database server, start a SQL*Plus session and connect to the OLAP database as the TGT user.

    ```
    sqlplus TGT/TGT@OLAP

    SQL>
    ```

4. Query the DEPT table to see if the new row exists.

    ```
    SQL> SELECT * FROM dept WHERE deptno = 50;


        DEPTNO DNAME          LOC
    ---------- -------------- -------------
            50 TEST           LONDON
    ```

The row exists! We have successfully configured and tested GoldenGate real-time data replication.

We can generate and view a report for a given process by issuing the following GGSCI commands:

```
SEND <PROCESS_TYPE> <PROCESS_GROUP_NAME>, REPORT

VIEW REPORT < PROCESS_GROUP_NAME>
```

The following example shows the runtime statistics section of the Replicat process ROLAP01 report:

```
GGSCI (dbserver2) 1> send REPLICAT ROLAP01, report

Sending REPORT request to REPLICAT ROLAP01 …

Request processed.

GGSCI (dbserver2) 2> view report ROLAP01


*****************************************************************
*                 ** Run Time Statistics **                    *
*****************************************************************


Last record for the last committed transaction is the following:


Trail name :   ./dirdat/ta000001

Hdr-Ind     :    E   (x45)     Partition   :    .   (x04)

UndoFlag    :    .   (x00)     BeforeAfter:     A   (x41)

RecLength   :   38   (x0026)   IO Time     : 2010-06-26 20:25:49.000368

IOType      :    5   (x05)     OrigNode    :   255   (xff)

TransInd    :    .   (x03)     FormatType  :    R   (x52)

SyskeyLen   :    0   (x00)     Incomplete  :    .   (x00)

AuditRBA    :        78        AuditPos    : 44639248

Continued   :    N   (x00)     RecCount    :    1   (x01)


2010-06-26 20:25:49.000368 Insert            Len     38 RBA 577

Name: SRC.DEPT


Reading ./dirdat/ta000001, current RBA 726, 1 records
```

```
Report at 2010-06-26 20:26:44 (activity since 2010-06-26 20:25:58)


From Table SRC.DEPT to TGT.DEPT:
      #                   inserts:          1
      #                   updates:          0
      #                   deletes:          0
      #                   discards:         0
```

Sure enough, our one record insert is reported. From the runtime statistics we see the SQL operation was an INSERT, which is an After image.

Stopping GoldenGate processes

We have seen how to start the Manager, Extract, and Replicat processes using GGSCI commands. Let's take a look at stopping them. Issuing a stop command will gracefully shutdown the GoldenGate processes.

1. Firstly check which processes are running.

   ```
   GGSCI (dbserver1) 1> info all

   Program      Status      Group       Lag         Time Since Chkpt

   MANAGER      RUNNING

   EXTRACT      RUNNING     EOLTP01     00:00:00    00:00:01

   EXTRACT      RUNNING     EPMP01      00:00:00    00:00:02
   ```

2. Stop ALL processes, using a wildcard.

   ```
   GGSCI (dbserver1) 2> stop *

   Sending STOP request to EXTRACT EOLTP01 ...
   Request processed.

   Sending STOP request to EXTRACT EPMP01 ...
   Request processed.
   ```

3. Check the processes again.

   ```
   GGSCI (dbserver1) 3> info all

   Program      Status      Group       Lag         Time Since Chkpt

   MANAGER      RUNNING
   EXTRACT      STOPPED     EOLTP01     00:00:00    00:00:01
   EXTRACT      STOPPED     EPMP01      00:00:00    00:00:02
   ```

4. Note that the Manager process is still running. This has to be stopped explicitly.

```
GGSCI (dbserver1) 4> stop MGR

Manager process is required by other GGS processes.

Are you sure you want to stop it (y/n)? y


Sending STOP request to MANAGER ...

Request processed.

Manager stopped.
```

The GoldenGate support for wildcards is very useful and available in some administrative GGSCI commands such as START, STOP, and INFO. Should a process already be in a **RUNNING** or **STOPPED** state, the command will succeed, but a warning message will be echoed to the screen. This is illustrated in the following screenshot:

One of the main components of the CDC process is the Trail file. Let's take a look at their role and how we can configure GoldenGate to manage them.

More about trail files

Trail files are used by Extract and Replicat processes, and their primary role is for data persistence. One could argue that writing files to what could be deemed as a "staging area" is wasteful and suboptimal. That said, GoldenGate writes to trail files in large blocks minimizing I/O. Furthermore, the architecture provides a guaranteed no data loss solution that is not to be underestimated.

The trail

By default, trail files are in canonical format being unstructured with a header record. Each record is of a variable record length containing the changed data. A trail can contain numerous trail files each having a two-character prefix with a 6 digit sequence number suffix.

An Extract process can write data to many trails. A Replicat can process data from one trail. However, it is possible to configure multiple Replicat processes to handle the workload.

Trail file purging

To "clean up" the processed trail files from a given trail to reduce disk space usage, configure the Manager process to delete consumed trail files. Although it is possible to add the PURGEOLDEXTRACTS parameter to Extract and Replicat parameter files, it is recommended that the Manager process controls the deletion of trail files centrally, thus preventing a process deleting files that are required by another process. The example MGR.prm file below illustrates this:

```
GGSCI (dbserver1) 1> VIEW PARAMS MGR

-- GoldenGate Manager parameter file

PORT 7809

PURGEOLDEXTRACTS /ggs/dirdat/sa*, USECHECKPOINTS, MINKEEPHOURS 1
```

The USECHECKPOINT option tells the Manager not to delete trail files until the checkpoint confirms the file as processed. This is based on the checkpoints of both Extract and Replicat processes before purging. An additional option is the MINKEEPHOURS which ensures the check pointed trail files are kept on disk for a minimum period (in hours).

Configuring the Manager process

In *Chapter 2, Installing and Preparing GoldenGate*, we discussed the PORT parameter that is mandatory to the GoldenGate Manager process communication. In the previous section we learnt how to set a retention period for trail files in the Manager configuration. Let's take a look at some additional, highly useful Manager parameters, AUTOSTART and AUTORESTART.

In the following example, AUTOSTART tells the Manager to start the Extract and Replicat processes when the Manager process starts. AUTORESTART instructs the Manager process to restart just the Extract process(es) after two minutes, should the Extract process(es) fail. In this instance, the Manager will retry five times before abending the processes.

```
AUTOSTART ER *
AUTORESTART EXTRACT *, WAITMINUTES 2, RETRIES 5
```

Summary

The examples given in this chapter are of the most basic form. However, they illustrate the configuration process, providing a greater understanding of the GoldenGate architecture.

We have learnt how to configure the Extract and Replicat processes for different load methods from Initial Load to Change Data Capture and Delivery. We understand the importance of data synchronization between a source and target database in a replication environment. Also the starting point, known as "instantiation", which defines the point in time where you wish to start data replication.

We have discovered that there are many parameters and options, together with the available functions, offering enormous scope and flexibility. In the next chapter, we look at the different configuration options available to GoldenGate, such as data encryption, data compression, batch loading, and DDL replication, including heterogeneous environments.

5
Configuration Options

This chapter is dedicated to the additional configuration options available in Oracle GoldenGate 10.4. These are powerful options allowing your configuration to extend in functionality and performance. We start with a performance enhancing option, allowing SQL statements to be grouped and applied as a batch against a target database. Later, we explore the security features, including data compression and encryption, take a look at heterogeneous environments, and finally discuss the tools available to monitor DDL replication.

This chapter explains the following configuration options:

- Batching SQL by operation type
- Understanding the GoldenGate SQL cache
- Data compression techniques
- Data and password encryption methods
- Triggering an action from an event
- Loop and conflict detection
- DDL replication

Using BATCHSQL

In default mode the Replicat process will apply SQL to the target database, one statement at a time. This often causes a performance bottleneck where the Replicat process cannot apply the changes quickly enough, compared to the rate at which the Extract process delivers the data. Despite configuring additional Replicat processes, performance may still be a problem.

GoldenGate has addressed this issue through the use of the BATCHSQL Replicat configuration parameter. As the name implies, BATCHSQL organizes similar SQLs into batches and applies them all at once. The batches are assembled into arrays in a memory queue on the target database server, ready to be applied.

Similar SQL statements would be those that perform a specific operation type (insert, update, or delete) against the same target table, having the same column list. For example, multiple inserts into table A would be in a different batch from inserts into table B, as would updates on table A or B. Furthermore, referential constraints are considered by GoldenGate where dependant transactions in different batches are executed first, depicting the order in which batches are executed. Despite the referential integrity constraints, BATCHSQL can increase Replicat performance significantly.

SQL cache

The GoldenGate SQL cache is very similar in operation to the Oracle RDBMS Library cache, where SQL statements are parsed and retained in memory for numerous subsequent executions. In GoldenGate, SQL statements are processed by BATCHSQL and also cached in memory. Similarly, each statement type is prepared once, cached, and executed many times with different values. Old statements are recycled using a least-recently-used algorithm, controlled by the MAXSQLSTATEMENTS parameter. This Replicat parameter has a default and maximum size of 250, which is deemed sufficient to store open cursors for both normal and BATCHSQL processing.

It is possible to manage the memory allocation further through Replicat parameters that control the number of batches, the number of allowed operations, and the maximum available memory per queue. The associated parameters are listed as follows:

- BATCHESPERQUEUE: Specifies the maximum number of batches per queue. The default is 50.

- BYTESPERQUEUE: Specifies the maximum number of bytes per queue. The default is 20 MB.

- OPSPERBATCH: Specifies the maximum number of row operations per batch. The default is 1200.

- OPSPERQUEUE: Specifies the maximum number of row operations a memory queue containing multiple batches can contain. The default is also 1200.

When any of the above maximum values is reached, the batched transaction must fire, releasing memory for new transactions to be queued.

The following is an example extract from a Replicat parameter file. Here, BATCHSQL is configured with optional parameters BATCHESPERQUEUE and OPSPERBATCH:

```
REPLICAT ROLAP01
SETENV (ORACLE_SID=OLAP)
USERID ggs_admin, PASSWORD ggs_admin
DISCARDFILE ./dirrpt/rolap01.dsc, PURGE
BATCHSQL BATCHESPERQUEUE 100, OPSPERBATCH 2000
```

 Although the BATCHSQL optional parameters can be tuned, very little gain in performance can result from adjusting these from their default settings.

Exceptions

When using BATCHSQL, exceptions are handled automatically in two distinct ways. Should an exception occur, the Replicat process rolls back the entire batch and replays the transactions in "normal" mode within the transaction boundaries set by the GROUPTRANSOPS parameter. If this fails, the Replicat replays the SQL transactions in the order they occurred on the source database.

In addition, when using BATCHSQL with the BATCHERRORMODE parameter, exception handling is enhanced. GoldenGate will automatically convert INSERT to UPDATE statements that fail due to duplicate data errors, such as ORA-00001: "unique constraint violated". Also, DELETE statements are ignored if the Primary Key for the target table is not found, such as ORA 1403: "no data found" error.

Oracle Large Objects (LOBs) and rows greater than 25KB are not supported by BATCHSQL. If found in a batch queue, they are treated as exceptions. In this case; GoldenGate flushes the whole batch, the Replicat process replays the exceptions in normal mode, and then resumes in batch mode. Therefore, ensure BATCHSQL is disabled for LOB data to avoid the potential performance overhead.

When to use BATCHSQL

The highest performance gains are achieved with BATCHSQL working on high throughput, but with very small transactions. Ideally, individual data changes of less than 100 bytes per row. Oracle quote that up to 300 percent performance gains are possible, but this is largely dependent on your application and hardware footprint.

BATCHSQL is supported for Initial Loads as well as Data Change Capture.

If you find your Replicat processes are a bottleneck then it is worth configuring BATCHSQL as it is self managed, able to fall back to normal mode, and above all maintains data integrity.

Data compression

Oracle GoldenGate offers data compression at the network layer, enhancing data transfer rates. Once configured in the Extract or Data Pump process parameter file, the Server Collector process on the target machine automatically decompresses the data before writing to the remote trail files.

Compressing the Data Stream

Depending on your data, the maximum compression ratio can exceed 5:1, which will help transfer speeds on low bandwidth networks. However, additional CPU utilization is possible when compared to no data compression, which is the default.

If compression is enabled, the following statistics are available in the Extract process report, requested via the GGSCI SEND command with the GETTCPSTATS argument:

- **Compression CPU time**: The time in seconds the process used the CPU resource.

- **Compress time**: The overall time the compression tool takes including waits on CPU resource.

- **Uncompressed bytes and compressed bytes**: Includes detail on the amount of compression taking place. It is worth using this metric to compare the compression ratio with the compression rate (compressed bytes per second) to determine if data compression is beneficial in terms of CPU resource verses network throughput.

The following example shows TCP/IP statistics from the GGSCI command:

```
GGSCI (dbserver1) 1> send EXTRACT EPMP01, gettcpstats

Sending GETTCPSTATS request to EXTRACT EPMP01 ...

RMTTRAIL ./dirdat/ta000039, RBA     5845374

OK

Session Index    0

Stats started 2010/08/28 15:06:19.585484          0:21:01.819545

Local address 192.168.1.65:7100    Remote address 192.168.1.66:41502

Inbound Msgs        12186    Bytes        145496,       115 bytes/second

Outbound Msgs       12187    Bytes      22088920,     17516 bytes/second
```

```
Recvs                   24372
Sends                   12187
Avg bytes per recv          5, per msg     11
Avg bytes per send       1812, per msg   1812
Recv Wait Time       22785734, per msg   1869, per recv   934
Send Wait Time        4199929, per msg    344, per send   344
Data compression is enabled
Compress CPU Time       0:00:00.000000
Compress time           0:00:05.027419, Threshold 512
Uncompressed bytes         296386887
Compressed bytes           22016692, 58958998 bytes/second
```

The COMPRESS option

The following example Data Pump process parameter file has the COMPRESS option configured:

```
EXTRACT EPMP01
PASSTHRU
RMTHOST dbserver2, MGRPORT 7809, COMPRESS, COMPRESSTHRESHOLD 512
RMTTRAIL ./dirdat/ta
```

The additional associated COMPRESSTHRESHOLD parameter specifies the minimum number of bytes in a block at which compression occurs.

The block size can be derived from the report generated by the following **GGSCI INFO** command (in the "Write Checkpoint" section):

```
GGSCI (dbserver1) 1> INFO EPMP01, SHOWCH

..

Write Checkpoint #1

  GGS Log Trail

  Current Checkpoint (current write position):
    Sequence #: 28
    RBA: 8832166
    Timestamp: 2010-08-28 15:17:16.674431
    Extract Trail: ./dirdat/ta

Header:
```

```
  Version = 2
  Record Source = A
  Type = 1
  # Input Checkpoints = 1
  # Output Checkpoints = 1

File Information:
  Block Size = 2048
  Max Blocks = 100
  Record Length = 2048
  Current Offset = 0

Configuration:
  Data Source = 0
  Transaction Integrity = 1
  Task Type = 0

Status:
  Start Time = 2010-08-28 15:06:14
  Last Update Time = 2010-08-28 15:17:16
  Stop Status = A
  Last Result = 400
```

The SHOWCH argument of the INFO command displays checkpoint information.

Oracle table compression

It's worth mentioning in this section that Oracle GoldenGate 10.4 does not support data replication from compressed tables, partitions or tablespaces. Nor does it support the use of Hybrid Columnar Compression, which is a new compression technology featured in Oracle 11*g* Release 2 that utilizes Exadata storage. This is because Oracle compresses data by eliminating duplicate values within a data-block. Currently, GoldenGate cannot extract the duplicate data from the redo stream.

Security features

GoldenGate offers the following security features to protect both data and passwords:

- Data encryption
- Password encryption

In this section, you will learn what these encryption methods are and how to configure them.

Data encryption

GoldenGate offers two data encryption options: Message encryption and Trail file encryption.

Message encryption uses Blowfish, a symmetric 64-bit block cipher that encrypts the individual messages sent over TCP/IP. The data is automatically decrypted by the Server Collector process running on the target machine. The Server Collector process is normally started automatically with default parameters on the remote system, so on this occasion, we need to start this manually. Once configured, the Server Collector process will start automatically in encrypted mode when you start the Extract and Replicat. It dynamically chooses a port in the available range specified by the Manager process parameters.

Trail file encryption uses 256 key byte substitution. The data record in the Trail or Extract file is automatically decrypted by the Data Pump or Replicat process. For completely secure data transmission, it is necessary to configure both Message and Trail file encryption.

To enable data encryption in GoldenGate, we first need to generate keys. This is achieved through the keygen Linux utility. The configuration steps are as follows.

1. Generate a key or multiple keys using the keygen Linux utility on both source and target database servers. The following command creates a 128 bit key. Blowfish accepts keys of lengths between 32 and 128 bits.

   ```
   [oracle@dbserver1 ggs]$ keygen 128 1
   0x2FC65F7E6339F70F466807493EA8C003
   ```

2. Create a file named ENCKEYS in the GoldenGate home on both servers using a text editor such as vi and add the following text (including the newly generated keys).

   ```
   # Encryption keys
   # Key name          Key value
   ```

```
MessageKey1
0x2FC65F7E6339F70F466807493EA8C003
```

3. Copy the ENCKEYS file from the source to the target's GoldenGate home directory.

4. Start GGSCI and add the ENCRYPT and KEYNAME parameters to RMTHOST in the source Extract or Data Pump parameter file. For example:

```
RMTHOST dbserver2, MGRPORT 7809, ENCRYPT BLOWFISH, KEYNAME
MessageKey1
```

5. Obtain the existing port number for the Server Collector process on the target machine.

```
[oracle@dbserver2 ggs]$ ps -ef | grep ora | grep server
oracle    3682  3583  0 15:31 ?        00:00:00 ./server -p 7843
-k -l /home/oracle/ggs/ggserr.log
```

6. From GGSCI on each server, stop the respective Extract and Replicat processes.

7. On the target machine, configure a static Server Collector process and manually start it as a background process using the port number obtained in step 5.

```
oracle@dbserver2 ggs]$ server -p 7843 -ENCRYPT BLOWFISH -KEYNAME
MessageKey1 &

2010-08-30 17:30:06  GGS INFO     373  Oracle GoldenGate
Collector, port 7843:  Listening for requests.
```

8. Now start the Extract and Replicat processes.

```
GGSCI (dbserver1) 1> start extract *

Sending START request to MANAGER ...
EXTRACT EOLTP01 starting

Sending START request to MANAGER ...
EXTRACT EPMP01 starting

GGSCI (dbserver2) 1> start replicat *

Sending START request to MANAGER ...
REPLICAT ROLAP01 starting
```

9. Exit GGSCI on the target machine and check the Server Collector process.

```
[oracle@dbserver2 ggs]$ ps -ef | grep ora | grep server

oracle    4824  3583  0 17:30 ?        00:00:00 ./server -encrypt
BLOWFISH -keyname MESSAGEKEY1-p 7842 -k -l /home/oracle/ggs/
ggserr.log
```

10. Finally check the Extract and Replicat processes are running using the GGSCI INFO ALL command.

```
GGSCI (dbserver2) 2> info all

Program     Status      Group       Lag         Time Since Chkpt

MANAGER     RUNNING

REPLICAT    RUNNING     ROLAP01     00:00:00    00:00:04
```

The system event log is a good source of information for GoldenGate processes. The following example shows details of the Data Pump process starting, including the data encryption method:

```
[root@dbserver1 ~]# tail -f /var/log/messages

Sep 12 14:26:54 dbserver1 Oracle GoldenGate Capture for Oracle[3579]:
2010-09-12 14:26:54  GGS INFO        310  Oracle GoldenGate Capture for
Oracle, epmp01.prm:  EXTRACT EPMP01 started.

Sep 12 14:26:54 dbserver1 Oracle GoldenGate Manager for Oracle[3396]:
2010-09-12 14:26:54  GGS INFO        301  Oracle GoldenGate Manager for
Oracle, mgr.prm:  Command received from EXTRACT on host 192.168.1.65
(START SERVER CPU -1 PRI -1 PARAMS  -encrypt BLOWFISH -keyname
MESSAGEKEY1).
```

Additional information regarding the starting and stopping of processes including the Server Collector process is also written to the system event log, as shown in the following example on the target machine:

```
[root@dbserver2 ~]# view /var/log/messages

Sep 12 14:26:09 dbserver2 Oracle GoldenGate Manager for Oracle[3396]:
2010-09-12 14:26:09  GGS INFO        302  Oracle GoldenGate Manager for
Oracle, mgr.prm:  Manager started collector process (Port 7842).

Sep 12 14:26:09 dbserver2 Oracle GoldenGate Delivery for Oracle[3566]:
2010-09-12 14:26:09  GGS INFO        320  Oracle GoldenGate Delivery for
Oracle, rolap01.prm:  REPLICAT ROLAP01 starting.

Sep 12 14:26:10 dbserver2 Oracle GoldenGate Collector[3567]: Waiting for
connection (started dynamically)
```

Password encryption

In previous chapters that have shown example Extract and Replicat parameter files, you may have noticed the database password entered as free text. Obviously, this is a potential security risk, allowing unauthorized users to read the database user password. It is possible to prevent access to the parameter files via the OS. For example, by default GoldenGate creates parameter files in the `dirprm` subdirectory with read-write permission for all users, as shown in the following example:

```
[oracle@ dbserver1 dirprm]$ ls -l
-rw-rw-rw- 1 oracle oinstall 214 Aug 28 14:43 defgen.prm
-rw-rw-rw- 1 oracle oinstall 158 Jun 19 17:09 eload01.prm
-rw-rw-rw- 1 oracle oinstall 242 Aug 28 14:28 eoltp01.prm
-rw-rw-rw- 1 oracle oinstall 254 Aug 28 15:22 epmp01.prm
-rw-rw-rw- 1 oracle oinstall 172 Jun 13 10:21 mgr.prm
-rw-rw-rw- 1 oracle oinstall 196 Jun 19 16:58 rload01.prm
-rw-rw-rw- 1 oracle oinstall 370 Aug 28 14:29 rolap01.prm
```

We can change this using the `chmod` Unix command, allowing only the Oracle user read-write access.

```
[oracle@dbserver1 dirprm]$ chmod 600 *prm
[oracle@ dbserver1 dirprm]$ ls -l
total 64
-rw------- 1 oracle oinstall 214 Aug 28 14:43 defgen.prm
-rw------- 1 oracle oinstall 158 Jun 19 17:09 eload01.prm
-rw------- 1 oracle oinstall 242 Aug 28 14:28 eoltp01.prm
-rw------- 1 oracle oinstall 254 Aug 28 15:22 epmp01.prm
-rw------- 1 oracle oinstall 172 Jun 13 10:21 mgr.prm
-rw------- 1 oracle oinstall 196 Jun 19 16:58 rload01.prm
-rw------- 1 oracle oinstall 370 Aug 28 14:29 rolap01.prm
```

Default method

The alternative and preferred method would be to encrypt the database password in each parameter file. This is configured as follows:

1. Start GGSCI and execute the following command:

    ```
    GGSCI (dbserver1) 1> ENCRYPT PASSWORD ggs_admin

    No key specified, using default key...

    Encrypted password:
    AACAAAAAAAAAAJACGQGJBXFPCHBOJWASBUJOGBBBDKCEBMA
    ```

2. Simply copy and paste the encrypted password into each Extract and Replicat parameter file, for example:

```
USERID ggs_admin@oltp, PASSWORD
AACAAAAAAAAAAAJACGQGJBXFPCHBOJWASBUJOGBBBDKCEBMA, ENCRYPTKEY
DEFAULT
```

Named method

Another password encryption option is the named method. Here we supply a key name to the ENCRYPTKEY argument, rather than using DEFAULT. The following steps guide you through the configuration:

1. If not already done, generate a key or multiple keys using the keygen Linux utility on both source and target database servers. The following command creates two 128 bit keys:

```
[oracle@dbserver1 ggs]$ keygen 128 2

0x2FC65F7E6339F70F466807493EA8C003

0xA0BAA517FD66E44EC071F22CF66AFE68
```

2. Create a file named ENCKEYS in the GoldenGate home on the source server using a text editor such as vi and add the following text (including the newly generated keys):

```
# Encryption keys
# Key name            Key value
Key1                     0x2FC65F7E6339F70F466807493EA8C003
Key2                     0xA0BAA517FD66E44EC071F22CF66AFE68
```

3. Copy the ENCKEYS file to the GoldenGate Home directory on the remote server.

4. Start GGSCI and encrypt the database password using a named key you created in step 2.

```
GGSCI (dbserver1) 1> ENCRYPT PASSWORD ggs_admin, ENCRYPTKEY Key1

Encrypted password:
AACAAAAAAAAAAAKAGEDHWCRJYGAAZDJEDAYIMEUGVEHEBGOC
```

5. If using ASM, repeat the same command for the SYS password using the other named key you also created in step 2.

```
GGSCI (dbserver1) 2> ENCRYPT PASSWORD change_on_install,
ENCRYPTKEY Key2

Encrypted password:   AACAAAAAAAAAAAIATDGCUDDFOITJSCRD
```

6. Add the encrypted password for each key to your Extract parameter file on the source machine and Replicat on the target. For example:

```
USERID ggs_admin@oltp, PASSWORD
AACAAAAAAAAAAAKAGEDHWCRJYGAAZDJEDAYIMEUGVEHEBGOC, ENCRYPTKEY Key1
TRANLOGOPTIONS ASMUSER SYS@ASM, ASMPASSWORD
AACAAAAAAAAAAIATDGCUDDFOITJSCRD, ENCRYPTKEY Key2
```

Event Actions

It is important in any data replication environment to capture and manage events such as Trail records containing specific data or operations, or maybe the occurrence of a certain error. These are known as Event Markers.

GoldenGate provides a mechanism to perform an action on a given event or condition, these are known as Event Actions and are triggered by Event Records. If you are familiar with Oracle Streams, Event Actions are like Rules.

Event Records

An Event Record can be either a trail record that satisfies a condition evaluated by a WHERE or FILTER clause, or a record written to an event table enabling an action to occur. Typical actions are to write status information, report errors, ignore certain records in a trail, invoke a Shell script, or perform an administrative task.

The following Replicat example helps to describe the function of capturing an event and performing an action by logging DELETE operations made against the CREDITCARD_ACCOUNTS_DIM table using the EVENTACTIONS parameter:

```
MAP SRC.CREDITCARD_ACCOUNTS, TARGET TGT.CREDITCARD_ACCOUNTS_DIM;

TABLE SRC.CREDITCARD_ACCOUNTS, &
FILTER (@GETENV ("GGHEADER", "OPTYPE") = "DELETE"), &
EVENTACTIONS (LOG INFO);
```

By default, all logged information is written to the process' report file, the GoldenGate error log, and to the system messages file.

The following example Report file shows the DELETE operation against the CREDITCARD_ACCOUNTS table in the **Run Time Statistics** section.

```
******************************************************************
*                   ** Run Time Statistics **                   *
******************************************************************
```

```
Last record for the last committed transaction is the following:
```

```
Trail name :  ./dirdat/ta000071

Hdr-Ind      :      E   (x45)     Partition  :      .  (x04)
UndoFlag     :      .   (x00)     BeforeAfter:      B  (x42)
RecLength    :     10   (x000a)   IO Time    : 2010-09-12 17:12:44.000490
IOType       :      3   (x03)     OrigNode   :    255  (xff)
TransInd     :      .   (x03)     FormatType :      R  (x52)
SyskeyLen    :      0   (x00)     Incomplete :      .  (x00)
AuditRBA     :          128       AuditPos   : 46104080
Continued    :      N   (x00)     RecCount   :      1  (x01)

2010-09-12 17:12:44.000490 Delete              Len     10 RBA 10062
Name: SRC.CREDITCARD_ACCOUNTS
```

```
Reading ./dirdat/ta000071, current RBA 10198, 2 records

Report at 2010-09-12 17:13:31 (activity since 2010-09-12 16:28:31)

From Table SRC.CREDITCARD_ACCOUNTS to TGT.CREDITCARD_ACCOUNTS:
    #                   inserts:        0
    #                   updates:        0
    #                   deletes:        1
    #                   discards:       0
```

 Note that the TABLE parameter is also used in the Replicat's parameter file. This is a means of triggering an Event Action to be executed by the Replicat when it encounters an Event Marker.

The next example shows the use of the IGNORE option that prevents certain records from being extracted or replicated, which is particularly useful for filtering out system type data. When used with the TRANSACTION option, the whole transaction and not just the Event Record is ignored.

The following example extends the previous example by stopping the Event Record itself from being replicated:

```
TABLE SRC.CREDITCARD_ACCOUNTS, &
FILTER (@GETENV ("GGHEADER", "OPTYPE") = "DELETE"), &
EVENTACTIONS (LOG INFO, IGNORE);
```

Another Event Action could include triggering a database backup, an ETL process, or even a DR switchover, based on an Event Marker in a Trail record. Such an Event Marker could be a record inserted into a trigger table on the source database that is subsequently written to the online redologs, extracted, and written to a Trail file on the remote system. Here, the Replicat process reads the trail and detects the "key word" in the data record, based on the FILTER clause and EVENTACTIONS parameter configuration. Finally, it calls a Unix Shell script to start the batch process.

The key words in the following example are **"START FULL BACKUP"**, which was inserted into the JOB column of the SRC.TRIGGER_TABLE table to trigger the event:

```
MAP SRC.TRIGGER_TABLE, TARGET TGT. TRIGGER_TABLE, &
FILTER (ON INSERT, JOB = "START FULL BACKUP"), &
EVENTACTIONS (SHELL /home/oracle/scripts/run_rman_level0.sh);
```

On successful completion, the Shell command or script writes information to the process report file and the GoldenGate error log.

Other EVENTACTIONS can be combined with the SHELL option, such as REPORT. Specifying REPORT with EVENTACTIONS is the same as invoking the SEND REPLICAT command on the GGSCI command line.

 When developing a Shell script to be called by GoldenGate, ensure that it returns a zero status on successful completion, otherwise the Replicat process will abend.

Bi-directional configuration options

When implementing a bi-directional configuration, you must consider the following areas to avoid data integrity issues. These are as follows:

- Loop detection
- Conflict detection
- Conflict resolution
- Replicating Oracle sequences
- Oracle triggers

Let's take a look at the first potential problem, data looping, and how to detect it.

Loop detection

GoldenGate has built-in loop detection, which is configured through the IGNOREREPLICATES and GETAPPLOPS parameters to prevent local transactions from being replicated and causing endless loops. Another solution would be the TRANLOGOPTIONS EXCLUDEUSER parameters in the Extract process configuration, effectively blocking the GGS_ADMIN user on the target system (the user associated with the Replicat process). However, loop detection is only half the battle in a bi-directional environment. We must also consider conflict detection and resolution.

 Truncate table operations cannot be detected by the loop detection scheme. To combat this, ensure the GETTRUNCATES is ON in only one direction, that is, source to target.

Loop detection is discussed in more detail in *Chapter 7, Advanced Configuration*.

Conflict detection

Conflicts occur in a bi-directional environment when the same row in a given table is updated around the same time on both sites. GoldenGate does not have a built-in conflict detector and must be hand crafted if you wish to address this issue.

Which transaction will succeed? Should they both fail? These are both valid questions and must be answered before you go ahead and code your conflict handler.

GoldenGate is renowned for its low latency, which helps to alleviate any conflicts. However, the best solution would be at the application level, segregating users at the different locations, only allowing each group to update specific ranges of records in tables and thus avoiding conflicts. This is sometimes not possible and conflict detection and resolution must be employed.

The key to conflict detection is the before image in an UPDATE operation. As we know, GoldenGate can store the before image and evaluate it against the existing value in the target row. The following example shows the use of SQLEXEC, which is used initially to obtain the existing value in the target table, and then compared to the before image from the source table by the BEFORE and CHECK parameters of the FILTER clause:

```
REPERROR (9999, EXCEPTION)
MAP SRC.CREDITCARD_PAYMENTS, TARGET TGT.CREDITCARD_PAYMENTS, &
SQLEXEC (ID CHECK_CONFLICT, ON UPDATE, BEFOREFILTER, &
QUERY "SELECT PAYMENT FROM TGT.CREDITCARD_PAYMENTS &
WHERE ID = :P1", &
PARAMS (P1 = ID)), &
```

```
FILTER (ON UPDATE, BEFORE.PAYMENT <> CHECK.PAYMENT, &
RAISEERROR 9999);
INSERTALLRECORDS
MAP SRC.CREDITCARD_PAYMENTS, TARGET TGT.EXCEPTIONS, EXCEPTIONSONLY, &
COLMAP (USEDEFAULTS, ERRTYPE = "Conflict Detected");
```

The `BEFOREFILTER` parameter of `SQLEXEC` allows the SQL to execute before the `FILTER` statement, enabling the results to be used in the filter.

Conflict resolution

The method behind conflict detection and resolution is discussed in *Chapter 10, Troubleshooting GoldenGate* in the "Exception Handling" section. Once you have a mechanism to detect conflicts, you need to resolve them based on your business rules. The following is a list of four possible options:

1. Apply the net difference instead of the after image.
2. Map the data to an exception table for manual resolution.
3. Apply the latest update from either source.
4. Discard the change.

All the above can be configured to execute automatically via GoldenGate parameter files except option 2. This has to be manually determined quickly as subsequent updates may also suffer conflicts. It is therefore good practice to have an Event Action to alert the GoldenGate Administrator when an `INSERT` operation on the Exceptions table occurs. This is shown in the following Replicat configuration example:

```
TABLE TGT.EXCEPTIONS, &
FILTER (@GETENV ("GGHEADER", "OPTYPE") = "INSERT"), &
EVENTACTIONS (SHELL /home/oracle/scripts/email_alert.sh);
```

Oracle sequences

GoldenGate does not support the replication of Oracle database sequence values in a bi-directional configuration. The database sequences must generate values on the target database independent to the source. Therefore, to ensure that the source and target database sequence numbers are unique across the environment, it is best practice to assign odd and even values to each.

Oracle triggers

Another consideration in a bi-directional environment is Oracle triggers. Having triggers firing on your primary source database may not be a problem, but when the related transactions are applied to your target, where the same triggers are enabled, data duplication may result. Furthermore, should the triggered transactions on the target be replicated back to the source, you have a real problem, as the IGNOREREPLICATES and EXCLUDEUSER parameter would not work in this case.

One solution would be to disable triggers on the target during replication. This can be achieved through an SQLEXEC parameter statement that calls bespoke stored procedures, initially disabling, then re-enabling the triggers. The individual procedure calls are shown in the following example of a Replicat parameter file:

```
REPLICAT ROLAP01
SOURCEDEFS ./dirdef/oltp.def
SETENV (ORACLE_SID=OLAP)
USERID ggs_admin, PASSWORD
AACAAAAAAAAAAAJACGQGJBXFPCHBOJWASBUJOGBBBDKCEBMA, ENCRYPTKEY DEFAULT
DISCARDFILE ./dirrpt/rolap01.dsc, PURGE
SQLEXEC "call disable_triggers ()"
MAP SRC.CHECK_PAYMENTS, TARGET TGT.CHECK_PAYMENTS;
MAP SRC.CHECK_PAYMENTS_STATUS, TARGET TGT.CHECK_PAYMENTS_STATUS;
MAP SRC.CREDITCARD_ACCOUNTS, TARGET TGT.CREDITCARD_ACCOUNTS;
SQLEXEC "call enable_triggers ()"
```

Heterogeneous environments

Although not heavily discussed in this book, one of the main features of GoldenGate is its support for heterogeneous databases. GoldenGate's decoupled architecture, plus its trail file universal data format, enables heterogeneity. This is a main selling feature for Oracle, as GoldenGate does not require additional gateways or conversion software in order to extract and replicate data across environments.

DEFGEN is an essential step in the GoldenGate configuration of heterogeneous environments. It provides the source definitions for the Replicat process to lookup. Without these, GoldenGate cannot replicate data between non-identical tables.

Specific options

So what specific configuration options are available to non-Oracle databases?

To help answer that question, the following paragraphs describe the options available to the most common alternative database types.

Microsoft SQL Server

GoldenGate has the ability to capture data from native SQL Server backups, not just the transaction logs. It can also coexist with Microsoft's SQL Server Replication too, although SQL Server Replication components are not required.

One of the main features is the support for tables having no unique key. This is not currently supported by SQL Server Replication. Other supported options are bi-directional replication, computed columns, and identity columns.

IBM DB2

For DB2, GoldenGate supports the following options:

- Multi Dimensional Clustered Tables (MDC)
- Materialized Query Tables (MQT)
- Bi-directional replication
- Data compression on tablespaces

Data compression is not supported by GoldenGate for Oracle databases. This is because of the way Oracle achieves the data compression through its unique compression algorithm. The compressed data information is not written to the redo logs and therefore cannot be extracted.

The DEFGEN utility

The **DEFGEN** utility creates a data definitions file for the tables in your source or target database schema. It defines the column structure, datatypes, field length, and offset. Originally designed for heterogeneous environments, DEFGEN provides an easy method of map configuration between non-identical schemas.

An extension to DEFGEN utility is the `DEF` option of the `MAP` parameter. `DEF` enables new table definitions to be added "on the fly" to a trail, based on a template created by the DEFGEN utility. As long as the new target tables have identical definitions to the table in the template, they can be added without having to rerun DEFGEN. Also there is no need to stop and start the Replicat process, which is ideal when downtime cannot be tolerated.

DDL replication

GoldenGate supports the replication of all DDL commands operating at schema level. By default DDL replication is enabled on the target (Replicat) for data integrity and disabled on the source (Extract). Should you wish to perform DDL and DML replication from your source database, the DDL part must be explicitly configured through a single DDL parameter statement.

> GoldenGate does not support DDL only replication. DDL replication must accompany DML replication and is enabled or disabled via the GETTRUNCATES and IGNORETRUNCATES parameters respectively.

The DDL parameter

DDL replication is configured and enabled on the Extract and Replicat process by passing multiple options to the DDL parameter. Not only can DDL operations be filtered for specific schemas and objects, but also operation types. The filtering is essentially driven through both the MAP statement and the use of wildcards in the configuration options.

Filtering

Starting with wildcards, the following DDL parameter statement would "catch all" DDL from a source schema when placed in the Extract process' parameter file.

```
DDL INCLUDE OBJNAME "SRC.*"
```

Similarly, specific operation types can also be captured, but wildcards are not supported here.

```
DDL INCLUDE OPTYPE CREATE
```

As well as INCLUDE, GoldenGate offers an EXCLUDE option, which is ideal for filtering out specific schemas.

```
DDL INCLUDE ALL EXCLUDE "SCRATCH.*"
```

Certain GoldenGate parameters and options have priority over others. To take the above statement as an example, we could achieve the same result using the following configuration options of the TRANLOGOPTIONS parameter, which may be more appropriate due to its global nature:

- EXCLUDEUSER (Extract)
- EXCLUDEUSERID (Replicat)

```
TRANLOGOPTIONS EXCLUDEUSER scratch
```

To exclude DDL operations for a given schema, type, or object, we must have a preceding INCLUDE option. However, in cases where DDL is performed on the target database by another mechanism, and for GoldenGate to maintain its knowledge of the source data dictionary, we can use the EXCLUDE ALL option of the DDL parameter. This will ensure that all DDL operations are not replicated, but allow data dictionary metadata to be sent to the target.

```
DDL EXCLUDE ALL
```

To prevent all DDL metadata being replicated, omit the DDL parameter from the Extract process' configuration.

Mapping options

Now let's discuss mapping with DDL replication. The DDL parameter offers a MAPPED or UNMAPPED option. This allows the DDL parameter to extend its configuration options to those specified in the MAP parameter of a Replicat process. For example, the following DDL operation creates an index on the CREDITCARD_HISTORY table in the PROD schema, the DDL statement is replicated to the target database and applied to the schema and object configured by the Replicat's MAP parameter.

```
CREATE INDEX prod.creditcard_history_idx ON TABLE prod.creditcard_
history(payment_date);
```

The following configuration exists on the source:

```
DDL INCLUDE MAPPED OBJNAME "PROD.*"
TABLE prod.*;
```

The following configuration exists on the target:

```
MAP prod.creditcard*, TARGET archive.creditcard*;
```

The CREATE INDEX statement is executed by the Replicat process on the target as the following:

```
CREATE INDEX archive.creditcard_history_idx ON TABLE archive.creditcard_
history(payment_date);
```

The index is actually created on the CREDITCARD_HISTORY table in the ARCHIVE schema!

The same behavior also applies to CREATE TABLE AS SELECT commands.

```
CREATE TABLE prod.creditcard_acct_bkup AS SELECT * FROM prod.creditcard_
accounts;
```

The `CREDITCARD_ACCT_BKUP` table will be created in the `ARCHIVE` schema based on the `MAP` parameter configuration. If you don't want this to occur, we can override the `MAP` parameter using the `UNMAPPED` option.

```
DDL INCLUDE UNMAPPED OBJNAME "PROD.*"
TABLE prod.*;
```

It is possible to create complex filter options through the DDL parameter, including the conversion of target names. The following example converts all object names created on the source to the equivalent name, but with a prefix of `hist_` on the target.

```
MAP src.*, TARGET tgt.hist_*;
```

Initial setup

Before your GoldenGate installation can support DDL replication, two setup scripts must be run in turn, as SYSDBA on the source database to install the necessary software components. Firstly run `marker_setup.sql` and then `ddl_setup.sql` found in the GoldenGate home.

The following example shows the setup process, the prompts, and responses:

```
SQL> @marker_setup.sql


Marker setup script


You will be prompted for the name of a schema for the GoldenGate database
objects.
NOTE: The schema must be created prior to running this script.
NOTE: Stop all DDL replication before starting this installation.


Enter GoldenGate schema name:GGS_ADMIN



Marker setup table script complete, running verification script...
Please enter the name of a schema for the GoldenGate database objects:
Setting schema name to GGS_ADMIN


MARKER TABLE
-------------------------------
```

OK

MARKER SEQUENCE

OK

Script complete.
SQL> @ddl_setup.sql

GoldenGate DDL Replication setup script

Verifying that current user has privileges to install DDL Replication...

You will be prompted for the name of a schema for the GoldenGate database objects.
NOTE: The schema must be created prior to running this script.
NOTE: On Oracle 10g and up, system recycle bin must be disabled.
NOTE: Stop all DDL replication before starting this installation.

Enter GoldenGate schema name:GGS_ADMIN

You will be prompted for the mode of installation.
To install or reinstall DDL replication, enter INITIALSETUP
To upgrade DDL replication, enter NORMAL
Enter mode of installation:INITIALSETUP

Working, please wait ...
Spooling to file ddl_setup_spool.txt

Using GGS_ADMIN as a GoldenGate schema name, INITIALSETUP as a mode of installation.

Working, please wait ...

RECYCLEBIN must be empty.

```
This installation will purge RECYCLEBIN for all users.
To proceed, enter yes. To stop installation, enter no.


Enter yes or no:yes



DDL replication setup script complete, running verification script...
Please enter the name of a schema for the GoldenGate database objects:
Setting schema name to GGS_ADMIN



LOCATION OF DDL TRACE FILE
----------------------------------------------------------------------------
-------
/opt/oracle/diag/rdbms/oltp/oltp/trace/ggs_ddl_trace.log


Analyzing installation status...


..
STATUS OF DDL REPLICATION
----------------------------------------------------------------------------
-------
SUCCESSFUL installation of DDL Replication software components


Script complete.
```

Known issues

When enabling DDL replication on the source, be aware that the Recycle Bin functionality in Oracle 10*g* and above must be disabled. This mechanism is not supported by GoldenGate and will cause the following error (and solution) to be written to the report file, when starting the Extract process:

```
2010-09-20 09:23:35  GGS ERROR      2003  RECYCLEBIN must be turned off.
For 10gr2 and up, set RECYCLEBIN in parameter file to OFF. For 10gr1,
set _RECYCLEBIN in parameter file to FALSE. Then restart database and
extract.


2010-09-20 09:23:35  GGS ERROR      190  PROCESS ABENDING.
```

To disable the Recycle Bin, log on to the source database as SYSDBA and execute the following command, then shutdown and startup.

```
SQL> alter system set recyclebin=off scope=spfile;


System altered.


SQL> shutdown immediate
Database closed.
Database dismounted.
ORACLE instance shut down.
SQL> startup
ORACLE instance started.
```

Using DUMPDDL

The GoldenGate DDL solution for Oracle installs a trigger named GGS_DDL_
TRIGGER_BEFORE, owned by the SYS user. This trigger writes information about
the captured DDL operations into the GGS_MARKER and GGS_DDL_HIST tables. Data
stored in the GGS_DDL_HIST table is in proprietary format and can only be viewed
using the GGSCI DUMPDDL command.

The basic DUMPDDL command dumps data to the following tables that can be
subsequently queried through standard SQL. Each table has the SEQNO as its primary
key, making it is easy to reconcile the DDL operations against the Extract and
Replicat report files.

- GGS_DDL_OBJECTS
- GGS_DDL_COLUMNS
- GGS_DDL_LOG_GROUPS
- GGS_DDL_PARTITIONS
- GGS_DDL_PRIMARY_KEYS

To view historical DDL operation information on the screen, use the SHOW option of
the DUMPDDL command. Note that you must log in to the source database from GGSCI
for the command to succeed.

```
GGSCI (dbserver1) 1> dblogin userid ggs_admin@oltp, password ggs_admin
Successfully logged into database.


GGSCI (dbserver1) 2> DUMPDDL SHOW
```

```
*** Dumping DDL Metadata for DDL sequence [1]...
Time of capture                = Before DDL
Time of DDL operation          = 2010-09-26 20:19:51
DDL operation (maybe partial)  = [create table my_new_table ( coll
number )]
Start SCN of DDL operation     = 2530002
DDL operation type             = CREATE
Object type                    = TABLE
DB Blocksize                   = 8192

Object owner                   = SRC
Object name                    = MY_NEW_TABLE
Object ID                      =
Base object owner              = SRC
Base object name               = MY_NEW_TABLE

Object valid                   = VALID
Log group exists               = 0
Subpartition                   = NO
Partition                      = NO
Total number of columns        = 0
Number of columns used         = 0
Finished displaying metadata information (sequence number [1], DDL
history table [GGS_ADMIN.GGS_DDL_HIST]).
```

The output shows that supplemental logging is automatically added to the new table upon creation; this is because DDLOPTIONS ADDTRANDATA is configured in the Extract parameter file. DDLOPTIONS are discussed in the next section.

There are two limitations we need to be aware of when using DUMPDDL -

a) The DDL metadata written to the GGS_DDL_HIST table relates to the "before" image of the DDL operation and

b) is restricted to 4000 bytes.

DDL OPTIONS

As the name suggests, the DDLOPTIONS parameter controls additional options and functionality for DDL replication. For example, we discussed the IGNOREAPPLOPS and GETREPLICATES options in Chapter 4 that ignore local DML, but capture Replicated DML. When configured as DDL options for Extract processes only, they prove useful for Cascade environments.

```
DDLOPTIONS IGNOREAPPLOPS GETREPLICATES
```

Another useful option is ADDTRANDATA that automatically adds supplemental logging to tables created on the source database. This option is also supported for ALTER TABLE commands where the supplemental log data is updated accordingly. Be aware that the ADD SUPPLEMENTAL LOGGING operation will not be replicated on the target unless the GETREPLICATES option is configured.

```
DDLOPTIONS ADDTRANDATA
```

It is also worth configuring the REPORT option in your DDL options. This will allow detail of replicated DDL operations to be written to the process' report file, when generated by the SEND command. The following example extends the previous configuration by including the REPORT option:

```
DDLOPTIONS ADDTRANDATA REPORT


DDL replication statistics:


                 Operations:          3
         Mapped operations:          3
       Unmapped operations:          0
          Other operations:          0
       Excluded operations:          0
                    Errors:          0
            Retried errors:          0
          Discarded errors:          0
            Ignored errors:          0
```

From the output we see the DDL operations are clearly visible in the runtime statistics section of the report.

Summary

Oracle GoldenGate 10.4 is a highly configurable product. Obtaining the optimal configuration for your application may be a challenge, but you will be rewarded with a robust, scalable, secure, and high performance data replication solution. Furthermore, additional options allow you to build on the existing configuration when the system requirements change with time.

Also in this chapter we discovered that the configuration options provide detailed reporting and monitoring capabilities, enabling the automatic execution of a script to alert the GoldenGate Administrator or maybe stop a process based on an event in the source database's redo stream.

In the next chapter. *Chapter 6, Configuring GoldenGate for HA* is a natural progression from this chapter, having an appreciation of design importance, configuration options, and the potential of knowing what can be achieved when building GoldenGate environments.

6
Configuring GoldenGate for HA

High Availability (HA) has become an important factor in computer system design in recent years. Systems can't afford to be down, not even for a minute, as they may be mission critical, life supporting, regulatory, or the financial impact may be too great to bear. Oracle has played a major role in developing a number of HA solutions, one of which is **Real Application Clusters** (**RAC**). Oracle Streams is heavily integrated with RAC out of the box and requires no additional configuration. This is not true for GoldenGate, where the Manager process has to be made "RAC aware".

In this chapter, we learn how to configure GoldenGate in a RAC environment and explore the various components that effectively enable HA for data replication and integration.

This includes the following discussion points:

- Shared storage options
- Configuring clusterware for GoldenGate
- GoldenGate on Exadata
- Failover

We also touch upon the new features available in Oracle 11*g* Release 2, including the Database Machine, that provides a "HA solution in a box".

GoldenGate on RAC

A number of architectural options are available to Oracle RAC, particularly surrounding storage. Since Oracle 11*g* Release 2, these options have grown, making it possible to configure the whole RAC environment using Oracle software, whereas in earlier versions, third party clusterware and storage solutions had to be used. Let's start by looking at the importance of shared storage.

Shared storage

The secret to RAC is "share everything" and this also applies to GoldenGate. RAC relies on shared storage in order to support a single database having multiple instances, residing on individual nodes. Therefore, as a minimum the GoldenGate checkpoint and trail files must be on the shared storage so all Oracle instances can "see" them. Should a node fail, a surviving node can "take the reins" and continue the data replication without interruption.

Since Oracle 11*g* Release 2, in addition to ASM, the shared storage can be an ACFS or a DBFS.

Automatic Storage Management Cluster File System (ACFS)

ACFS is Oracle's multi-platform, scalable file system, and storage management technology that extends ASM functionality to support files maintained outside of the Oracle Database. This lends itself perfectly to supporting the required GoldenGate files. However, any Oracle files that could be stored in regular ASM diskgroups are not supported by ACFS. This includes the OCR and Voting files that are fundamental to RAC.

Database File System (DBFS)

Another Oracle solution to the shared filesystem is DBFS, which creates a standard file system interface on top of files and directories that are actually stored as SecureFile LOBs in database tables. DBFS is similar to Network File System (NFS) in that it provides a shared network file system that "looks like" a local file system.

On Linux, you need a DBFS client that has a mount interface that utilizes the **Filesystem in User Space (FUSE)** kernel module, providing a file-system mount point to access the files stored in the database.

This mechanism is also ideal for sharing GoldenGate files among the RAC nodes. It also supports the **Oracle Cluster Registry (OCR)** and Voting files, plus Oracle homes.

DBFS requires an Oracle Database 11*g*R2 (or higher) database. You can use DBFS to store GoldenGate recovery related files for lower releases of the Oracle Database, but you will need to create a separate Oracle Database 11*g*R2 (or higher) database to host the file system.

Configuring Clusterware for GoldenGate

Oracle Clusterware will ensure that GoldenGate can tolerate server failures by moving processing to another available server in the cluster. It can support the management of a third party application in a clustered environment. This capability will be used to register and relocate the GoldenGate Manager process.

Once the GoldenGate software has been installed across the cluster and a script to start, check, and stop GoldenGate has been written and placed on the shared storage (so it is accessible to all nodes), the GoldenGate Manager process can be registered in the cluster. Clusterware commands can then be used to create, register and set privileges on the virtual IP address (VIP) and the GoldenGate application using standard Oracle Clusterware commands.

The Virtual IP

The VIP is a key component of Oracle Clusterware that can dynamically relocate the IP address to another server in the cluster, allowing connections to failover to a surviving node. The VIP provides faster failovers compared to the TCP/IP time-out based failovers on a server's actual IP address. On Linux this can take up to 30 minutes using the default kernel settings!

The prerequisites are as follows:

1. The VIP must be a fixed IP address on the public subnet.
2. The interconnect must use a private non-routable IP address, ideally over Gigabit Ethernet.

Use a VIP to access the GoldenGate Manager process to isolate access to the Manager process from the physical server. Remote data pump processes must also be configured to use the VIP to contact the GoldenGate Manager.

The following diagram illustrates the RAC architecture for 2 nodes (rac1 and rac2) supporting 2 Oracle instances (oltp1 and oltp2). The VIPs are 11.12.1.6 and 11.12.1.8 respectively, in this example:

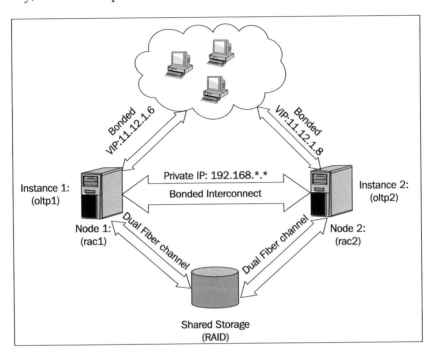

The user community or application servers connect to either instance via the VIP and a load balancing database service, that has been configured on the database and in the client's SQL*Net tnsnames.ora file or JDBC connect string.

The following example shows a typical tnsnames entry for a load balancing service. Load balancing is the default and does not need to be explicitly configured. Hostnames can replace the IP addresses in the tnsnames.ora file as long as they are mapped to the relevant VIP in the client's system hosts file.

```
OLTP =
  (DESCRIPTION =
    (ADDRESS_LIST =
      (ADDRESS = (PROTOCOL = TCP)(HOST = 11.12.1.6)(PORT = 1521))
      (ADDRESS = (PROTOCOL = TCP)(HOST = 11.12.1.8)(PORT = 1521))
    )
    (CONNECT_DATA =
```

```
         (SERVICE_NAME = oltp)
    )
  )
```

This is the recommended approach for scalability and performance and is known as active-active. Another HA solution is the active-passive configuration, where users connect to one instance only leaving the passive instance available for node failover.

 The term active-active or active-passive in this context relates to 2-node RAC environments and is not to be confused with the GoldenGate topology of the same name.

On Linux systems, the database server hostname will typically have the following format in the /etc/hosts file.

For Public VIP: <hostname>-vip

For Private Interconnect: <hostname>-pri

The following is an example hosts file for a RAC node:

```
127.0.0.1            localhost.localdomain localhost
::1                  localhost6.localdomain6 localhost6

#Virtual IP Public Address
11.12.1.6 rac1-vip          rac1-vip
11.12.1.8 rac2-vip          rac2-vip

#Private Address
192.168.1.33    rac1-pri           rac1-pri
192.168.1.34    rac2-pri           rac2-pri
```

Creating a GoldenGate application

The following steps guide you through the process of configuring GoldenGate on RAC. This example is for an Oracle 11*g* Release 1 RAC environment:

1. Install GoldenGate as the Oracle user on each node in the cluster or on a shared mount point that is visible from all nodes. If installing the GoldenGate home on each node, ensure the checkpoint and trails files are on the shared filesystem.

2. Ensure the GoldenGate Manager process is configured to use the AUTOSTART and AUTORESTART parameters, allowing GoldenGate to start the Extract and Replicat processes as soon as the Manager starts.

3. Configure a VIP for the GoldenGate application as the Oracle user from 1 node.

```
<CLUSTERWARE_HOME>/bin/crs_profile -create ggsvip \
-t application \
-a <CLUSTERWARE_HOME>/bin/usrvip \
-o oi=bond1,ov=11.12.1.6,on=255.255.255.0
```

> **CLUSTERWARE_HOME** is the oracle home in which Oracle Clusterware is installed. E.g. `/u01/app/oracle/product/11.1.0/crs`
>
> **ggsvip** is the name of the application VIP that you will create.
>
> **oi=bond1** is the public interface in this example.
>
> **ov=11.12.1.6** is the virtual IP address in this example.
>
> **on=255.255.255.0** is the subnet mask. This should be the same subnet mask for the public IP address.

4. Next, register the VIP in the Oracle Cluster Registry (OCR) as the Oracle user.

```
<CLUSTERWARE_HOME>/bin/crs_register ggsvip
```

5. Set the ownership of the VIP to the root user who assigns the IP address. Execute the following command as the root user:

```
<CLUSTERWARE_HOME>/bin/crs_setperm ggsvip -o root
```

6. Set read and execute permissions for the Oracle user. Execute the following command as the root user:

```
<CLUSTERWARE_HOME>/bin/crs_setperm ggsvip -u user:oracle:r-x
```

7. As the Oracle user, start the VIP.

```
<CLUSTERWARE_HOME>/bin/crs_start ggsvip
```

8. To verify the the VIP is running, execute the following command then ping the IP address from a different node in the cluster.

```
<CLUSTERWARE_HOME>/bin/crs_stat ggsvip -t
Name            Type          Target    State     Host
------------------------------------------------------------
ggsvip          application    ONLINE    ONLINE    rac1


ping -c3 11.12.1.6
64 bytes from 11.12.1.6: icmp_seq=1 ttl=64 time=0.096 ms
```

```
64 bytes from 11.12.1.6: icmp_seq=2 ttl=64 time=0.122 ms
64 bytes from 11.12.1.6: icmp_seq=3 ttl=64 time=0.141 ms
--- 11.12.1.6 ping statistics ---
3 packets transmitted, 3 received, 0% packet loss, time 2000ms
rtt min/avg/max/mdev = 0.082/0.114/0.144/0.025 ms
```

9. Oracle Clusterware supports the use of "Action" scripts within its configuration, allowing bespoke scripts to be executed automatically during failover. Create a Linux shell script named `ggs_action.sh` that accepts 3 arguments: start, stop or check. Place the script in the `<CLUSTERWARE_HOME>/crs/public` directory on each node or if you have installed GoldenGate on a shared mount point, copy it there.

   ○ Ensure that `start` and `stop`: returns 0 if successful, 1 if unsuccessful.

   ○ `check`: returns 0 if GoldenGate is running, 1 if it is not running.

10. As the Oracle user, make sure the script is executable.

```
chmod 754 ggs_action.sh
```

11. To check the GoldenGate processes are running, ensure the action script has the following commands. The following example can be expanded to include checks for Extract and Replicat processes:

    ○ First check the Linux process ID (PID) the GoldenGate Manager process is configured to use.

```
GGS_HOME=/mnt/oracle/ggs                    # Oracle GoldenGate
home
pid=`cut -f8 ${GGS_HOME}/dirpcs/MGR.pcm`
```

    ○ Then, compare this value (in variable `$pid`) with the actual PID the Manager process is using. The following example will return the correct PID of the Manager process if it is running.

```
ps -e |grep ${pid} |grep mgr |cut -d " " -f2
```

12. The code to start and stop a GoldenGate process is simply a call to `ggsci`.

```
ggsci_command=$1
ggsci_output=`${GGS_HOME}/ggsci << EOF
${ggsci_command}
exit
EOF`
```

13. Create a profile for the GoldenGate application as the Oracle user from 1 node.

```
<CLUSTERWARE_HOME>/bin/crs_profile \
-create goldengate_app \
-t application \
-r ggsvip \
-a <CLUSTERWARE_HOME>/crs/public/ggs_action.sh \
-o ci=10
```

> **CLUSTERWARE_HOME** is the Oracle home in which Oracle Clusterware is installed. For example: `/u01/app/oracle/product/11.1.0/crs`
>
> **-create** goldengate_app the application name is goldengate_app.
>
> **-r specifies** the required resources that must be running for the application to start. In this example, the dependency is the VIP ggsvip must be running before Oracle GoldenGate starts.
>
> **-a** specifies the action script. For example: `<CLUSTERWARE_HOME>/crs/public/ggs_action.sh`
>
> **-o** specifies options. In this example the only option is the Check Interval which is set to 10 seconds.

14. Next, register the application in the Oracle Cluster Registry (OCR) as the oracle user.

```
<CLUSTERWARE_HOME>/bin/crs_register goldengate_app
```

15. Now start the Goldengate application as the Oracle user.

```
<CLUSTERWARE_HOME>/bin/crs_start goldengate_app
```

16. Check that the application is running.

```
<CLUSTERWARE_HOME>/bin/crs_stat goldengate_app -t
```

Name	Type	Target	State	Host
goldengate_app	application	ONLINE	ONLINE	rac1

17. You can also stop GoldenGate from Oracle Clusterware by executing the following command as the oracle user:

```
CLUSTERWARE_HOME/bin/crs_stop goldengate_app
```

Oracle has published a White Paper on "Oracle GoldenGate high availability with Oracle Clusterware". To view the Action script mentioned in this chapter, refer to Appendices 1 and 2 of the document, which can be downloaded in PDF format from the Oracle Website at the following URL:

`http://www.oracle.com/technetwork/middleware/`
`goldengate/overview/ha-goldengate-whitepaper-128197.pdf`

Increasing system resilience

Implementing Oracle RAC is a step toward high availability. For a RAC environment to be totally resilient to outages, all single points of failure must be removed from all elements. For example, the network infrastructure, storage solution, and power supply. To facilitate this, the recommendation is as follows:

- Dual fibre channels to shared storage (SAN)
- RAID disk subsystem (striped and mirrored)
- Mirrored OCR and Voting disks
- Bonded network on high speed interconnect via two physically connected switches
- Bonded network on public network (VIP) via two physically connected switches
- Dual power supply to each node, switch, and storage solution via UPS

When using ASM as your storage manager, Oracle recommends configuring a redundant diskgroup. However, if you have a RAID disk subsystem, you can configure ASM to use external redundancy. It is also best practice to "stripe on stripe" where ASM stripes the data across the LUNs, thus reducing I/O contention and increasing performance.

GoldenGate on Exadata

Already mentioned in the previous chapter is the Oracle Sun Database Machine. This purpose built machine features a number of Oracle 11gR2 database servers configured for RAC offering highly parallel processing on Exadata storage and high speed Infiniband network interfaces. The environment also supports GoldenGate, enabling real-time data integration.

Depending on the machine size, the database servers and storage cells can be configured in a number of ways to provide more than one RAC cluster. If your source and target database reside in the same Database Machine, there is no need to configure a Data Pump process. Data can be transmitted directly from Extract to Replicat at very high speeds.

Configuration

Configuring GoldenGate on Exadata is a similar process to 11gR1 RAC environments except we use DBFS as the shared mount point supporting the persistent GoldenGate files.

The GoldenGate Manager must only run on one node in a RAC cluster. To prevent Extract and Replicat processes being started concurrently, mount DBFS on a single RAC node will deny access to the checkpoint files from other nodes. Ensure the mount point detail is written to the node's /etc/fstab file.

For example:

```
/sbin/mount.dbfs#/@DBConnectString /mnt/oracle/dbfs fuse rw,user,
noauto 0 0
```

If the GoldenGate home is not on the shared storage, ensure that GoldenGate is installed on each node in the cluster and that the parameter files exist in the local subdirectories. Checkpoint and trail files must reside on the shared storage.

Parameter files may also reside on the shared storage. However, in this case the Oracle environment variables must be set in the Oracle user profile on each node. This removes the need to set the Oracle environment in the GoldenGate Extract and Replicat parameter files. Furthermore, should you wish to make changes to your GoldenGate configuration, this can be done in one place without having to copy parameter files to each node.

Creating the Extract process

The following example steps you through the creation of an Extract process on the source database using DBFS to store the trail files:

1. Ensure the DBFS file system is already mounted. As the root user create the dirchk and dirdat GoldenGate subdirectories on top of the mount point (/mnt/oracle/dbfs). For example:

   ```
   mkdir /mnt/oracle/dbfs/ggs/dirchk
   mkdir /mnt/oracle/dbfs/ggs/dirdat
   ```

2. As root, grant the oracle user read-write privileges to the ggs directory.

```
chown -R oracle:oinstall /mnt/oracle/dbfs/ggs
```

3. As the oracle user, remove the GoldenGate subdirectories, `dirchk` and `dirdat`, from the GoldenGate home on each node in the cluster.

```
rmdir $GGS_HOME/dirchk
rmdir $GGS_HOME/dirdat
```

4. Now create symbolic links to the newly created DBFS mount point directories on each node in the cluster.

```
cd $GGS_HOME
ln -s /mnt/oracle/dbfs/ggs/dirchk dirchk
ln -s /mnt/oracle/dbfs/ggs/dirdat dirdat
```

5. Now that the DBFS mount point and GoldenGate subdirectories have been created on the shared filesystem, we can create the Extract process. Firstly, create an Extract parameter file using EDIT PARAMS command in ggsci.

> The ASM connect details allow GoldenGate to access the online redo logs for all database instances (threads). The symlinks simplify the Extract parameter files by not having to specify the full path to the shared trail file directory.

In the following example, Extract parameter file snippet, the Oracle SID is set by the SETENV parameter. For local parameter files, ensure the Oracle SID is set appropriately for the node you are configuring.

```
EXTRACT EOLTP01
SETENV (ORACLE_SID=OLTP1)
USERID ggs_admin, PASSWORD ggs_admin
EXTTRAIL ./dirdat/aa
TRANLOGOPTIONS ASMUSER SYS@ASM, ASMPASSWORD Password1
```

1. Then create the Extract process from GGSCI.

```
GGSCI (rac1) 1> add extract EOLTP01, tranlog, begin now, threads 4
EXTRACT added.
```

2. Finally create the EXTTRAIL from GGSCI.

```
GGSCI (rac1) 2> add exttrail ./dirdat/aa, extract EOLTP01,
megabytes 500
EXTTRAIL added.
```

Creating the Replicat process

Now that the DBFS mount point and GoldenGate subdirectories have been created on the shared filesystem, we can create the Replicat process.

1. Firstly, create a Replicat parameter file using EDIT PARAMS command in GGSCI. The discard directory need not be on the shared DBFS filesystem as the files are not required for GoldenGate process recovery.

   ```
   REPLICAT ROLAP01
   SETENV (ORACLE_SID=OLAP1)
   USERID ggs_admin, PASSWORD ggs_admin
   DISCARDFILE ./dirrpt/rolap01.dsc, PURGE
   ```

2. Now create the Replicat process. Note the Replicat uses the same EXTTRAIL as the source.

   ```
   GGSCI (dbolap1) 1> add replicat ROLAP01, exttrail ./dirdat/aa

   REPLICAT added.
   ```

We have looked at some of the Oracle 11*g* Release 2 new features, including the Exadata Database Machine. Now let's look at failover, ensuring availability.

Failover

By default VIPs and database services automatically failover to a surviving instance in the case of a crash or node eviction. The VIP will automatically failback to its "home" node once the failed database instance restarts. VIPs and database services can also be manually relocated for maintenance reasons using the Oracle Server Control utility's srvctl relocate command, allowing a node to be taken off-line without affecting user connections to the database.

Automatic failover

What does this mean to the GoldenGate Manager process running on one node in a clustered environment?

To help answer this question, Oracle Clusterware can also be installed on other servers apart from the database servers to form a single cluster. For example, you can use four database servers and two additional Oracle GoldenGate servers in the single cluster. The Oracle Database would run on the four database servers and GoldenGate would run on one of the two remaining servers, with failover to its dedicated twin. Because the Goldengate Manager and Data Pump processes (if any) are configured to use the VIP, the failover will be automatic.

You may however, wish to install GoldenGate on every database server in a cluster with no dedicated GoldenGate servers. In this configuration, the automatic failover using the VIP is still supported.

Manual failover

The following sections discuss the various methods of manual failover.

Relocating a service

For maintenance reasons, it is sometimes necessary to relocate a database service from one RAC instance to another. The following example shows how to relocate the database service using `srvctl`:

```
srvctl status service -d OLTP -s ACTIVE_SRV

Service ACTIVE_SRV is running on instance(s) OLTP2

srvctl relocate service -d OLTP -s ACTIVE_SRV -i OLTP2 -t OLTP1

$ srvctl status service -d OLTP -s ACTIVE_SRV

Service ACTIVE_SRV is running on instance(s) OLTP1
```

Relocating a VIP

When GoldenGate is running, you may want to move GoldenGate to run on a different server, again for maintenance reasons. The following Oracle Clusterware command executed by the Oracle user allows you to do this. Use the `crs_relocate` program with the force option to move the VIP as well.

```
<CLUSTERWARE_HOME>/bin/crs_relocate -f goldengate_app

Attempting to stop `goldengate_app` on member `rac2`

Stop of `goldengate_app` on member `rac2` succeeded.

Attempting to stop `ggatevip` on member `rac2`

Stop of `ggatevip` on member `rac2` succeeded.

Attempting to start `ggatevip` on member `rac1`

Start of `ggatevip` on member `rac1` succeeded.

Attempting to start `goldengate_app` on member `rac1`

Start of `goldengate_app` on member `rac1` succeeded.
```

This is exactly what happens automatically when a node crashes or gets evicted from the cluster. The GoldenGate Manager process is restarted on a surviving node where its configuration auto-starts the Extract and Replicat processes.

Summary

Oracle RAC is one of the most popular database configurations, first introduced in Oracle 9*i*, superseding Oracle Parallel Server. GoldenGate has recently played a major role in the Oracle 11*g* Release 2 RAC environment with the advent of Exadata and the Database Machine. In fact both are commonly sold together to provide a robust OLTP and OLAP solution in the same Oracle-Sun equipment rack.

In this chapter, we learnt how to configure GoldenGate on Oracle RAC, leveraging HA through Clusterware configuration techniques, and explored the new shared storage solutions available in Oracle 11*g* Release 2.

We discovered the importance of automatic relocation and startup of the GoldenGate Manager and processes on the new instance to restore data replication to downstream systems, all in the name of HA.

In the next chapter, we look at configuration in more detail - starting with data mapping and filtering, and finally discussing data transformation and error handling, all of which help to create a robust GoldenGate environment.

7
Advanced Configuration

In this chapter, you will gain a deeper understanding of GoldenGate configuration. The topics covered in this chapter include data selection, mapping, and transformation. One could argue that this sounds remarkably like Extract, Transform and Load (ETL) in concept. One would be right. However, combining GoldenGate's real-time Change Data Capture (CDC) with an ETL tool, known as Extract, Load and Transform (ELT), decreases data latency and eliminates the need for batch processing. This poses two questions:

1. How much data transformation should GoldenGate do?
2. Should the Replicat process load the production tables directly?

The answers to the above questions would decide whether or not an ETL tool is required, thus illustrating the power of GoldenGate's advanced configuration.

This chapter discusses the following in detail:

- Data mapping at column level to deal with different source and target table structures
- Data selection and filtering using a **WHERE** clause or **FILTER** statement
- Data replication loop detection and prevention
- Using data transformation functions
- Configuring GoldenGate to replicate DDL operations
- Including SQL in your mapping for data lookup
- Defining Macros and Tokens to automate events at runtime
- Calling external programs and routines

The above tasks are all configurable through Extract or Replicat parameter specification. By the time you are done with this chapter, you will be able to explore and realize each parameter specification and further develop your GoldenGate configuration.

Let's start by looking at data mapping.

Mapping your data

In Chapter 4, Configuring Oracle GoldenGate you performed data replication with identical source and target tables. You'll remember that the GoldenGate Replicat parameter ASSUMETARGETDEFS defines this. In the real world, it is unlikely that your target tables will be exactly the same as the source, having some additional columns or maybe different datatypes. You may even wish to transform the data, or omit certain rows from being replicated.

With GoldenGate, it is possible to map and transform your column data using the TABLE parameter in an Extract's configuration, or the MAP parameter for a Replicat.

Due to the length of some of the multi-line parameter statements, an ampersand character (&) is required as a "continuation" character at the end of each line.

When changing Extract or Replicat process parameters, be sure to stop and start the process to allow the new configuration to be read into memory. This requirement is not to be confused with zero downtime migrations. Once you are happy that your GoldenGate environment is configured appropriately, then you can start the data transfer with no interruptions.

Should a process abend due to its new configuration, GoldenGate will "replay" failed transactions on a successful restart, once the configuration error is resolved.

Column mapping

So far we have discussed table mapping. Although part of the TABLE or MAP statement, column mapping defined by the COLMAP option provides greater flexibility. For example, we can add additional columns to target tables or maybe change column names between source and target tables. Let's see how this can be configured.

Using the COLMAP option

Used without additional options, the TABLE parameter purely selects the tables for replication from the source database schema. However, should you wish to explicitly map source columns to target columns that have different names, you can include the COLMAP option.

The COLMAP option can also be used with the MAP parameter for the Replicat process, but both configurations are dependent on the source table definitions file. This file is generated by the DEFGEN utility and must be referenced using the SOUCREDEFS parameter.

 Never use the COLMAP option in a Data Pump's configuration when using the PASSTHRU parameter. The concept of PASSTHRU does not allow any mapping or transformation.

The following example shows the use of the TABLE parameter with COLMAP option in the Extract EOLTP01 parameter file:

```
TABLE SRC.SERVICECHARGE, TARGET TGT.SERVICECHARGE_DIM, &
COLMAP (USEDEFAULTS, &
ID = SERVICECHARGE_ID, &
MODIFIED_AT=TIMESTAMP);
```

The USEDEFAULTS option enables mapping of identical columns that have not been explicitly mapped.

Source Table	Target Table
ID	SERVICECHARGE_ID
VERSION	VERSION
EXTERNAL_KEY	EXTERNAL_KEY
SERVICE_AGREEMENT_ID	SERVICE_AGREEMENT_ID
CHARGE_TYPE_ID	CHARGE_TYPE_ID
MODIFIED_AT	TIMESTAMP

COLMAP also supports the use of GoldenGate functions to enhance data transformation operations. This is discussed in the next section—*Data Selection and Filtering*.

The COLMATCH option

Another powerful mapping feature is the COLMATCH option. Defined in an Extract or Replicat parameter file, it creates global rules for column mapping. Tables of a similar structure but have different column names for the same sets of data are ideal candidates for COLMATCH.

Similar to COLMAP, column names can be explicitly mapped, as shown in the following example.

```
COLMATCH NAMES ID = SERVICECHARGE_ID
```

In addition, it is possible to configure a global column name prefix or suffix to be ignored. The following example maps a target column having a _PK suffix to a source column with the same name, such as COL1 to COL1_PK. The syntax in the parameter file would be:

```
COLMATCH SUFFIX _PK
```

Use the RESET keyword after COLMATCH to turn off the global mapping rules for subsequent tables defined in an Extract or Replicat parameter file.

Using the DEFGEN utility

The DEFGEN utility creates a data definitions file for the tables in your source or target database schema. It defines the column structure, datatypes, field length, and offset. Originally designed for heterogeneous environments, DEFGEN provides an easy method of map configuration between non-identical schemas.

The following table shows the field descriptions for each column entry in the DEFGEN data definitions file:

Column position	Field description
1	Name
2	Data Type
3	External Length
4	Fetch Offset
5	Scale
6	Level
7	Null
8	Bump if Odd
9	Internal Length
10	Binary Length

Column position	Field description
11	Table Length
12	Most Significant Data Type
13	Least Significant Data Type
14	High Precision
15	Low Precision
16	Elementary Item
17	Occurs
18	Key Column
19	Sub Data Type

To configure GoldenGate to use a data definitions file includes the following main steps:

- Creating a parameter file for the DEFGEN utility
- Running the DEFGEN utility to generate the file
- Configuring the GoldenGate process to reference the definitions file

An example procedure for creating a source definitions file is described next:

1. Log on to the database server (as the Oracle user).

2. Change directory to the GoldenGate Home.

   ```
   cd /home/oracle/ggs
   ```

3. Run GGSCI.

   ```
   ggsci
   ```

4. Execute the following commands to create a DEFGEN parameters file:

   ```
   GGSCI (dbserver1) 1> EDIT PARAMS DEFGEN

   DEFSFILE ./dirdef/oltp.def

   USERID ggs_admin@oltp, PASSWORD ggs_admin

   TABLE SRC.CHECK_PAYMENTS;

   TABLE SRC.CHECK_PAYMENTS_STATUS;

   TABLE SRC.CREDITCARD_ACCOUNTS;

   TABLE SRC.CREDITCARD_PAYMENTS;
   ```

5. Exit GGSCI.

   ```
   GGSCI (dbserver1) 2> EXIT
   ```

6. From the GoldenGate Home, run the DEFGEN utility on the Linux command line to create the oltp.def file.

```
defgen paramfile dirprm/defgen.prm
******************************************************************

        Oracle GoldenGate Table Definition Generator for Oracle
                    Version 10.4.0.19 Build 002

    Linux, x86, 32bit (optimized), Oracle 11 on Sep 29 2009
08:55:42


Copyright (C) 1995, 2009, Oracle and/or its affiliates.  All
rights reserved.



               Starting at 2010-07-11 12:22:12

******************************************************************


Operating System Version:

Linux

Version #1 SMP Tue Jun 5 23:11:13 EDT 2007, Release 2.6.18-8.el5

Node: dbserver1

Machine: i686
                          soft limit    hard limit
Address Space Size    :    unlimited     unlimited
Heap Size             :    unlimited     unlimited
File Size             :    unlimited     unlimited
CPU Time              :    unlimited     unlimited


Process id: 8063


******************************************************************
**           Running with the following parameters
**
******************************************************************
DEFSFILE ./dirdef/oltp.def
USERID ggs_admin@oltp, PASSWORD ********
TABLE SRC.CHECK_PAYMENTS;
Retrieving definition for SRC.CHECK_PAYMENTS
```

```
TABLE SRC.CHECK_PAYMENTS_STATUS;

Retrieving definition for SRC.CHECK_PAYMENTS_STATUS

TABLE SRC.CREDITCARD_ACCOUNTS;

Retrieving definition for SRC.CREDITCARD_ACCOUNTS

TABLE SRC.CREDITCARD_PAYMENTS;

Retrieving definition for SRC.CREDITCARD_PAYMENTS

Definitions generated for 4 tables in ./dirdef/oltp.def
```

- As this example shows the DEFGEN parameter file creation on the source system, ftp (in ASCII mode) dirdef/oltp.def file to the same location on the target system

- On the target system, configure the Replicat process to reference the `dirprm/defoltp.prm` file by including the `SOURCEDEFS` parameter specification as shown in the following example:

```
GGSCI (dbserver2) 1> EDIT PARAMS ROLAP01

REPLICAT ROLAP01

SOURCEDEFS ./dirdef/oltp.def

SETENV (ORACLE_SID=OLAP)

USERID ggs_admin, PASSWORD ggs_admin

DISCARDFILE ./dirrpt/rolap01.dsc, PURGE

MAP SRC.CHECK_PAYMENTS, TARGET TGT.CHECK_PAYMENTS_DIM;
MAP SRC.CHECK_PAYMENTS_STATUS, TARGET TGT.CHECK_PAYMENTS_STATUS_
DIM;
MAP SRC.CREDITCARD_ACCOUNTS, TARGET TGT.CREDITCARD_ACCOUNTS_FACT;

MAP SRC.CREDITCARD_PAYMENTS, TARGET TGT.CREDITCARD_PAYMENTS_FACT;
```

The example also includes MAP statements. You will need to add the source tables to your Extract and Data Pump parameter files to enable replication.

Even though the table structures may be identical, a source-definitions file is required when the semantics of a source Oracle database are configured as bytes and the target semantics are configured as characters.

Although it's possible to manually add new schema tables to the data definitions file, it is not advisable as an error could potentially corrupt the existing system generated configuration.

Data selection and filtering

In addition to column mapping, GoldenGate offers two data filtering options:

- Complex
- Non-complex

Non-complex filtering is achieved through the WHERE clause in a TABLE (Extract) or MAP (Replicat) statement, while complex data evaluations use the FILTER clause. FILTER can select rows and columns for a given operation, whereas WHERE just selects rows. FILTER can also use GoldenGate built-in functions.

The Extract and Replicat parameter files can be modified without stopping the process. However, care should be taken to avoid syntax errors causing the process to abend. Remember that once saved, the new configuration in the parameter file is adopted immediately by the running process.

The WHERE clause

Configuring a WHERE clause is much like the WHERE clause in an SQL statement. In this case we add it at the end of the TABLE or MAP statement. The following example will filter out from the source trail, those records that have an amount greater than 1000 in the CREDITCARD_PAYMENTS table:

```
MAP SRC.CREDITCARD_PAYMENTS, TARGET TGT.CREDITCARD_PAYMENTS_FACT, &
WHERE (AMOUNT > 1000);
```

An extension to the above example would be the use of GoldenGate's built-in conditional tests. These are @PRESENT, @ABSENT, and @NULL, and are the only GoldenGate functions compatible with the WHERE clause.

The @PRESENT and @ABSENT functions test for the existence of columns in a data record. The @NULL function tests for nulls in data only. When used in conjunction with <> (not equals) the test is not null.

 All GoldenGate functions are expressed with the "@" prefix in parameter files.

The following example mapping succeeds if the AMOUNT column exists in the source data record as long as it is not null:

```
MAP SRC.CREDITCARD_PAYMENTS, TARGET TGT.CREDITCARD_PAYMENTS_FACT, &
WHERE (AMOUNT = @PRESENT AND AMOUNT <> @NULL);
```

Adding the @PRESENT function to the WHERE clause causes the record not to be discarded when AMOUNT is absent.

```
MAP SRC.CREDITCARD_PAYMENTS, TARGET TGT.CREDITCARD_PAYMENTS_FACT, &
WHERE (AMOUNT = @PRESENT AND AMOUNT > 1000);
```

 Arithmetic operators and floating-point datatypes are NOT supported by the WHERE clause.

The FILTER clause

Having the ability to evaluate row data and column names for a given DML operation; UPDATE, INSERT and DELETE, the FILTER clause is a very powerful feature. To use the example from the previous section, adding the following FILTER clause will allow UPDATE or DELETE operations only on the CREDITCARD_PAYMENTS target table. It will also filter on records having AMOUNT greater than 1000.

```
MAP SRC.CREDITCARD_PAYMENTS, TARGET TGT.CREDITCARD_PAYMENTS_FACT, &
FILTER (ON UPDATE, ON DELETE, AMOUNT > 1000);
```

You may prefer to set the filter at the source, selecting only "updates and deletes" for replication. The IGNORE keyword provides the inverse to ON.

```
TABLE SRC.CREDITCARD_PAYMENTS, FILTER (ON UPDATE, ON DELETE, AMOUNT >
1000);
```

Equally, the use of GoldenGate's global parameters; IGNOREUPDATES, IGNOREINSERTS and IGNOREDELETES can be used before a list of TABLE or MAP statements to filter out respective DML records. GETUPDATES, GETINSERTS and GETDELETES are the default, they have to be explicitly declared in the Extract or Replicat's parameter file to reset the previous configuration.

FILTER can use GoldenGate functions to provide complex data comparison and evaluation. The following example demonstrates the @STRFIND function that provides string comparison within the row data, selecting only records from the CREDITCARD_PAYMENTS table having "JOHN" in the NAME column.

```
TABLE SRC.CREDITCARD_PAYMENTS, FILTER (@STRFIND(NAME, "JOHN")>0);
```

We can also perform calculations for FILTER to evaluate using the @COMPUTE function. The following example selects data records from the CREDITCARD_ACCOUNT table having a remaining credit balance of over 10,000:

```
TABLE SRC.CREDITCARD_ACCOUNTS, FILTER (@COMPUTE(CREDIT_LIMIT-CREDIT_
BALANCE) > 10000);
```

It is also possible to filter data on a range of values, such as date or number. In addition, GoldenGate provides a @RANGE function that can implicitly divide data for parallel replication, maintaining data integrity. This is similar in concept to Oracle's Hash algorithm for table partitioning.

The following example shows the use of FILTER with the @RANGE function to "split" the source data for the BLOB_RECORDS table across three Replicats, based on the Primary Key:

Replicat 1

```
MAP SRC.BLOB_RECORDS, TARGET TGT.BLOB_RECORDS, FILTER (@RANGE (1, 3, ID));
```

Replicat 2

```
MAP SRC.BLOB_RECORDS, TARGET TGT.BLOB_RECORDS, FILTER (@RANGE (2, 3, ID));
```

Replicat 3

```
MAP SRC.BLOB_RECORDS, TARGET TGT.BLOB_RECORDS, FILTER (@RANGE (3, 3, ID));
```

When multiple filters are specified per TABLE or MAP statement, each one is executed in turn until one fails. The failure of any filter results in a failure for all filters.

Loop detection

There are times when you need to detect and prevent data replication loops occurring in your GoldenGate environment. We are going to look at the specific configurations that prevent, and those that allow replicated data to be re-extracted and propagated to a given target database.

Active-active

When configuring bi-directional data replication, known as active-active, you must prevent data looping. Data looping can occur when a transaction is replicated on the target database only to be extracted and propagated back to the source database. The source database's replicat process applies the data and the loop continues endlessly.

GoldenGate includes parameters to tell the local Extract process to ignore transactions created by the local Replicat process. These being the IGNOREREPLICATES, GETREPLICATES, IGNOREAPPLOPS, and GETAPPLOPS parameters.

To configure the Extract process to ignore Replicat operations but include application data in the trail file, set IGNOREREPLICATES and GETAPPLOPS together in the Extract parameter file as follows. For Oracle databases this is the default.

```
EXTRACT EOLTP01
SETENV (ORACLE_SID=OLTP)
USERID ggs_admin, PASSWORD ggs_admin
EXTTRAIL ./dirdat/sa
GETAPPLOPS
IGNOREREPLICATES
TRANLOGOPTIONS ASMUSER SYS@ASM, ASMPASSWORD Password1
TABLE SRC.CHECK_PAYMENTS;
TABLE SRC.CHECK_PAYMENTS_STATUS;
TABLE SRC.CREDITCARD_ACCOUNTS;
TABLE SRC.CREDITCARD_PAYMENTS;
```

Cascade

When configuring a GoldenGate cascade topology, it may be appropriate to replicate the data from Replicat operations. For example, at an intermediate site where you want the Extract process to capture all the operation data and pass it on to the next system in the architecture.

In this case, configure the Extract process to include Replicat operations by specifying GETREPLICATES and GETAPPLOPS in the Extract parameter file.

GETAPPLOPS must be configured to capture sequences that are replicated by Replicat. A Replicat issues sequence updates in an autonomous transaction, so the sequence update appears as if it is an application operation. GETAPPLOPS is the default.

Data transformation

Now that we understand data mapping, we can perform data transformation in our GoldenGate configuration. Using the built-in string manipulation and number conversion functions, with the COLMAP option, it is possible to achieve the most common data transformations: truncation, concatenation, substitution, conversion, and case changes. Note that the target column is always on the left in the COLMAP statement.

Data transformation does come at a price though—performance. When conducting complex or numerous simple transformations with high data volume and throughput, latency will prevail. It may not be as significant a bottleneck as a serial process, but the CPU consumption on the target system will increase.

Truncation and extraction

Starting with truncation, Oracle performs implicit data type conversion between a source and target column. However, should the target column scale be smaller than its source, the data is truncated on the right.

GoldenGate offers the @SUBEXT function for string truncation and character extraction. Although the function will extract any characters from a string based on begin and end character positions, it lends itself to truncating the string to a certain length, as shown in the following example. Here we are splitting the 12 digit telephone number from the source table into AREA_CODE and PHONE_NO fields on the target:

```
MAP SRC. CREDITCARD_ACCOUNTS, TARGET TGT. CREDITCARD_ACCOUNTS, &COLMAP
(USEDEFAULTS, &
AREA_CODE = @STREXT(PHONE_NUMBER,1,5), &
PHONE_NO = @STREXT(PHONE_NUMBER,6,11));
```

Concatenation

The @STRCAT function provides string concatenation by joining two or more separate strings together. In the following example, we concatenate the FIRST_NAME and SURNAME fields from the source table into the NAME field on the target table:

```
MAP SRC. CREDITCARD_ACCOUNTS, TARGET TGT. CREDITCARD_ACCOUNTS, &
COLMAP (USEDEFAULTS, &
NAME = @STRCAT(FIRST_NAME," ",SURNAME));
```

Substitution

The @STRSUB function provides string substitution, allowing a pattern of characters to be replaced with a new string. The following example converts the TITLE field from the source table into an abbreviated form on the target:

```
MAP SRC. CREDITCARD_ACCOUNTS, TARGET TGT. CREDITCARD_ACCOUNTS, &
COLMAP (USEDEFAULTS, &
TITLE = @STRSUB(TITLE, "DOCTOR","DR","MISTER","MR"));
```

Case changing

Although you could use the @STRSUB function to perform case change transformations, the preferred method is to use the @STRUP function. The following example illustrates the function's simplicity:

```
MAP SRC. CREDITCARD_ACCOUNTS, TARGET TGT. CREDITCARD_ACCOUNTS, &
COLMAP (USEDEFAULTS, &
TITLE = @STRUP(TITLE));
```

Numeric conversions

In addition to string manipulation, GoldenGate supports numeric conversions through two functions.

The @NUMSTR function converts a string to a number for arithmetic calculations. Similarly the @STRNUM converts a number to a string, but with the additional option of padding characters. The following example will convert the CREDIT_BALANCE value from the source table to a string, padded with zeros to a maximum of five characters:

```
MAP SRC.CREDITCARD_PAYMENTS, TARGET TGT.CREDITCARD_PAYMENTS, &
COLMAP (USEDEFAULTS, &
CREDIT_BALANCE = @STRNUM(CREDIT_BALANCE,RIGHTZERO, 5));
```

It is also possible to convert a binary string of 8 or less bytes to a number using the @NUMBIN function.

Date conversions

Valid numeric strings can be converted into a number of different formats, compatible with SQL. The default date format for GoldenGate is 'YYYY-MM-DD HH:MI:SS', this being generated by the @DATENOW function.

To perform a conversion on a numeric string, use the @DATE function, choosing the relevant format options, which are similar to SQL. The following example converts the DATE_KEY column numeric values on the source to a date on the target:

```
MAP SRC. CREDITCARD_ACCOUNTS, TARGET TGT. CREDITCARD_ACCOUNTS, &
COLMAP (USEDEFAULTS, &
CREATED_AT = @DATE ("YYYY-MM-DD:HH:MI:SS", "YYYYMMDDHHMISS", DATE_KEY)
&);
```

The @DATENOW function can be used to populate a MODIFIED_AT column on the target table.

```
MAP SRC. CREDITCARD_ACCOUNTS, TARGET TGT. CREDITCARD_ACCOUNTS, &
COLMAP (USEDEFAULTS, &
MODIFIED_AT = @DATENOW);
```

DDL support

GoldenGate allows DDL replication for Oracle databases, which is important when structural changes are made to your source tables. You would not want your Replicat process to abend because it can no longer insert a record into the respective target table. Before we can perform DDL replication, two setup scripts must be run in turn, as SYSDBA on the source database to install the necessary software components; `setup.sql` and then `ddl_setup.sql` both of which can be found in the GoldenGate Home directory.

GoldenGate will replicate the majority of ALTER TABLE commands including TRUNCATE. Commands that operate at database level, such as ALTER DATABASE and ALTER SYSTEM are not supported.

The following table lists all supported DDL commands at object level:

Operation	Object type
CREATE	TABLE (includes AS SELECT)
ALTER	INDEX
DROP	TRIGGER
RENAME	SEQUENCE
COMMENT ON TABLE	MATERIALIZED VIEW
COMMENT ON COLUMN	VIEW
	FUNCTION
	PACKAGE
	PROCEDURE
	SYNONYM
Permission	**Object type**
GRANT	TABLE
REVOKE	SEQUENCE
	MATERIALIZED VIEW

DDL replication must be explicitly defined for the Extract process in its parameter file. By default, DDL replication is disabled for Extract and enabled for Replicat processes.

The following examples show the configuration options for the DDL parameter. Here all DDL will be replicated for non-system schemas in the source database, except the HR schema.

```
DDL INCLUDE ALL, EXCLUDE OBJNAME "hr.*"
```

To enable DDL replication for the SRC schema:

```
DDL INCLUDE MAPPED "SRC.*"
```

It is also possible to filter on operation and object type. Let's exclude ALTER operations:

```
DDL INCLUDE MAPPED "SRC.*", EXCLUDE OPTYPE ALTER
```

Or maybe exclude index creation on the target:

```
DDL INCLUDE MAPPED "SRC.*", EXCLUDE OPTYPE INDEX
```

Another related parameter in an Extract or Replicat parameter file is DDLOPTIONS. Should you decide to replicate DDL operations, you can fine tune the delivery by adding additional options. The following example for the Extract process enables DDL replication for Replicat operations only:

```
DDLOPTIONS GETREPLICATES, IGNOREAPPLOPS
```

The SQLEXEC parameter

Another powerful feature of GoldenGate is the SQLEXEC parameter. We will discuss when and how to use it as a standalone statement, or in a TABLE or MAP statement to fulfill your data transformation requirements. SQLEXEC is valid for Extract and Replicat processes.

Data lookups

On the target database, the SQLEXEC parameter in a MAP statement allows external calls to be made through an SQL interface that support s the execution of native SQL and PL/SQL stored procedures. This option is typically invoked to perform database lookups to obtain data required to resolve a mapping and can only be executed by the GoldenGate (GGS_ADMIN) database user.

Executing stored procedures

The following example maps data from the CREDITCARD_ACCOUNT table to NEW_ ACCOUNT table. The Extract process executes the LOOKUP_ACCOUNT stored procedure prior to executing the column map. This stored procedure has two parameters: an **IN** and an **OUT**. The **IN** parameter accepts an Account Code and is named CODE_ IN_PARAM. The value returned by the stored procedure's **OUT** parameter is obtained by the @GETVAL function and used in the COLMAP statement to populate the NEW_ ACCOUNT_NAME field.

The SPNAME Replicat parameter specifies the name of the PL/SQL stored procedure, while PARAMS specifies its parameters.

```
MAP SRC.CREDITCARD_ACCOUNTS, TARGET TGT.NEW_ACCOUNT, &
SQLEXEC (SPNAME LOOKUP_ACCOUNT, &
PARAMS (CODE_IN_PARAM = ACCOUNT_CODE)), &
COLMAP (USEDEFAULTS, &
NEW_ACCOUNT_ID = ACCOUNT_ID, &
NEW_ACCOUNT_NAME = @GETVAL(LOOKUP_ACCOUNT.CODE_OUT_PARAM));
```

To pass values from a stored procedure or query as input to a FILTER or COLMAP clause, we must specify the stored procedure name followed by the **OUT** parameter name.

Executing SQL

It is also possible to perform the same "lookup" operation using SQL. The following example illustrates this using the same logic and parameter names:

```
MAP SRC.CREDITCARD_ACCOUNTS, TARGET TGT.NEW_ACCOUNT, &
SQLEXEC (ID LOOKUP_ACCOUNT, &
QUERY "SELECT ACCOUNT_NAME FROM ACCOUNT WHERE ACCOUNT_CODE = ,:CODE_
IN_PARAM", &
PARAMS (CODE_IN_PARAM = ACCOUNT_CODE)), &
COLMAP (NEW_ACCOUNT_ID = ACCOUNT_ID, &
NEW_ACCOUNT_NAME = @GETVAL (LOOKUP_ACCOUNT.CODE_OUT_PARAM));
```

:CODE_IN_PARAM becomes a bind variable as the input to the SQL query that drives the lookup based on Account Code, while the CODE_OUT_PARAM remains as the **OUT** parameter that populates the NEW_ACCOUNT_NAME field.

Since we have referenced the LOOKUP_ACCOUNT procedure in both examples, here is the source code:

```
CREATE OR REPLACE PROCEDURE LOOKUP_ACCOUNT
        (CODE_IN_PARAM IN VARCHAR2, CODE_OUT_PARAM OUT VARCHAR2)
BEGIN
        SELECT ACCOUNT_NAME
        INTO CODE_OUT_PARAM
        FROM ACCOUNT
        WHERE ACCOUNT_CODE = CODE_IN_PARAM;
END;
```

Executing DML

Rather than having GoldenGate apply the data changes to the target database, it is possible to have SQLEXEC do this via INSERT, UPDATE, or DELETE commands. Using SQLEXEC in standalone mode to execute DML against the target database necessitates the DBOP keyword in the configuration to commit the changes, else the transaction will rollback.

The following example calls the AUDIT_TXN procedure that inserts a record into an audit table, keeping a history of GoldenGate transactions. On successful execution, the DBOP keyword ensures the transaction is committed to the target database.

```
SQLEXEC (SPNAME audit_txn, &
PARAMS (hostname = @GETENV ("GGENVIRONMENT","HOSTNAME"), &
@GETENV("GGENVIRONMENT","OSUSERNAME"), &
@GETENV ("GGHEADER", "OPTYPE"), &
@GETENV("GGHEADER","COMMITTIMESTAMP"), &
@GETENV ("GGHEADER", "TABLENAME"), &
ALLPARAMS REQUIRED, ERROR REPORT, DBOP)
```

> Note the use of the ALLPARAMS and REQUIRED keywords that enforce that all parameters must be present or else the procedure call will fail. Also, ERROR REPORT ensures all execution errors are reported by GoldenGate to the process' discard file.

Let's take a closer look at error handling within an SQLEXEC procedure call.

Handling errors

When using SQLEXEC, database errors must be handled, otherwise GoldenGate will abend the process regardless of the severity. Fortunately, this is made easy via the ERROR option of the SQLEXEC parameter. For calls to stored procedures, the error handling logic must be included in the procedure's PL/SQL EXCEPTION block to only raise those errors that you want GoldenGate to handle.

The following options will help you decide what GoldenGate will do when a database error is raised:

- IGNORE
    - GoldenGate does not handle any errors returned by the query or stored procedure. This is the default.

- REPORT
  - All errors returned by the query or stored procedure are reported to the discard file. GoldenGate continues processing after reporting the error.

- RAISE
  - Handles errors set by a REPERROR parameter specified in the process' parameter file. However, GoldenGate continues processing other stored procedures or queries.

- FINAL
  - Acts in the same manner as RAISE except that the error is processed immediately.

- FATAL
  - GoldenGate abends the process immediately.

It is recommended to record the error to assist with troubleshooting. This is achieved through the REPORT, RAISE and FINAL options. That said, should a process abend, GoldenGate will always write the error to the process' report file.

Scheduling jobs

SQL and stored procedures can be executed from GoldenGate as one-off statements, or scheduled to run periodically. Although you would probably leave any job scheduling to the DBMS_SCHEDULER package in the Oracle 11g database, the following examples show; a one-off SQL execution, a procedure call scheduled to run daily, and another to run every 30 seconds from within the GoldenGate environment.

```
SQLEXEC "select sysdate from dual"
SQLEXEC "call etl_proc ()" EVERY 1 DAYS
SQLEXEC "call check_exceptions_table ()" EVERY 30 SECONDS
```

Note that SQLEXEC is a parameter and not a command. SQLEXEC and its associated expressions must exist in a parameter file and cannot be called directly from the GGSCI command prompt. Also, SQL statements are expressed in double quotes with no terminating semi-colon and are executed in the order they appear after the DBLOGIN specification.

Using and defining macros

As in many programmable software products, defining a macro allows for automation of repetitive tasks. This can be very useful when configuring a GoldenGate process. For example, trapping an exception for each MAP statement in a Replicat parameter file is both necessary and repetitive. However, defining the macro at the start of the parameter file allows the code to be called by an alias multiple times in the configuration.

The following example code block defines the `#exception_handler()` macro in a Replicat parameter file. All macros have a hash '#' character prefix in their name.

```
-- This starts the macro
MACRO #exception_handler
BEGIN
, TARGET ggs_admin.exceptions
, COLMAP ( rep_name = "ROLAP01"
, table_name = @GETENV ("GGHEADER", "TABLENAME")
, errno = @GETENV ("LASTERR", "DBERRNUM")
, dberrmsg = @GETENV ("LASTERR", "DBERRMSG")
, optype = @GETENV ("LASTERR", "OPTYPE")
, errtype = @GETENV ("LASTERR", "ERRTYPE")
, logrba = @GETENV ("GGHEADER", "LOGRBA")
, logposition = @GETENV ("GGHEADER", "LOGPOSITION")
, committimestamp = @GETENV ("GGHEADER", "COMMITTIMESTAMP"))
, INSERTALLRECORDS
, EXCEPTIONSONLY ;
END;
-- This ends the macro
```

It populates a target table named EXCEPTIONS with all the necessary information it derives from the GoldeGate environment via the @GETENV function. The macro can then be called in each MAP statement as follows:

```
MAP SRC.CHECK_PAYMENTS, TARGET TGT.CHECK_PAYMENTS_DIM, REPERROR
(-1403, EXCEPTION);
MAP SRC.CHECK_PAYMENTS #exception_handler()
MAP SRC.CHECK_PAYMENTS_STATUS, TARGET TGT.CHECK_PAYMENTS_STATUS_DIM,
REPERROR (-1403, EXCEPTION);
MAP SRC.CHECK_PAYMENTS_STATUS #exception_handler()
MAP SRC.CREDITCARD_ACCOUNTS, TARGET TGT.CREDITCARD_ACCOUNTS_FACT,
REPERROR (-1403, EXCEPTION);
MAP SRC.CREDITCARD_ACCOUNTS #exception_handler()
MAP SRC.CREDITCARD_PAYMENTS, TARGET TGT.CREDITCARD_PAYMENTS_FACT,
REPERROR (-1403, EXCEPTION);
MAP SRC.CREDITCARD_PAYMENTS #exception_handler()
```

We will discuss exception handling in greater detail in *Chapter 10, Troubleshooting GoldenGate.*

It is also possible to invoke other macros from within a macro, pass external parameters, and create macro libraries for all Manager, Extract, or Replicat parameter files to reference. Expanding on the previous example, the following Replicat parameter file references a macro library named `excep_handler.mac` stored in the `dirprm` sub-directory under the GoldenGate Home. The `#exceptions_handler()` macro can then be called multiple times without its definition existing in the same parameter file. Furthermore, it's now shared code within the GoldenGate environment.

```
INCLUDE ./dirprm/excep_handler.mac
REPLICAT ROLAP01
SOURCEDEFS ./dirdef/oltp.def
SETENV (ORACLE_SID=OLAP)
USERID ggs_admin, PASSWORD ggs_admin
DISCARDFILE ./dirrpt/rolap01.dsc, PURGE
REPERROR (DEFAULT, EXCEPTION)
MAP SRC.CHECK_PAYMENTS, TARGET TGT.CHECK_PAYMENTS_DIM, REPERROR
(-1403, EXCEPTION);
MAP SRC.CHECK_PAYMENTS #exception_handler()
..
```

User tokens

User tokens are GoldenGate environment variables that are captured and stored in the trail record for replication. They can be accessed via the @GETENV function which we have already touched upon the @GETENV function in the previous section, *Using and Defining macros*. You can use token data in column maps, stored procedures called by SQLEXEC, and of course macros.

A vast array of user tokens exists, too many to list in this book. You can use the TOKENS option of the Extract TABLE parameter to define a user token and associate it with GoldenGate environment data. For example:

```
TABLE SRC.CREDITCARD_ACCOUNTS, &
TOKENS (TKN_OSUSER = @GETENV("GGENVIRONMENT","OSUSERNAME"), &
TKN_DBNAME = @GETENV ("DBENVIRONMENT","DBNAME"), &
TKN_HOSTNAME = @GETENV ("GGENVIRONMENT","HOSTNAME"), &
TKN_COMMITTIME = @GETENV("GGHEADER","COMMITTIMESTAMP")  &
TKN_BEFOREAFTERIND = &
@GETENV(("GGHEADER","BEFOREAFTERINDICATOR"));
```

The defined user tokens can then be called within a MAP statement using the @ TOKEN function. User tokens are particularly useful for auditing data and trapping exceptions. The following example populates a record in the target database TGT. CREDITCARD_ACCOUNTS_FACT table having the four additional columns defined: OSUSER, DBNAME, HOSTNAME, and TIMESTAMP.

```
MAP SRC.CREDITCARD_ACCOUNTS, TARGET&&
TGT.CREDITCARD_ACCOUNTS_FACT &
COLMAP (USEDEFAULTS, &
OSUSER = @TOKEN ("TKN_OSUSER"), &
DBNAME = @TOKEN ("TKN_DBNAME"), &
HOSTNAME = @TOKEN ("TKN_HOSTNAME"), &
TIMESTAMP = @TOKEN ("TKN_COMMITTIME"), &
BEFOREAFTERIND = @TOKEN("TKN_BEFOREAFTERIND");
```

The BEFOREAFTERINDICATOR environment variable is particularly useful for providing a status flag showing whether the data was from a before or after image of an UPDATE or DELETE operation. By default, GoldenGate provides after images. To enable before image extraction, the GETUPDATEBEFORES Extract parameter must be used on the source database.

User Exits

If you find that your application requires arithmetic calculation or data transformation beyond that provided by GoldenGate functions and SQLEXEC, it is possible to invoke User Exits. These are user defined C or C++ function calls, extending the capabilities of GoldenGate. Typical applications for user exits are housekeeping tasks, data normalization, and conflict detection and handling.

Calling C routines

The user-defined functions may be called from either an Extract or Replicat process via the CUSEREXIT parameter.

To use user exits, create a shared object in C and create a routine to be called from Extract or Replicat.

The routine must accept the following parameters that provide the communication between GoldenGate and your C program:

EXIT_CALL_TYPE

EXIT_CALL_RESULT

EXIT_PARAMS

The following is an example C function header for `cleanup_task`, defining the required parameters:

```
void cleanup_task (exit_call_type_def exit_call_type,
        exit_result_def *exit_call_result,
        exit_params_def *exit_params)
```

And here is an example call to the `cleanuptask` C library routine specified in the Extract parameter file:

```
CUSEREXIT cleanup.so cleanup_task
```

In your C routine be sure to include the `usrdecs.h` library file that is located in the GoldenGate install directory. Call the `ERCALLBACK` function from your C routine to retrieve record and application context information.

Sample User Exits

GoldenGate provides a subdirectory named `UserExitExamples` beneath the installation directory (GoldenGate Home) that contains a number of examples. The source code and make files exist in the following subdirectories:

```
ls -l /home/oracle/ggs/UserExitExamples
drwxr-xr-x 2 oracle oinstall 4096 Sep 18  2009 ExitDemo
drwxr-xr-x 2 oracle oinstall 4096 Sep 18  2009 ExitDemo_lobs
drwxr-xr-x 2 oracle oinstall 4096 Sep 18  2009 ExitDemo_more_recs
drwxr-xr-x 2 oracle oinstall 4096 Sep 18  2009 ExitDemo_passthru
drwxr-xr-x 2 oracle oinstall 4096 Sep 18  2009 ExitDemo_pk_befores
```

Source files explained

The following table lists and describes the sample User Exit C programs that ship with Oracle GoldenGate 10.4:

C Program Name	Description
exitdemo.c	Shows how to initialize the user exit, issue callbacks at given exit points, and modify data.
exitdemo_passthru.c	Shows how the PASSTHRU option of the CUSEREXIT parameter can be used in an Extract Data Pump.
exitdemo_more_recs.c	Shows an example of how to use the same input record multiple times to generate several target records.
exitdemo_lob.c	Shows an example of how to get read access to LOB data.

C Program Name	Description
`exitdemo_pk_` `befores.c`	Shows how to access the before and after image portions of a primary key update record, as well as the before images of non primary key updates. Another method shows how to get target row values with SQLEXEC in the Replicat parameter file to provide the before image for conflict detection.

All the User Exit examples are based on the GoldenGate demo tables that must be created first by executing the following SQL scripts found in the GoldenGate Home directory:

```
ls -1 /home/oracle/ggs/demo*create*sql
```

```
demo_more_ora_create.sql
```

```
demo_ora_create.sql
```

```
demo_ora_lob_create.sql
```

```
demo_ora_pk_befores_create.sql
```

Using logic in data replication

GoldenGate has a number of functions that enable the administrator to program logic into the Extract and Replicat process configuration. These provide generic functions found in all programming languages, such as; IF and CASE. In addition, the @COLTEST function enables conditional calculations by testing for one or more column conditions. This is typically used with the @IF function as shown in the following example. Here the @COLTEST function tests the AMOUNT column in the source data to see if it is "MISSING" or "INVALID". The @IF function returns a 0 if @ COLTEST returns TRUE and the value of AMOUNT if FALSE.

```
MAP SRC.CREDITCARD_PAYMENTS, TARGET TGT.CREDITCARD_PAYMENTS_FACT, &
COLMAP (USEDEFAULTS, &
AMOUNT = @IF(@COLTEST(AMOUNT, MISSING, INVALID), 0, AMOUNT));
```

The target AMOUNT column is therefore set to 0 when the equivalent source is found to be missing or invalid, or else a direct mapping occurs.

The @CASE function tests a list of values for a match, and then returns a specified value. If no match is found, @CASE can return a default value. There is no limit to the number of cases to test, although if the list is very large a database lookup may be more appropriate. The following example shows the simplicity of the @CASE statement. Here the country name is returned from the country code.

```
MAP SRC.CREDITCARD_STATEMENT, TARGET TGT.CREDITCARD_STATEMENT_DIM, &
COLMAP (USEDEFAULTS, &
COUNTRY = @CASE(COUNTRY_CODE, "UK", "United Kingdom", "USA", "United
States of America"));
```

Other GoldenGate functions exist that perform tests: @EVAL and @VALONEOF. Similar to @CASE, @VALONEOF compares a column or string to a list of values. The difference being it evaluates more than one value against a single column or string. In the following example, when used with @IF it returns "EUROPE" when TRUE and "UNKNOWN" when FALSE:

```
MAP SRC.CREDITCARD_STATEMENT, TARGET TGT.CREDITCARD_STATEMENT_DIM, &
COLMAP (USEDEFAULTS, &
REGION = @IF(@VALONEOF(COUNTRY_CODE, "UK","E", "D"),"EUROPE",
"UNKNOWN"));
```

The @EVAL function evaluates a list of conditions and returns a specified value. Optionally, if none are satisfied it returns a default value. There is no limit to the number of evaluations you can list. However, it is best to list the most common at the beginning to enhance performance.

The following example includes the BEFORE option that compares the before value of the replicated source column to the current value of the target column. @EVAL will return "PAID MORE", "PAID LESS", or "PAID SAME" depending on the evaluation.

```
MAP SRC. CREDITCARD_ PAYMENTS, TARGET TGT.CREDITCARD_PAYMENTS, &
COLMAP (USEDEFAULTS, &
STATUS = @EVAL(AMOUNT < BEFORE.AMOUNT, "PAID LESS", AMOUNT > BEFORE.
AMOUNT, "PAID MORE", AMOUNT = BEFORE.AMOUNT, "PAID SAME"));
```

The BEFORE option can be used with other GoldenGate functions including the WHERE and FILTER clauses. However, in order for the before image to be written to the trail and to be available, the GETUPDATEBEFORES parameter must be enabled in the source database's Extract parameter file, or the target database's Replicat parameter file, but not both. The GETUPDATEBEFORES parameter can be set globally for all tables defined in the Extract or individually per table using GETUPDATEBEFORES and IGNOREUPDATEBEFORES as seen in the following example:

```
EXTRACT EOLTP01
SETENV (ORACLE_SID=OLTP)
```

```
USERID ggs_admin, PASSWORD ggs_admin
EXTTRAIL ./dirdat/sa
GETAPPLOPS
IGNOREREPLICATES
TRANLOGOPTIONS ASMUSER SYS@ASM, ASMPASSWORD Password1
GETUPDATEBEFORES
TABLE SRC.CHECK_PAYMENTS;
IGNOREUPDATEBEFORES
TABLE SRC.CHECK_PAYMENTS_STATUS;
TABLE SRC.CREDITCARD_ACCOUNTS;
TABLE SRC.CREDITCARD_PAYMENTS;
```

In the code examples given in this section, the parameter specification is sometimes seen to wrap over multiple lines because of the width of the page. In an actual parameter file, a multi-line parameter specifications must contain an ampersand (&) character at the end of each line. Parameter specifications are terminated with a semi-colon (;) character and do not require an additional ampersand.

Licensing

At the time of writing this book, Oracle bundled their Active Data Guard DR solution within the GoldenGate license, clearly expressing the close functionality of both products. As a Disaster Recovery solution, a Physical Standby database provides an exact copy of its Primary database, which is superlative. GoldenGate however, can easily replace a Logical Standby solution, offering more than just schema replication.

The Physical Standby element of Data Guard is quite different to GoldenGate's Changed Data Capture and Delivery. Although both solutions have a target database that is OPEN, the Standby database is READ ONLY and in "managed recovery mode". This means that data changes are applied at block level via Oracle's Database Recovery mechanism and not via SQL. The Primary and Physical Standby databases can also be automatically switched or failed over as both databases are mirrored copies sharing the same database name.

Summary

This chapter has provided an overview of the advanced configuration options that GoldenGate has to offer. We started with data selection using the WHERE and FILTER clauses before moving onto data mapping, exploring the COLMAP option and the DEFGEN utility. Finally, we discussed data transformation and the vast array of functions and tools available.

We also discovered that should GoldenGate not provide a function or mapping specific to our requirements, we can write our own in PL/SQL, C or C++. The GoldenGate software provides the necessary call interface to stored procedures and external routines.

In the next chapter, we learn how to measure and report on your GoldenGate performance. Here, we will discover the on demand and automated procedures for statistics gathering and process monitoring, enabling effective system management.

8
Managing Oracle GoldenGate

Managing a computer system can be a challenge, especially when there are multiple sites and distributed databases. We need to keep a close eye on things, ensuring that systems remain operational and efficient, checking that; the databases are open, data replication is running with minimal lag, adequate space is available in both the databases and file-systems, the list goes on.

Although Oracle offers a web-based product called Director, for managing and configuring GoldenGate instances, this chapter focuses on the management features already built in to the GoldenGate Command Interpreter (GGSCI). We will discuss and implement a number of utilities, including tips and tricks that allow us to manage our GoldenGate environment effectively at no extra cost. This includes the following:

- Command level security
- Trail File management
- Managing process startup
- Monitoring system health
- Managing TCP/IP errors
- Monitoring performance
- Gathering and reporting on statistics

Let's begin with Command level security.

Command level security

In the previous chapters, we discussed GoldenGate's Command Interpreter (GGSCI) in detail, conveying many useful commands, some of which are information only whilst others change or add to the configuration. This could be deemed as a security risk, allowing users to misconfigure or even delete valid processes, potentially breaking your GoldenGate environment.

To avoid this risk, GoldenGate has a security feature that protects your environment at the command level. Here, users are restricted in the commands they can execute from GGSCI.

The CMDSEC file

To enable Command Level Security, we must first create a CMDSEC file in the GoldenGate home directory. This text file should be created by the user responsible for the central administration of GoldenGate. It contains the security rules and controls which users have access to certain GGSCI commands.

Open the file using a text editor and specify one rule per line in the following format:

<command name> <command object> <OS group> <OS user> <YES |NO>

The following shows an example CMDSEC file, allowing the ggs_user access to STATUS and INFO commands on Extract and Replicat processes only, whilst the ggs_admin user has full access to all commands for all objects. It is important to order the configuration of entries from the most specific to the least specific (those with wildcards), because rules are always processed from the top down.

```
-- Command Line Security File
INFO EXTRACT ggs_grp ggs_user YES
INFO REPLICAT ggs_grp ggs_user YES
STATUS EXTRACT ggs_grp ggs_user YES
STATUS REPLICAT ggs_grp ggs_user YES
* * ggs_grp ggs_user NO
* * ggs_grp ggs_admin YES
```

The administrator (Oracle) must grant read access to anyone allowed access to GGSCI, but restrict write and purge access to everyone but the administrator. This is achieved using the Linux command chmod. If no entry is made for a given user, that user has full access to all GGSCI commands.

```
[oracle@dbserver1 ggs]$ chmod 644 CMDSEC
```

Here we see the file permissions are read-write for the Oracle user, but read only for groups and other users.

```
[oracle@dbserver1 ggs]$ ls -l CMDSEC

-rw-r--r-- 1 oracle oinstall 223 Nov  8 13:38 CMDSEC
```

When an attempt is made to execute a command that is not authorized, an appropriate error is echoed to the screen. Note in the following example, that despite the `ggs_user` user having been granted access to the `INFO` command, executing `INFO ALL` is prohibited. This is because the grants to the `INFO` command are specified in the CMDSEC file for Extract and Replicat only.

```
GGSCI (dbserver2) 1> info all

ERROR: Command not authorized for this user.


GGSCI (dbserver2) 2> info REPLICAT REPLCAT1


REPLICAT    REPLCAT1  Last Started 2010-11-08 13:26    Status RUNNING

Checkpoint Lag         00:00:00 (updated 00:00:08 ago)

Log Read Checkpoint    File ./dirdat/ta0000199

                       2010-11-08 13:26:08.029660  RBA 580


GGSCI (dbserver2) 3> stop mgr

ERROR: Command not authorized for this user.
```

By now, you know how to secure your environment. Let's now look at how to manage the daily volume of data being generated by GoldenGate Trail files.

Trail file management

In a busy database environment, redo data generation can increase significantly, particularly with the required supplemental logging enabled on your source tables. As we know, an Oracle database will "recycle" its redo logs in a round-robin fashion, switching to the next log when full. GoldenGate scans the redo logs and writes its own Trail files to the `dirdat` subdirectory. Although the Trail file data is typically a quarter the size of its equivalent redo data, if left unmanaged, the volume of files in `dirdat` can be significant. In the worst case, filling the filesystem to 100% utilized. Obviously this is not ideal, so GoldenGate has provided an automated mechanism for purging Trail files from this area.

This is achieved by configuring the PURGEOLDEXTRACTS parameter in the GoldenGate Manager parameter file as follows:

```
-- GoldenGate Manager parameter file
PORT 7809
PURGEOLDEXTRACTS ./dirdat/sa*, USECHECKPOINTS, MINKEEPHOURS 1
```

The USECHECKPOINTS option preserves the Trail files in the dirdat subdirectory until the last record in a file is check-pointed. This ensures that no files are deleted that are still required for replication. Additionally, MINKEEPHOURS retains the check-pointed Trail files for the specified number of hours.

Another option of the PURGEOLDEXTRACTS parameter is MINKEEPFILES that allows GoldenGate to maintain a minimum number of Trail files over and above the MINKEEPHOURS specified. This particular option is rarely used in production environments. However, a warning is written to the GoldenGate error log as shown in the following example:

```
2010-11-09 13:58:40  GGS WARNING     201  Oracle GoldenGate Manager
for Oracle, mgr.prm:  PURGEOLDEXTRACTS ./dirdat/tb*, USECHECKPOINTS,
MINKEEPHOURS 1 (MINKEEPFILES option not used.).
```

It is important to configure Trail file management on both the source and the target to ensure adequate free space is maintained in your local and remote file systems, even at peak times.

The purging operation is written to the ggserr.log as an informational message, as seen in the following example output:

```
2010-10-13 16:17:21  INFO    OGG-00957  Oracle GoldenGate Manager for
Oracle, mgr.prm:  Purged old extract file /u01/app/oracle/product/ggs/
dirdat/sa000020, applying UseCheckPoints purge rule: Oldest Chkpt Seqno
23 > 20.
```

Managing process startup

In a near real-time data replication environment, we don't want to incur high latencies nor outages due to process failure. GoldenGate has a mechanism to automatically restart Extract or Replicat processes should they fail. The AUTORESTART parameter of the Manager process governs this and provides additional options on retry attempts.

```
-- GoldenGate Manager parameter file
PORT 7809
AUTORESTART EXTRACT *, RETRIES 3, WAITMINUTES 1, RESETMINUTES 60
```

In addition, the AUTOSTART parameter enables automatic start up of either the Extract or Replicat processes when the Manager process starts. The following example configuration is for the Extract processes:

```
AUTOSTART EXTRACT *
```

For Replicat processes:

```
AUTOSTART REPLICAT *
```

For both:

```
AUTOSTART ER *
```

Once manually stopped by executing the GGSCI STOP command, the Extract or Replicat processes will not auto-start. This is important for planned maintenance operations.

The Manager process report file MGR.rpt contains information regarding the configuration and process startup and shutdown, including the TCP port number the Server Collector process is using.

We have learnt the importance of configuring AUTORESTART to restart failed processes following an error. Let's now take a closer look at the network layer and understand how TCP/IP errors are handled by GoldenGate.

Managing TCP/IP errors

GoldenGate automatically handles TCP/IP network related errors. The actual response, delay in responding and the maximum number or retries are configured in a text parameter file named tcperrs. This file can be found in the GoldenGate home directory.

Any errors occurring at the network layer are written to the GoldenGate log file ggserr.log located in the GoldenGate Home directory. These errors are categorized as WARNINGS.

The tcperrs file

The following is the default configuration held in the tcperrs file:

```
# Error          Response      Delay (csecs)    Max Retries

ECONNABORTED     RETRY         1000             10
#ECONNREFUSED    ABEND         0                0
ECONNREFUSED     RETRY         1000             12
```

ECONNRESET	RETRY	500	10
ENETDOWN	RETRY	3000	50
ENETRESET	RETRY	1000	10
ENOBUFS	RETRY	100	60
ENOTCONN	RETRY	100	10
EPIPE	RETRY	500	10
ESHUTDOWN	RETRY	1000	10
ETIMEDOUT	RETRY	1000	10
NODYNPORTS	RETRY	100	10

In GoldenGate, the default response to errors is to abend the process suffering the condition. This is not ideal for network errors, where a network glitch could stop a process from running altogether. TCP/IP errors are handled separately, allowing processes to retry a number of times before failing.

Reporting and statistics

An important part of any computer system is its ability to report and provide statistics on the availability and performance. GoldenGate offers a number of options to monitor status, latency, and throughput using its command line interface.

To monitor for errors and warnings, we must look beyond the GGSCI tool and into the log files.

Monitoring errors

It is important to note that errors detected by GoldenGate are not automatically alerted to Network Managers, SMS gateways, or Email servers. Therefore, the GoldenGate administrator must proactively monitor the logs generated by GoldenGate, the OS, and the Database. This includes the following file list (Linux):

- `<GoldenGate_Home>/ggserr.log`
  - Provides all GoldenGate **INFO, WARNING**, and **ERROR** messages

- `/var/log/messages`
  - Provides all Operating System **INFO, WARNING**, and **ERROR** messages, including GoldenGate processes.

- `$ORACLE_BASE/diag/rdbms/$ORACLE_SID/trace/alert_$ORACLE_SID.log`
  - Provides all Oracle **INFO, WARNING,** and **ORA-** error messages relating to the Oracle database instance.

To access the system messages file `/var/log/messages` you must be logged in as root, the Linux super user.

As a simple health check solution, run a **tail** against the `ggserr.log` to provide real-time monitoring of system status. For example, the Linux command to achieve this is as follows:

```
[oracle@dbserver2 ggs]$ tail -f ggserr.log | egrep 'WARNING|ERROR'

2010-10-29 17:12:38  ERROR   OGG-00665  Oracle GoldenGate Delivery for
Oracle, replcat1.prm:  OCI Error calling OCITransCommit (status = 3114-
ORA-03114: not connected to ORACLE), SQL<UPDATE "GGS_ADMIN"."GGSCHKPT"
SET last_update_ts = sysdate,          seqno = :seqno,        rba = :rba,
audit_ts = :audit_ts  WHERE group_name = :group_name AND        group_key
= :key>.
```

 Simple Network Management Protocol (SNMP) *Traps would need to be developed and integrated with a Network Manager to enable automatic GoldenGate error notification.*

Monitoring latency

One of the key measurements in your GoldenGate environment is Lag. You will want to know the time taken from a transaction being committed on the source database to the time it is committed on the target. This gives an overall picture of performance against each process.

Lag information can be measured automatically at intervals by adding the following parameters to the Manager process parameter file:

```
LAGINFOMINUTES 0
LAGREPORTMINUTES 1
```

The Lag information is subsequently written to the GoldenGate error log every minute. A value of zero for the `LAGINFOMINUTES` parameter forces an informational message to be written to the log at the frequency specified by the `LAGREPORTMINUTES` parameter.

The following example shows the Lag and Checkpoint data for three Replicat processes:

```
[oracle@dbserver2 ggs]$ tail -f ggserr.log

2010-11-09 13:50:01  GGS INFO        260  Oracle GoldenGate Manager for
Oracle, mgr.prm:  Lag for REPLICAT REPLCAT1 is 00:00:00 (checkpoint
updated 00:00:23 ago).
```

```
2010-11-09 13:50:01  GGS INFO        260  Oracle GoldenGate Manager for
Oracle, mgr.prm:  Lag for REPLICAT REPLCAT2 is 00:00:00 (checkpoint
updated 00:00:05 ago).
2010-11-09 13:50:01  GGS INFO        260  Oracle GoldenGate Manager for
Oracle, mgr.prm:  Lag for REPLICAT REPLCAT3 is 00:00:00 (checkpoint
updated 00:00:05 ago).
```

Another option is to use the following GGSCI commands:

```
GGSCI (dbserver2) 1> LAG REPLICAT *
```

Or

```
GGSCI (dbserver2) 2> SEND REPLICAT *, GETLAG
```

Or

```
GGSCI (dbserver2) 3> INFO ALL
```

Lag reported by the LAG or SEND commands is more accurate than that reported by INFO ALL, as the statistic is taken from the last record that was check-pointed, not the current record that is being processed. However, in reality the difference is minimal.

A bespoke solution to monitoring and reporting

The INFO ALL command provides a complete summary of process status, lag, and checkpoint times. Furthermore, to collect this information every minute would be useful not only for monitoring purposes, but also for reporting.

The following two example scripts provide the necessary solution:

- info_all.sh
    - A Shell script () that, when scheduled via a crontab job, captures the output of the GGSCI INFO ALL command periodically including a timestamp of each execution.

- format_info.pl
    - A Perl script that formats the data from the Shell script into a pipe (|) delimited text file.

The code for the `info_all.sh` script is shown next:

```
#!/bin/sh

# info_all.sh

export ORACLE_SID=OLAP
export ORACLE_BASE=/u01/app/oracle
export ORACLE_HOME=/u01/app/oracle/product/11.1.0/db_1
export GGS_HOME=/u01/app/oracle/product/ggs
export PATH=$PATH:$HOME/bin:$ORACLE_HOME/bin:/usr/local/bin:/bin
export LD_LIBRARY_PATH=$ORACLE_HOME/lib

echo
echo "###########################################################"
echo `date +%d/%m/%Y\ %k:%M:%S`

$GGS_HOME/ggsci <<EOF
info all
exit
EOF
```

The `info_all.sh` script can have its output redirected to a text file and scheduled to execute every minute, as specified in the following crontab example entry:

```
* * * * * /home/oracle/ggs/ggs_scripts/info_all.sh >> /home/oracle/ggs/
output/info_all.txt 2>&1
```

An example of the output data is shown next:

```
###########################################################
12/10/2010 10:09:01

Oracle GoldenGate Command Interpreter for Oracle
Version 11.1.1.0.0 Build 078
Linux, x64, 64bit (optimized), Oracle 11 on Jul 28 2010 13:13:42

Copyright (C) 1995, 2010, Oracle and/or its affiliates. All rights
reserved.

GGSCI (dbserver2) 1>
Program     Status      Group       Lag         Time Since Chkpt

MANAGER     RUNNING
```

REPLICAT	RUNNING	RTGTMSG1	00:00:07	00:00:01
REPLICAT	RUNNING	RTGTMSG2	00:00:07	00:00:00
REPLICAT	RUNNING	RTGTRNG1	00:00:00	00:00:00
REPLICAT	RUNNING	RTGTRNG2	00:00:00	00:00:00
REPLICAT	RUNNING	RTGTRNG3	00:00:06	00:00:00
REPLICAT	RUNNING	RTGTRNG4	00:00:06	00:00:00

Running a `tail -f info_all.txt` in a terminal session would provide us with an up to date mechanism that monitors (in this case) the target system's GoldenGate processes. To report on a full hour or more of running and to load the results into Microsoft Excel for further analysis, we need to format the data appropriately. Microsoft Excel is able to load text files that have their data contents delimited by a special character, typically a comma. These text files are known as **Comma Separated Values (CSV)** files. The example Perl script (`format_info.pl`) extracts the timestamp from the data produced by the Shell script (`info_all.sh`) and formats the text into delimited values. In the following example, a pipe (|) delimiter character has been used to achieve this. The code for the `format_info.pl` script is shown next:

```perl
#!/usr/bin/perl

# format_info.pl
#
# Script to format output from GoldenGate GGSCI INFO ALL
# command into pipe delimited text

# Author: John Jeffries

use strict;
use warnings;
# read each line, tag with timestamp, pipe delimit each element and
print
our($timestamp) = "";
my(@lines) = ();
open (FILE,"<", "info_all.txt") or die "Could not read file: $!";
LINE: while( <FILE> )
    {
    my($line) = $_;
    chomp($line);

    if($line =~ m|^\d\d/\d\d/\d\d\d\d \d\d:\d\d:\d\d$| ) # timestamp
line
        {
    $timestamp = $line;
            next LINE;
```

```
            }
      elsif($_ =~ m/REPLICAT/)
          {
    print "$timestamp\|";
    $_ =~ s/\s+/\|/g;
    @lines = ($_);
         print "@lines\n";
         next LINE;
         }
      else
        {
         next LINE;
         }
      }

   close (FILE);
```

The input file to the Perl script is `info_all.txt`, the output file is `output.txt` as is invoked on the Linux command line as follows:

```
$ ./format_info.pl > output.txt
```

The output looks similar to the following:

```
12/10/2010 12:49:01|REPLICAT|RUNNING|RTGTMSG1|00:00:09|00:00:22|
12/10/2010 12:49:01|REPLICAT|RUNNING|RTGTMSG2|00:00:09|00:00:22|
12/10/2010 12:49:01|REPLICAT|RUNNING|RTGTRNG1|00:00:08|00:00:01|
12/10/2010 12:49:01|REPLICAT|RUNNING|RTGTRNG2|00:00:08|00:00:01|
12/10/2010 12:49:01|REPLICAT|RUNNING|RTGTRNG3|00:00:08|00:00:01|
12/10/2010 12:49:01|REPLICAT|RUNNING|RTGTRNG4|00:00:08|00:00:01|
```

Graphing the results using Microsoft Excel

Now it is possible to produce graphs from the output data against the date/time (column 1 x-axis) and lag (column 5 y-axis) columns. The following steps walk through the process of using the Microsoft Excel 2007 text import wizard to achieve this:

1. From within Excel, open the pipe delimited text file (`output.txt`) as shown in the following screenshot:

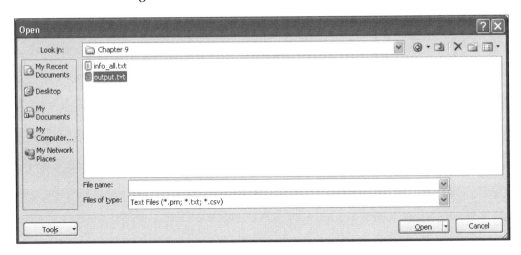

2. In step 1 of 3 shown in the wizard dialog box, select the **Delimited** radio button and then click the **Next** button

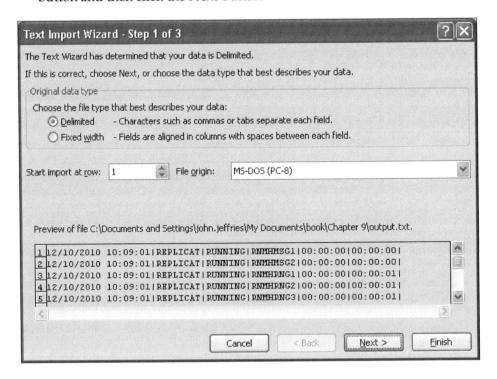

3. Type the pipe (|) character into the **Other** field and click the **Next** button.

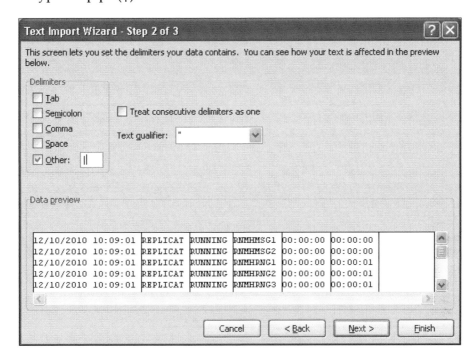

4. Change the first column from **General** to **Date** format and click the **Finish** button.

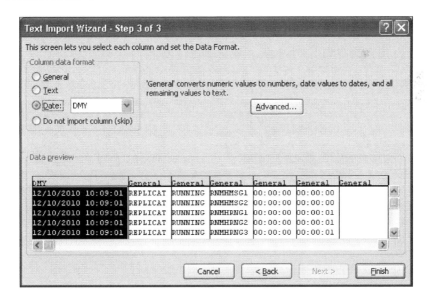

5. Now with the data loaded and presented in the spreadsheet, select the first and the fifth columns before clicking on the **2-D Line** graphing wizard to generate the graph.

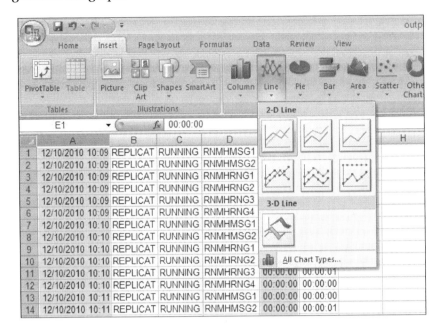

The following line graph was produced from the output data using the Microsoft Excel 2007 Graphing Wizard:

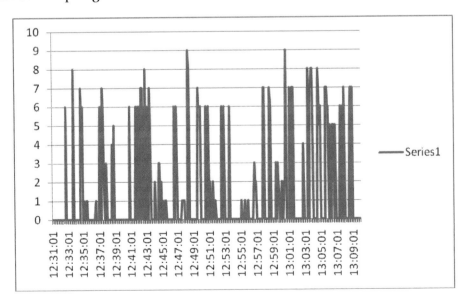

Although Oracle provides tools such as Oracle Management Pack, (formerly known as GoldenGate Director) for monitoring and reporting, this simple solution satisfies the requirement at no additional cost to your GoldenGate implementation.

Measuring throughput

Your lag figures may be good, but what about your throughput? In a replication environment it is important to measure the amount of data replicated in a given time period. After all, bandwidth is always quoted in Gigabits per second (Gbit/s). Furthermore, the associated number and type of operation is also worth measuring and reporting on, collectively giving us an overall understanding of our GoldenGate environment performance.

Data throughput

To calculate the rate of throughput in GoldenGate, we can use the following parameter to automatically append relevant statistics to the process' report file:

```
REPORTCOUNT EVERY 1 MINUTES, RATE
```

REPORTCOUNT can be used in your Extract or Replicat parameter file. The RATE option provides additional performance statistics, calculating the total number of records divided by the total time elapsed since the process started, including a delta statistic on the number of records since the last report, divided by the time since the last report.

Here is example Extract report showing the RATE statistics for the 1 minute interval:

```
2010-10-13 11:24:58  INFO    OGG-01026  Rolling over remote file ./
dirdat/na000060.
          9334116 records processed as of 2010-10-13 11:25:24 (rate
3728,delta 9352)
          9907789 records processed as of 2010-10-13 11:26:24 (rate
3865,delta 9543)
          10492064 records processed as of 2010-10-13 11:27:26 (rate
3997,delta 9518)
          10975243 records processed as of 2010-10-13 11:28:26 (rate
4088,delta 8052)
```

To measure throughput per second, minute, or hour, we have to calculate the number of bytes transmitted over a given period. To achieve this, we must follow these simple steps for each Extract or Replicat process during a sustained load:

1. Log on to the source or target database server as the Oracle user and invoke GGSCI.

2. Execute the `INFO ALL` command to list the individual processes. Choose a process to measure throughput on and obtain its runtime details.

```
GGSCI (dbserver2) 2> info RTGTRNG1, detail


REPLICAT   RTGTRNG1 Last Started 2010-10-29 16:39   Status RUNNING
Checkpoint Lag       00:00:00 (updated 00:00:27 ago)
Log Read Checkpoint  File ./dirdat/nb000001
                     2010-10-29 17:07:15.993969  RBA 428715322


  Extract Source                            Begin          End


  ./dirdat/nb000001                         2010-10-29 16:37  2010-
10-29 17:07
  ./dirdat/nb000000                         * Initialized *  2010-
10-29 16:37
```

3. Wait for one minute and execute the same command from GGSCI.

```
GGSCI (dbserver2) 3> !
info RTGTRNG1, detail


REPLICAT   RTGTRNG1 Last Started 2010-10-29 16:39   Status RUNNING
Checkpoint Lag       00:00:00 (updated 00:00:07 ago)
Log Read Checkpoint  File ./dirdat/nb000001
                     2010-10-29 17:08:15.982789  RBA 485803675
```

4. Now calculate the throughput by subtracting the Relative Byte Address (RBA) of the second command output from the first.

```
485803675 - 428715322 = 57088353 bytes / minute
```

5. Convert bytes per minute to megabytes per minute.

```
57088353/(1024*1024) = 54.55 MB/minute
```

6. Convert megabytes per minute to megabytes per hour.

```
54.55 * 60 = 3266.62 MB/hour
```

7. Finally, calculate the rate in gigabytes per hour.

```
3266.62/1024 = 3.19 GB/hour
```

This procedure provides an excellent mechanism to calculate the data throughput accurately for each process and to quickly identify bottlenecks.

Operation throughput

We know how to measure and report on lag and data throughput in our GoldenGate environment. Let's now look at operation throughput. This is the total number of insert, update, delete, and discard operations per second that have occurred during a given period.

Thankfully, GoldenGate provides comprehensive statistics on operation throughput, which are used for confirming processes are working as well as reporting volumes and performance. This is achieved using the GGSCI STATS command against either an Extract or Replicat process. The following command provides statistics on the cumulative number of operations since process startup, including per day and per hour. It also supports wildcards.

```
GGSCI (dbserver2) 1> stats replicat  RTGTRNG1, totalsonly *, reportrate
sec
```

Another option of the STATS command is to report on the volume of operations over a given period, on this occasion, against an Extract process and specific table.

```
GGSCI (dbserver1) 1> stats EXTRACT ESRCNMSG, totalsonly SRC.ORDERS
```

To have operation volumes written to a process report file on demand, execute the GGSCI SEND command to create the report.

```
GGSCI (dbserver1) 2> send EXTRACT ESRCNMSG, report

Sending REPORT request to EXTRACT ESRCNMSG ...
Request processed.
```

The SEND command can be used with EVENTACTIONS to generate statistics on a specific event. To read the latest report file use the VIEW command.

```
GGSCI (dbserver1) 3> view report ESRCNMSG

..

Output to ./dirdat/na:


From Table SRC.SESSIONS:
        #                       inserts:       2526
        #                       updates:       2526
        #                       deletes:          0
        #                       discards:         0
From Table SRC.USERS:
        #                       inserts:          0
        #                       updates:       7534
```

```
   #                    deletes:         0
   #                    discards:        0
From Table SRC.ORDERS:
   #                    inserts:    476897
   #                    updates:    240484
   #                    deletes:         0
   #                    discards:        0
..
```

In addition to viewing log files and using OS tools, the GoldenGate Command
Interpreter (GGSCI) provides a comprehensive set of commands for managing and
monitoring your GoldenGate instance.

Summary

Having installed, configured, and tuned your GoldenGate environment, this chapter
has taught you how to manage and monitor it. Using the GoldenGate Command
Interpreter you have learnt the commands and options that allow historic and real-
time reports and statistics to be viewed against individual and collective processes.
Thus providing the information necessary to fully support and manage your
GoldenGate environment.

This chapter has also provided bespoke scripts for leveraging your own techniques
to collect and subsequently graph statistics.

The next chapter is dedicated to performance tuning, where we learn how to use
all of the configuration options and techniques described in this book to enable and
maintain real-time data replication.

9
Performance Tuning

Performance tuning is one of the main aspects of any IT project. Many leave it to the end and then realize that it is not possible to make the necessary changes without significant additional investment or time constraints. Performance must be considered at the beginning and throughout the lifetime of your project. Closely coupled to the design, this chapter hones in on individual performance tuning methods.

Oracle states that GoldenGate can achieve near real-time data replication. However, out of the box, GoldenGate may not meet your performance requirements. Here we focus on the main areas that lend themselves to tuning, especially parallel processing and load balancing, enabling high data throughput and very low latency.

In this chapter, we learn the following:

- Balancing load across multiple processes
- Splitting large or transaction intensive tables across parallel process groups
- Adding additional Replicats to a process group
- Improving Replicat throughput by reducing commit delay
- Exploring the GoldenGate 11.1.1 new features
- Tuning the network

Let's start by taking a look at some of the considerations before we start tuning Oracle GoldenGate.

Before tuning GoldenGate

There are a number of considerations we need to be aware of before we start the tuning process. For one, we must consider the underlying system and its ability to perform. Let's start by looking at the source of data that GoldenGate needs for replication to work the online redo logs.

Online redo

Before we start tuning GoldenGate, we must look at both the source and target databases and their ability to read/write data. Data replication is I/O intensive, so fast disks are important, particularly for the online redo logs. Redo logs play an important role in GoldenGate: they are constantly being written to by the database and concurrently being read by the Extract process. Furthermore, adding supplemental logging to a database can increase their size by a factor of 4!

Firstly, ensure that only the necessary amount of supplemental logging is enabled on the database. In the case of GoldenGate, the logging of the Primary Key is all that is required.

Next, take a look at the database wait events, in particular the ones that relate to redo. For example, if you are seeing "Log File Sync" waits, this is an indicator that either your disk writes are too slow or your application is committing too frequently, or a combination of both. RAID5 is another common problem for redo log writes. Ideally, these files should be placed on their own mirrored storage such as RAID1+0 (mirrored striped sets) or Flash disks. Many argue this to be a misconception with modern high speed disk arrays, but some production systems are still known to be suffering from redo I/O contention on RAID5.

An adequate number (and size) of redo groups must be configured to prevent "checkpoint not complete" or "cannot allocate new log" warnings appearing in the database instance alert log. This occurs when Oracle attempts to reuse a log file but the checkpoint that would flush the blocks in the DB buffer cache to disk are still required for crash recovery. The database must wait until that checkpoint completes before the online redolog file can be reused, effectively stalling the database and any redo generation.

Large objects (LOBs)

Know your data. LOBs can be a problem in data replication by virtue of their size and the ability to extract, transmit, and deliver the data from source to target. We discussed LOBs in *Chapter 5, Configuration Options*, expressing the importance of not using the BATCHSQL tuning parameter. Furthermore, tables containing LOB datatypes should be isolated from regular data to use a dedicated Extract, Data Pump, and Replicat process group to enhance throughput. Also ensure that the target table has a primary key to avoid Full Table Scans (FTS), an Oracle GoldenGate best practice. LOB INSERT operations can insert an empty (null) LOB into a row before updating it with the data. This is because a LOB (depending on its size) can spread its data across multiple Logical Change Records, resulting in multiple DML operations required at the target database.

Base lining

Before we can start tuning, we must record our baseline. This will provide a reference point to tune from. We can later look back at our baseline and calculate the percentage improvement made from deploying new configurations.

An ideal baseline is to find the "breaking point" of your application requirements. For example, the following questions must be answered:

1. What is the maximum acceptable end to end latency?
2. What are the maximum application transactions per second we must accommodate?

To answer these questions we must start with a single threaded data replication configuration having just one Extract, one Data Pump, and one Replicat process. This will provide us with a worst case scenario in which to build improvements on.

Ideally, our data source should be the application itself, inserting, deleting, and updating "real data" in the source database. However, simulated data with the ability to provide throughput profiles will allow us to gauge performance accurately Application vendors can normally provide SQL injector utilities that simulate the user activity on the system.

Balancing the load across parallel process groups

The GoldenGate documentation states "The most basic thing you can do to improve GoldenGate's performance is to divide a large number of tables among parallel processes and trails. For example, you can divide the load by schema".This statement is true as the bottleneck is largely due to the serial nature of the Replicat process, having to "replay" transactions in commit order. Although this can be a constraining factor due to transaction dependency, increasing the number of Replicat processes increases performance significantly. However, it is highly recommended to group tables with referential constraints together per Replicat.

The number of parallel processes is typically greater on the target system compared to the source. The number and ratio of processes will vary across applications and environments. Each configuration should be thoroughly tested to determine the optimal balance, but be careful not to over allocate, as each parallel process will consume up to 55MB. Increasing the number of processes to an arbitrary value will not necessarily improve performance, in fact it may be worse and you will waste CPU and memory resources.

The following data flow diagram shows a load balancing configuration including two Extract processes, three Data Pump, and five Replicats:

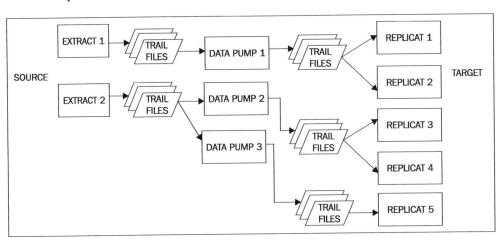

Considerations for using parallel process groups

To maintain data integrity, ensure to include tables with referential constraints between one another in the same parallel process group. It's also worth considering disabling referential constraints on the target database schema to allow child records to be populated before their parents, thus increasing throughput. GoldenGate will always commit transactions in the same order as the source, so data integrity is maintained.

Oracle best practice states no more than 3 Replicat processes should read the same remote trail file. To avoid contention on Trail files, pair each Replicat with its own Trail files and Extract process. Also, remember that it is easier to tune an Extract process than a Replicat process, so concentrate on your source before moving your focus to the target.

Splitting large tables into row ranges across process groups

What if you have some large tables with a high data change rate within a source schema and you cannot logically separate them from the remaining tables due to referential constraints? GoldenGate provides a solution to this problem by "splitting" the data within the same schema via the @RANGE function. The @RANGE function can be used in the Data Pump and Replicat configuration to "split" the transaction data across a number of parallel processes.

The Replicat process is typically the source of performance bottlenecks because, in its normal mode of operation, it is a single-threaded process that applies operations one at a time by using regular DML. Therefore, to leverage parallel operation and enhance throughput, the more Replicats the better (dependant on the number of CPUs and memory available on the target system).

The RANGE function

The way the @RANGE function works is it computes a hash value of the columns specified in the input. If no columns are specified, it uses the table's primary key. GoldenGate adjusts the total number of ranges to optimize the even distribution across the number of ranges specified. This concept can be compared to Hash Partitioning in Oracle tables as a means of dividing data.

With any division of data during replication, the integrity is paramount and will have an effect on performance. Therefore, tables having a relationship with other tables in the source schema must be included in the configuration. If all your source schema tables are related, you must include all the tables!

Adding Replicats with @RANGE function

The @RANGE function accepts two numeric arguments, separated by a comma:

1. **Range**: The number assigned to a process group, where the first is 1 and the second 2 and so on, up to the total number of ranges.

2. **Total number of ranges**: The total number of process groups you wish to divide using the @RANGE function.

The following example includes three related tables in the source schema and walks through the complete configuration from start to finish.

For this example, we have an existing Replicat process on the target machine (dbserver2) named ROLAP01 that includes the following three tables:

- ORDERS
- ORDER_ITEMS
- PRODUCTS

We are going to divide the rows of the tables across two Replicat groups. The source database schema name is SRC and target schema TGT. The following steps add a new Replicat named ROLAP02 with the relevant configuration and adjusts Replicat ROLAP01 parameters to suit.

 Note that before conducting any changes stop the existing Replicat processes and determine their **Relative Byte Address (RBA)** and Trail file log sequence number. This is important information that we will use to tell the new Replicat process from which point to start.

1. First check if the existing Replicat process is running:

   ```
   GGSCI (dbserver2) 1> info all
   ```

Program	Status	Group	Lag	Time Since Chkpt
MANAGER	RUNNING			
REPLICAT	RUNNING	ROLAP01	00:00:00	00:00:02

2. Stop the existing Replicat process:

   ```
   GGSCI (dbserver2) 2> stop REPLICAT ROLAP01

   Sending STOP request to REPLICAT ROLAP01...
   Request processed.
   ```

3. Add the new Replicat process, using the existing trail file.

```
GGSCI (dbserver2) 3> add REPLICAT ROLAP02, exttrail ./dirdat/tb
REPLICAT added.
```

4. Now add the configuration by creating a new parameter file for ROLAP02.

```
GGSCI (dbserver2) 4> edit params ROLAP02
```

```
--

-- Example Replicator parameter file to apply changes
-- to target tables
--
REPLICAT ROLAP02
SOURCEDEFS ./dirdef/mydefs.def
SETENV (ORACLE_SID= OLAP)
USERID ggs_admin, PASSWORD ggs_admin
DISCARDFILE ./dirrpt/rolap02.dsc, PURGE
ALLOWDUPTARGETMAP
CHECKPOINTSECS 30
GROUPTRANSOPS 2000

MAP SRC.ORDERS, TARGET TGT.ORDERS, FILTER (@RANGE (1,2));
MAP SRC.ORDER_ITEMS, TARGET TGT.ORDER_ITEMS, FILTER (@RANGE
(1,2));
MAP SRC.PRODUCTS, TARGET TGT.PRODUCTS, FILTER (@RANGE (1,2));
```

5. Now edit the configuration of the existing Replicat process, and add the @RANGE function to the FILTER clause of the MAP statement. Note the inclusion of the GROUPTRANSOPS parameter to enhance performance by increasing the number of operations allowed in a Replicat transaction.

```
GGSCI (dbserver2) 5> edit params ROLAP01
```

```
--

-- Example Replicator parameter file to apply changes
-- to target tables
--
REPLICAT ROLAP01
SOURCEDEFS ./dirdef/mydefs.def
SETENV (ORACLE_SID=OLAP)
```

```
USERID ggs_admin, PASSWORD ggs_admin

DISCARDFILE ./dirrpt/rolap01.dsc, PURGE

ALLOWDUPTARGETMAP

CHECKPOINTSECS 30

GROUPTRANSOPS 2000

MAP SRC.ORDERS, TARGET TGT.ORDERS, FILTER (@RANGE (2,2));

MAP SRC.ORDER_ITEMS, TARGET TGT.ORDER_ITEMS, FILTER (@RANGE
(2,2));

MAP SRC.PRODUCTS, TARGET TGT.PRODUCTS, FILTER (@RANGE (2,2));
```

6. Check that both the Replicat processes exist.

```
GGSCI (dbserver2) 6> info all
```

Program	Status	Group	Lag	Time Since Chkpt
MANAGER	RUNNING			
REPLICAT	STOPPED	ROLAP01	00:00:00	00:10:35
REPLICAT	STOPPED	ROLAP02	00:00:00	00:12:25

7. Before starting both Replicat processes, obtain the log **Sequence Number (SEQNO)** and **Relative Byte Address (RBA)** from the original trail file.

```
GGSCI (dbserver2) 7> info REPLICAT ROLAP01, detail

REPLICAT   ROLAP01  Last Started 2010-04-01 15:35   Status STOPPED

Checkpoint Lag       00:00:00 (updated 00:12:43 ago)

Log Read Checkpoint  File ./dirdat/tb000279 <- SEQNO

    2010-04-08 12:27:00.001016  RBA 43750979 <- RBA
```

Extract Source	Begin	End
./dirdat/tb000279	2010-04-01 12:47	2010-04-08 12:27
./dirdat/tb000257	2010-04-01 04:30	2010-04-01 12:47
./dirdat/tb000255	2010-03-30 13:50	2010-04-01 04:30
./dirdat/tb000206	2010-03-30 13:50	First Record
./dirdat/tb000206	2010-03-30 04:30	2010-03-30 13:50
./dirdat/tb000184	2010-03-30 04:30	First Record
./dirdat/tb000184	2010-03-30 00:00	2010-03-30 04:30
./dirdat/tb000000	* Initialized *	2010-03-30 00:00
./dirdat/tb000000	* Initialized *	First Record

8. Adjust the new Replicat process ROLAP02 to adopt these values, so that the process knows where to start from on startup.

```
GGSCI (dbserver2) 8> alter replicat ROLAP02, extseqno 279
REPLICAT altered.


GGSCI (dbserver2) 9> alter replicat ROLAP02, extrba 43750979
REPLICAT altered.
```

> Failure to complete this step will result in either duplicate data or ORA-00001 against the target schema, because GoldenGate will attempt to replicate the data from the beginning of the initial trail file (`./dirdat/tb000000`) if it exists, else the process will abend.

9. Start both Replicat processes. Note the use of the wildcard (*).

```
GGSCI (dbserver2) 10> start replicat ROLAP*

Sending START request to MANAGER ...
REPLICAT ROLAP01 starting

Sending START request to MANAGER ...
REPLICAT ROLAP02 starting
```

10. Check if both Replicat processes are running.

```
GGSCI (dbserver2) 11> info all
```

Program	Status	Group	Lag	Time Since Chkpt
MANAGER	RUNNING			
REPLICAT	RUNNING	ROLAP01	00:00:00	00:00:22
REPLICAT	RUNNING	ROLAP02	00:00:00	00:00:14

11. Check the detail of the new Replicat processes.

```
GGSCI (dbserver2) 12> info REPLICAT ROLAP02, detail

REPLICAT    ROLAP02   Last Started 2010-04-08 14:18    Status RUNNING
Checkpoint Lag          00:00:00 (updated 00:00:06 ago)
Log Read Checkpoint   File ./dirdat/tb000279
                        First Record   RBA 43750979

   Extract Source                Begin               End
```

```
./dirdat/tb000279        * Initialized *    First Record
./dirdat/tb000279        * Initialized *    First Record
./dirdat/tb000279        * Initialized *    2010-04-08 12:26
./dirdat/tb000279        * Initialized *    First Record
```

12. Generate a report for the new Replicat process ROLAP02.

```
GGSCI (dbserver2) 13> send REPLICAT ROLAP02, report


Sending REPORT request to REPLICAT ROLAP02 ...
Request processed.
```

13. Now view the report to confirm the new Replicat process has started from the specified start point. (RBA 43750979 and SEQNO 279). The following is an extract from the report:

```
GGSCI (dbserver2) 14> view report ROLAP02

2010-04-08 14:20:18  GGS INFO       379  Positioning with begin
time: Apr 08, 2010 14:18:19 PM, starting record time: Apr 08, 2010
14:17:25 PM at extseqno 279, extrba 43750979.
```

Configuring multiple parallel process groups

Taking the parallel concept one step further, we can not only add parallel process groups at the target, but also at the source. The diagram at the start of this chapter gives an overview configuration, showing multiple parallel processes from the Data Pumps on the source, feeding data to dedicated Replicat processes, where the data is "split" again into more parallel threads.

Based on the following diagram, we will be configuring multiple process groups from scratch for 1 Extract process to enhance transaction throughput and reduce lag times:

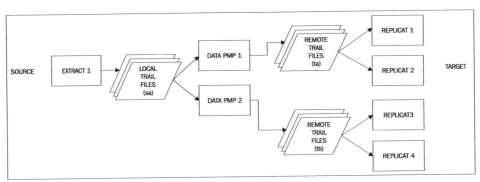

In the following configuration example, the source database name is OLTP and its source schema name is SRC. The target database name is OLAP and its target schema name is TGT.

Source system configuration

The following section specifies an example configuration for parallel data processing that will be used to leverage the performance of the GoldenGate data capture and routing process.

Parallel process parameter files

1. Place the following EXTRACT.prm file in the dirprm sub-directory of the GoldenGate home on the source system:

    ```
    -- EXTRACT1.prm
    --
    -- Change Capture parameter file to capture
    -- SRC table changes
    --
    EXTRACT EXTRACT1
    SETENV (ORACLE_SID=oltp)
    USERID ggs_admin, PASSWORD ggs_admin
    EXTTRAIL ./dirdat/sa
    TRANLOGOPTIONS ASMUSER SYS@ASM, ASMPASSWORD Welcome
    TABLE SRC.CREDITCARD_ACCOUNTS;
    TABLE SRC.CREDITCARD_PAYMENTS;
    TABLE SRC.CREDITCARD_PAYMENTS_HISTORY;
    TABLE SRC.CREDITCARD_PAYMENTS_STATUS;
    ```

2. Place the following DATAPMP1.prm and DATAPMP2.prm files in the dirprm sub-directory of the GoldenGate home on the source system:

    ```
    -- DATAPMP1.prm
    --
    -- Data Pump parameter file to read the local
    -- trail sa for SRC table changes and write to
    -- remote trail ta
    --
    EXTRACT DATAPMP1
    SETENV (ORACLE_SID=oltp)
    USERID ggs_admin, PASSWORD ggs_admin
    RMTHOST dbserver2, MGRPORT 7810
    RMTTRAIL ./dirdat/ta
    TABLE SRC.CREDITCARD_ACCOUNTS, FILTER (@RANGE (1,2));
    ```

```
TABLE SRC.CREDITCARD_PAYMENTS, FILTER (@RANGE (1,2));
TABLE SRC.CREDITCARD_PAYMENTS_HISTORY, FILTER (@RANGE (1,2));
TABLE SRC.CREDITCARD_PAYMENTS_STATUS, FILTER (@RANGE (1,2));


-- DATAPMP2.prm
--
-- Data Pump parameter file to read the local
-- trail sa for SRC table changes and write to
-- remote trail tb
--
EXTRACT DATAPMP2
SETENV (ORACLE_SID=oltp)
USERID ggs_admin, PASSWORD ggs_admin
RMTHOST dbserver2, MGRPORT 7810
RMTTRAIL ./dirdat/tb
TABLE SRC.CREDITCARD_ACCOUNTS, FILTER (@RANGE (2,2));
TABLE SRC.CREDITCARD_PAYMENTS, FILTER (@RANGE (2,2));
TABLE SRC.CREDITCARD_PAYMENTS_HISTORY, FILTER (@RANGE (2,2));
TABLE SRC.CREDITCARD_PAYMENTS_STATUS, FILTER (@RANGE (2,2));
```

Now that the Extract process parameter files have been created in the `dirprm` sub-directory, we can create the associated Extract process groups.

Creating extract parallel process groups

1. Use the following Obey file to prepare and configure your source system for multiple Data Pump process groups:

```
-- config_source.oby

-- Database Authentication Connection
DBLOGIN USERID ggs_admin@oltp, PASSWORD ggs_admin

-- Turning on Data Capture Changes on all Tables
ADD TRANDATA SRC.CREDITCARD_ACCOUNTS
ADD TRANDATA SRC.CREDITCARD_PAYMENTS
ADD TRANDATA SRC.CREDITCARD_PAYMENTS_HISTORY
ADD TRANDATA SRC.CREDITCARD_PAYMENTS_STATUS

-- Verify that supplemental log has been switched on
INFO TRANDATA SRC.CREDITCARD_ACCOUNTS
INFO TRANDATA SRC.CREDITCARD_PAYMENTS
INFO TRANDATA SRC.CREDITCARD_PAYMENTS_HISTORY
INFO TRANDATA SRC.CREDITCARD_PAYMENTS_STATUS
```

```
-- Adding the extract group for the capture
ADD EXTRACT extract1, TRANLOG, BEGIN NOW

-- Defining the local trail files for capture
ADD EXTTRAIL ./dirdat/sa, EXTRACT extract1, MEGABYTES 500

-- Check status of all running processes
INFO ALL

-- Adding the extract group for the pump
ADD EXTRACT datapmp1, EXTTRAILSOURCE ./dirdat/sa

-- Defining the remote trail files for pump
ADD RMTTRAIL ./dirdat/ta, EXTRACT datapmp1, MEGABYTES 500

-- Adding the extract group for the pump
ADD EXTRACT datapmp2, EXTTRAILSOURCE ./dirdat/sb

-- Defining the remote trail files for pump
ADD RMTTRAIL ./dirdat/tb, EXTRACT datapmp2, MEGABYTES 500

-- Start extract and data pump processes
START EXTRACT *

-- Check status of all running processes
INFO ALL
```

2. Place the `config_source.oby` file in the `dirprm` sub-directory of the GoldenGate home on the source system.

3. To execute the Obey file, call it from the GGSCI command line.

   ```
   GGSCI (dbserver1) 1> obey ./dirprm/config_source.oby
   ```

4. Check if the Extract processes are running.

   ```
   GGSCI (dbserver1) 93> info all
   ```

Program	Status	Group	Lag	Time Since Chkpt
MANAGER	RUNNING			
EXTRACT	RUNNING	DATAPMP1	00:00:00	00:00:03
EXTRACT	RUNNING	DATAPMP2	00:00:00	00:00:02
EXTRACT	RUNNING	EXTRACT1	00:00:00	00:00:03

That concludes the source system configuration. From the example output, we can see that the Extract processes have been started and are running. Let's now configure the target system.

Target system configuration

The following section specifies an example configuration for parallel data processing that will be used to leverage the performance of the GoldenGate data delivery process.

Parallel process parameter files

1. Place the following REPLCAT1.prm, REPLCAT2.prm, REPLCAT3.prm and REPLCAT4.prm files in the dirprm sub-directory of the GoldenGate home on the target system:

```
-- REPLCAT1.prm
--
-- Replicator parameter file to read remote trail ta
-- and apply changes to TGT tables
--
REPLICAT REPLCAT1
SOURCEDEFS ./dirdef/oltp.def
SETENV (ORACLE_SID=olap)
USERID ggs_admin, PASSWORD ggs_admin
DISCARDFILE ./dirrpt/replcat1.dsc, PURGE
ALLOWDUPTARGETMAP
CHECKPOINTSECS 30
GROUPTRANSOPS 2000
BATCHSQL
MAP SRC.CREDITCARD_ACCOUNTS, TARGET TGT.CREDITCARD_ACCOUNTS,
FILTER (@RANGE (1,2));
MAP SRC.CREDITCARD_PAYMENTS, TARGET TGT.CREDITCARD_PAYMENTS,
FILTER (@RANGE (1,2));
MAP SRC.CREDITCARD_PAYMENTS_HISTORY, TARGET TGT.CREDITCARD_
PAYMENTS_HISTORY, FILTER (@RANGE (1,2));
MAP SRC.CREDITCARD_PAYMENTS_STATUS, TARGET TGT.CREDITCARD_
PAYMENTS_STATUS, FILTER (@RANGE (1,2));

-- REPLCAT2.prm
--
-- Replicator parameter file to read remote trail ta
-- and apply changes to TGT tables
--
REPLICAT REPLCAT2
SOURCEDEFS ./dirdef/oltp.def
SETENV (ORACLE_SID=olap)
USERID ggs_admin, PASSWORD ggs_admin
DISCARDFILE ./dirrpt/replcat2.dsc, PURGE
```

```
ALLOWDUPTARGETMAP
CHECKPOINTSECS 30
GROUPTRANSOPS 2000
BATCHSQL
MAP SRC.CREDITCARD_ACCOUNTS, TARGET TGT.CREDITCARD_ACCOUNTS,
FILTER (@RANGE (2,2));
MAP SRC.CREDITCARD_PAYMENTS, TARGET TGT.CREDITCARD_PAYMENTS,
FILTER (@RANGE (2,2));
MAP SRC.CREDITCARD_PAYMENTS_HISTORY, TARGET TGT.CREDITCARD_
PAYMENTS_HISTORY, FILTER (@RANGE (2,2));
MAP SRC.CREDITCARD_PAYMENTS_STATUS, TARGET TGT.CREDITCARD_
PAYMENTS_STATUS, FILTER (@RANGE (2,2));

-- REPLCAT3.prm
--
-- Replicator parameter file to read remote trail tb
-- and apply changes to TGT tables
--
REPLICAT REPLCAT3
SOURCEDEFS ./dirdef/oltp.def
SETENV (ORACLE_SID=olap)
USERID ggs_admin, PASSWORD ggs_admin
DISCARDFILE ./dirrpt/replcat3.dsc, PURGE
ALLOWDUPTARGETMAP
CHECKPOINTSECS 30
GROUPTRANSOPS 2000
BATCHSQL
MAP SRC.CREDITCARD_ACCOUNTS, TARGET TGT.CREDITCARD_ACCOUNTS,
FILTER (@RANGE (1,2));
MAP SRC.CREDITCARD_PAYMENTS, TARGET TGT.CREDITCARD_PAYMENTS,
FILTER (@RANGE (1,2));
MAP SRC.CREDITCARD_PAYMENTS_HISTORY, TARGET TGT.CREDITCARD_
PAYMENTS_HISTORY, FILTER (@RANGE (1,2));
MAP SRC.CREDITCARD_PAYMENTS_STATUS, TARGET TGT.CREDITCARD_
PAYMENTS_STATUS, FILTER (@RANGE (1,2));

-- REPLCAT4.prm
--
-- Replicator parameter file to read remote trail tb
-- and apply changes to TGT tables
--
REPLICAT REPLCAT4
SOURCEDEFS ./dirdef/oltp.def
SETENV (ORACLE_SID=olap)
USERID ggs_admin, PASSWORD ggs_admin
```

```
DISCARDFILE ./dirrpt/replcat4.dsc, PURGE
ALLOWDUPTARGETMAP
CHECKPOINTSECS 30
GROUPTRANSOPS 2000
BATCHSQL
MAP SRC.CREDITCARD_ACCOUNTS, TARGET TGT.CREDITCARD_ACCOUNTS,
FILTER (@RANGE (2,2));
MAP SRC.CREDITCARD_PAYMENTS, TARGET TGT.CREDITCARD_PAYMENTS,
FILTER (@RANGE (2,2));
MAP SRC.CREDITCARD_PAYMENTS_HISTORY, TARGET TGT.CREDITCARD_
PAYMENTS_HISTORY, FILTER (@RANGE (2,2));
MAP SRC.CREDITCARD_PAYMENTS_STATUS, TARGET TGT.CREDITCARD_
PAYMENTS_STATUS, FILTER (@RANGE (2,2));
```

Now that we have created the Replicat parameter files and placed them in the `dirprm` sub-directory, we can create the associated Replicat process groups.

Creating Replicat parallel process groups

1. Use the following Obey file to prepare and configure your target system for multiple Replicat process groups:

```
-- config_target.oby

-- Login to Database
dblogin userid ggs_admin@olap, password ggs_admin

-- Adds Checkpoint Table
add checkpointtable GGS_ADMIN.GGSCHKPT

-- Adding the replicat group for the delivery
ADD REPLICAT replcat1, EXTTRAIL ./dirdat/ta, CHECKPOINTTABLE GGS_
ADMIN.GGSCHKPT

-- Adding the replicat group for the delivery
ADD REPLICAT replcat2, EXTTRAIL ./dirdat/ta, CHECKPOINTTABLE GGS_
ADMIN.GGSCHKPT

-- Adding the replicat group for the delivery
ADD REPLICAT replcat3, EXTTRAIL ./dirdat/tb, CHECKPOINTTABLE GGS_
ADMIN.GGSCHKPT

-- Adding the replicat group for the delivery
ADD REPLICAT replcat4, EXTTRAIL ./dirdat/tb, CHECKPOINTTABLE GGS_
ADMIN.GGSCHKPT
```

```
-- Starting the replicat groups
START REPLICAT *

-- Check status of all running processes
INFO ALL
```

2. Place the `config_target.oby` file in the `dirprm` sub-directory of the GoldenGate home on the target system.

3. To execute the Obey file, call it from the GGSCI command line.

   ```
   GGSCI (dbserver2) 1> obey ./dirprm/config_target.oby
   ```

4. Check if the Replicat processes are running.

   ```
   GGSCI (dbserver2) 119> info all
   ```

Program	Status	Group	Lag	Time Since Chkpt
MANAGER	RUNNING.			
REPLICAT	RUNNING	REPLCAT1	00:00:00	00:00:06
REPLICAT	RUNNING	REPLCAT2	00:00:00	00:00:06
REPLICAT	RUNNING	REPLCAT3	00:00:00	00:00:06
REPLICAT	RUNNING	REPLCAT4	00:00:00	00:00:06

That concludes the target system configuration. From the example output, we can see that the Replicat processes have been started and are running. You can now enjoy high performance data replication from the OLTP to OLAP databases.

Improving Replicat throughput

Replicat performance can be further improved by altering the way GoldenGate commits the transaction on the target database. By default, Oracle will wait for a commit to succeed before allowing the session to continue. However, this synchronous behavior can cause unnecessary delays when the workload is high.

To alleviate this bottleneck, we can configure our Replicat processes to commit asynchronously at session level by including the following SQLEXEC statement in each parameter file:

```
SQLEXEC "alter session set commit_wait = 'NOWAIT'";
```

Note that the specification of the NOWAIT allows a small window of vulnerability. These are as follows:

- If the database instance crashes, causing the database to lose redo that was buffered but not yet written to the online redo logs

- A file I/O problem prevents log writer from writing buffered redo to disk

Don't be alarmed; in both cases, GoldenGate will automatically "replay" the uncommitted transactions which would be driven by the information stored in the Checkpoint table, following database instance crash recovery.

New releases

At the time of writing this book, a new release of Oracle GoldenGate has become available:

Version 11.1.1.0.0 Build 078 for Oracle 11gR2

This version runs on the Oracle Sun Exadata2 Database Machine (11.2.0.1), but is not without some performance issues. A known bug causes slow write performance to a Database file system (DBFS), which would typically be used to store the GoldenGate persistent files in a RAC environment. During tests, the measured data pump write rate (with no Replicat processes running) into DBFS was 1.5 to 1.7 MB/sec. For comparison, the Data Pump write rate into a regular Linux file system on the same server was in the 30 MB/sec range and simple writes using the Linux dd utility into the same DBFS mount produced rates in the 30 to 50 MB/sec range.

Happily however, Oracle states this issue is fixed in the next release of GoldenGate: Version 11.1.1.0.5 Build 003.

DBFS enhancements

When configuring DBFS, it is highly recommended to adopt the following options:

- Create a separate database instance running in NOARCHIVELOG mode to support the DBFS.

- Create a DBFS tablespace in the dedicated Database, configured with NOLOGGING

- Create a SecureFile LOB segment defined with NOCACHE NOLOGGING

- Create the file system with the PARTITION option

- Mount the DBFS through `/etc/fstab`, using the following options:

    ○ `rw,user,direct_io,allow_other,wallet,noauto,max_
threads=64`

You may be concerned by having NOLOGGING set on your DBFS tablespace for recovery reasons. Rest assured, because GoldenGate can "pick up" from where it left off following a database crash, due to its check-pointing mechanism. GoldenGate will only checkpoint its Replicat process once it has committed data to the target. If you have had to conduct a point-in-time database recovery on your target, GoldenGate can replay the transactions by altering the Replicat process using the associated BEGIN option.

New redo log OCI API

A new option of the TRANLOGOPTIONS parameter is available in Oracle GoldenGate version 11.1.1, called DBLOGREADER. This alleviates the need to access ASM directly to read the redo logs. Now, via an OCI API, GoldenGate reads the redo and archived logs from the DB server, increasing Extract performance over the former PL/SQL API. There is, therefore, no need to specify the TRANLOGOPTIONS ASMUSER option when specifying DBLOGREADER.

Throughputs of over 75GB per hour are achievable with the new ASM API.

Tuning the network

Another key area to focus on is the network. A poorly performing network will cause high latencies and possible disconnections. One easy method to determine whether your GoldenGate implementation is suffering from network delays is to check that the process write checkpoints are increasing at the same rate. For example, if your primary Extract process is check-pointing frequently when compared to the Data Pump process, this indicates that the Data Pump process cannot write to the remote trail quickly enough. So what can be done about it?

We can look at increasing data throughput by adjusting OS TCP socket buffers, TCP packet sizes, transmission queue lengths, and so on. Let's take a look at some of the common network tuning parameters and tools.

Linux TCP tuning

Like most operating systems, the default maximum kernel parameter settings for networking are way too small. For example, Linux kernel 2.6 has a maximum TCP buffer size of 256KB for both send and receive. During high throughput, you will experience dropped packets when the buffer overflows. The protocol will retransmit these, thus incurring a performance overhead.

Oracle recommends setting the following kernel parameters to at least 4MB. In fact the Oracle 11*g* Universal Installer (OUI) pre-checks these before allowing the installer to continue. These adjustments must be done on both the source and the target database servers.

```
net.core.rmem_max=4194304
net.core.wmem_max=4194304
```

For Oracle GoldenGate, however, these setting may need to be increased further. To set these parameters dynamically, edit the system control configuration file as the root user. Then invoke the `sysctl -p` command to update the kernel as shown:

```
[root@dbserver1 ~]# vi /etc/sysctl.conf

net.core.rmem_max=8388608

net.core.wmem_max=8388608

[root@dbserver1 ~]# sysctl -p
```

Setting the TCP queue length to 5000 can also be beneficial for Gigabit Ethernet Network Interface Controllers (NIC). For networks with more than a 50 ms round trip time, a value of 5000-10000 is recommended. To increase the `txqueuelen` parameter, run the following command as the root user, where `eth2` is the name of your NIC device:

```
[root@dbserver1 ~]# ifconfig eth2 txqueuelen 5000
```

It is also worth experimenting with NIC flow control and TCP Segmentation Offload if performance is still an issue. **Large Segment Offload (LSO)** is a technique for increasing outbound throughput of high-bandwidth network connections by reducing the overhead on CPU. This technique is supported by most of today's NICs.

To check the current status of the NIC settings, execute the following commands as root.

```
[root@ dbserver1 ~]# ethtool -a eth3
Pause parameters for eth2:
Autonegotiate:  on
RX:             on
TX:             on
```

```
[root@dbserver1 ~]# ethtool -k eth2
Offload parameters for eth2:
rx-checksumming: on
tx-checksumming: on
scatter-gather: off
tcp segmentation offload: off
udp fragmentation offload: off
generic segmentation offload: off
```

To enable TCP Segmentation Offload, execute the following command as root. The setting is persistent across server reboots.

```
[root@dbserver1 ~]# ethtool -K eth2 tso on
```

Typically, the network between the source and target database servers is tuned first, but the local TNS connection to the database or ASM instance is often overlooked. For example, when using ASM as your storage solution, we can glean up to three times the performance from an Extract process by using a Bequeath connection and not TCP.

Configuring a Bequeath connection

As the Extract process runs locally on the database server, we can exploit the Bequeath connection, thus avoiding the database Listener altogether. TCP connections are managed by the Listener, whereas BEQ connections access the redo logs directly. It is possible to read up to 1MB per read operation from ASM. When TNS is used, the TCP layer will "chop up" the data into packets incurring the additional performance overhead.

The following steps describe how to configure a Bequeath connection to your ASM instance that will be used by the GoldenGate Extract process.

1. Using a text editor, add a TNS entry, similar to the following example, for the ASM instance, on your source database server:

    ```
    vi $ORACLE_HOME/network/admin/tnsnames.ora file

    ASM =
      (DESCRIPTION =
        (ADDRESS = (PROTOCOL = BEQ)
        (PROGRAM = /u01/app/oracle/product/11.1.0/asm/bin/oracle)
        (ARGV0 = oracle+ASM1)
        (ARGS = '(DESCRIPTION=(LOCAL=YES)(ADDRESS=(PROTOCOL=BEQ)))')
         (ENVS = 'ORACLE_HOME=/u01/app/oracle/product/11.1.0/
    asm,ORACLE_SID=+ASM1')
    ```

```
    )
    (CONNECT_DATA =
      (SERVICE_NAME = +ASM)
      (INSTANCE_NAME = +ASM1)
    )
  )
```

2. Open a terminal session to the server as the Oracle user and log on to the ASM instance using SQL*Plus with ASM TNS alias.

```
[oracle@dbserver1 ~]$ sqlplus sys/password@ASM as sysasm
```

3. Run the following query to identify the OS process ID.

```
SQL >select substr(s.sid,1,3) sid,substr(s.serial#,1,5) ser,
  2   substr(osuser,1,8) osuser,spid ospid,
  3   substr(status,1,3) stat,substr(command,1,3) com,
  4   substr(schemaname,1,10) schema,
  5   substr(type,1,3) typ
  6   from v$process p, v$SESSTAT t,v$sess_io i ,v$session s
  7   where i.sid=s.sid and p.addr=paddr(+) and s.sid=t.sid and
  8   t.statistic#=12
  9   and s.PROGRAM like '%sqlplus%';
```

SID	SER	OSUSER	OSPID	STAT	COM	SCHEMA	TYP
483	24067	oracle	25322	ACT	3	SYS	USE

4. Open a new terminal session to the same server and `grep` for the OS PID identified by the above query. The output confirms we are using the Bequeath connection to the +ASM1 instance.

```
[oracle@dbserver1 ~]$ ps -ef | grep 25322
oracle  25322    1  0 08:24 ?        00:00:00 oracle+ASM1
(DESCRIPTION=(LOCAL=YES)(ADDRESS=(PROTOCOL=BEQ)))
```

5. Ensure you have the following parameter configured in your Extract parameter file:

```
TRANLOGOPTIONS ASMUSER SYS@ASM, ASMPASSWORD Password
```

Summary

Computer System functionality is only as good as its performance. We have all experienced a slow user interface and given up waiting for a response, deferring to a later time when the system is less busy. Although Oracle GoldenGate has a reputation for being fast and efficient, we have learnt it may still require extensive tuning depending on the requirements and data volumes involved. From parallel processing configuration to tuning Linux kernel parameters, this chapter has provided the approach that should be adopted when implementing GoldenGate on Oracle 11*g*. We have also discussed the performance enhancements that are available in the latest release of GoldenGate, including tips and tricks associated with them.

In the next *Chapter 10, Troubleshooting GoldenGate* we will learn how to interpret and resolve some of the issues and errors raised from day to day operations as well as from system monitoring. This includes automatic exception handling and conflict resolution.

10
Troubleshooting GoldenGate

Troubleshooting is quite often the final chapter in most technical books, and for good reason; we need to understand how a product works before we can fix it. That said, readers with a sound knowledge of GoldenGate could dive into this chapter to find the key point or action that they seek.

This chapter covers the following elements to troubleshoot Oracle GoldenGate 10.4:

- Investigating Oracle errors
- Investigating and resolving network issues
- Handling Exceptions to avoid process abends
- Conflict detection and resolution
- Handling Oracle Sequences
- Using the LOGDUMP utility
- Upgrading Oracle GoldenGate

Starting with the section *"Troubleshooting tips"* we will learn how to investigate and resolve some of the common issues faced by the GoldenGate administrator.

Troubleshooting tips

So you have configured your GoldenGate environment, maybe in its simplest form, having one source and one target database. But despite starting the Manager, Extract, and Replicat processes, data is not being replicated.

The easiest way to determine that data replication is not working is to execute row counts against a given source and its target table. Then drill into the GoldenGate processes to obtain their status and statistics.

The following paragraphs provide the necessary troubleshooting tips to enable a quick resolution to the most common issues.

Replication not working?

Start your troubleshooting at the source. We need to determine that the Extracts are processing data before looking at the other components in the data stream. Two methods exist to confirm throughput, which we have already discussed in Chapter 8, *Managing Oracle GoldenGate* and Chapter 9, *Performance Tuning*. These are the GGSCI SEND and STATS commands, demonstrated in the following examples:

```
GGSCI (dbserver1) 1> send EXTRACT EXTRACT1, report


Sending REPORT request to EXTRACT EXTRACT1 ...
Request processed.


GGSCI (dbserver1) 2> stats EXTRACT EXTRACT1, totalsonly *


Sending STATS request to EXTRACT EXTRACT1 ...
```

Both commands produce similar output. In the case of the STATS command, this is real-time reporting at the command line giving totals per second. This is ideal for confirming the row counts against one or more tables. In particular, look for the "*Latest statistics*" section, running the same command again to confirm the totals increment.

```
*** Latest statistics since 2010-10-28 15:54:09 ***
        Total inserts/second:              1115.05
        Total updates/second:                 0.00
```

If all is well, the next place to look is the Data Pump process (assuming you have at least one configured). Use the same commands as previously suggested, ensuring you substitute the appropriate Extract name. You should STAT every Extract process to confirm data movement. This command can cause performance hits during processing at high data loads, but given that data replication is not working, this shouldn't pose a problem.

If the Data Pumps are doing their thing, then we must check the Replicat processes. Again use the STATS or SEND commands to generate reports to determine the throughput. If the row counts are zero for all Replicat processes during a period of load, then we need to investigate further.

The following example shows the output of the STATS command when no data has been replicated since process startup:

```
    GGSCI (dbserver2) 1> stats REPLICAT REPLCAT1, totalsonly *
```

```
Sending STATS request to REPLICAT REPLCAT1 ...

No active replication maps.
```

Knowing where to start troubleshooting is often the key to resolving the underlying problem. A good place to start is by looking at the GoldenGate process parameter files to confirm correct syntax and configuration.

The CHECKPARAMS parameter

One area where GoldenGate is very sensitive is its parameter files. The correct parameter syntax is crucial for the successful operation of a process. Happily however, GoldenGate offers a special parameter designed to check the validity of a parameter file. This is the CHECKPARAMS parameter, which you place at the beginning of the parameter file. When starting the process, CHECKPARAMS checks the file and provides a report, then stops the process without processing any data.

The following example goes through the procedure, finally confirming the validity of the REPLCAT1 parameter file:

1. Log on to GGSCI and edit the required Replicat.

    ```
    GGSCI (dbserver2) 1> edit params REPLCAT1
    ```

2. Insert the CHECKPARAMS parameter at the top of the parameter file.

3. Stop the Replicat process.

    ```
    GGSCI (dbserver2) 2> stop REPLICAT REPLCAT1

    Sending STOP request to REPLICAT REPLCAT1...

    Request processed.
    ```

4. Start the Replicat process.

    ```
    GGSCI (dbserver2) 3> start REPLICAT REPLCAT1

    Sending START request to MANAGER ...

    REPLICAT REPLCAT1 starting
    ```

5. Check the status of the Replicat process. Note that it is stopped.

    ```
    GGSCI (dbserver2) 4> info REPLCAT1

    REPLICAT    REPLCAT1  Last Started 2010-09-27 15:05    Status
    STOPPED

    Checkpoint Lag         00:00:00 (updated 00:00:17 ago)

    Log Read Checkpoint  File ./dirdat/ta000931

                         2010-09-27 15:05:24.642237  RBA 580
    ```

6. Now view the process report that gets automatically generated.

   ```
   GGSCI (dbserver2) 5> view report REPLCAT1
   ```

7. At the very end of the report you will see the following text if the file contents are valid:

   ```
   Parameters processed successfully.
   ```

8. Should CHECKPARAMS find a syntax error, a message similar to the following will be written to the process' report file. Note the error includes the name of the unrecognized parameter.

   ```
   2010-09-17 12:19:38  GGS ERROR     101  Unrecognized parameter:
   WRONGPARAMETER. Parameter could be misspelled or unsupported.


   2010-09-17 12:19:38  GGS ERROR     190  PROCESS ABENDING.
   ```

 I have tested what CHECKPARAMS actually reports and it is not foolproof. For example, a missing parenthesis or an additional space is not detected.

Adjusting the start point

So you have checked all the processes, but the Replicat's are still not processing any data despite the syntax check and status of **RUNNING**. The answer to the problem may be in the Trail files, that is, GoldenGate does not know where to begin processing data from. This is relevant for Extract processes only, where we need to tell each Extract from where to begin. The Data Pumps and Replicat processes will follow suit and process the data sent to them.

There are two options for adjusting the starting point of a process. These are as follows:

1. Providing a specific time or start immediately.
2. Providing a specific RBA and Sequence number.

The former option has a BEGIN NOW command which is often used for new installations. Valid commands are as follows:

```
GGSCI (dbserver1) 1> ADD EXTRACT extract1, TRANLOG, BEGIN NOW
```

Or:

```
GGSCI (dbserver1) 2> ADD EXTRACT extract1, TRANLOG, BEGIN 2010-09-17
10:05
```

Alternatively, you may wish to start your Extract process from the beginning of the trail to "replay" transactions (if the files are still available). This is achieved through the following GGSCI commands:

1. Stop the Extract process.

   ```
   GGSCI (dbserver1) 4> STOP EXTRACT extract1
   ```

2. Now adjust the Extract process' Sequence number and RBA.

   ```
   GGSCI (dbserver1) 5> ALTER EXTRACT extract1, EXTSEQNO 0, EXTRBA 0
   ```

3. Restart the Extract process.

   ```
   GGSCI (dbserver1) 6> START EXTRACT extract1
   ```

Altering Extract processes in RAC environments

The following example shows the differences between altering an Extract process in a RAC environment. Here, the THREAD option must be specified when altering the starting position in a trail, unless a timestamp is used, affecting all RAC instances.

```
GGSCI (rac1) 1> stop ENMMSG1

Sending STOP request to EXTRACT ENMMSG1 ...
Request processed.

 GGSCI (rac1) 2> alter EXTRACT ENMMSG1, extseqno 15471, extrba 76288
ERROR: Only timestamps may be altered for checkpoints of all RAC
instances. Use THREAD option to alter position per thread..

GGSCI (rac1) 3> alter EXTRACT ENMMSG1, extseqno 15471, extrba 76288,
thread 1 EXTRACT altered.

GGSCI (rac1) 4> start ENMMSG1
```

Checking process checkpoints

To verify that a process is working, we can check whether it is check-pointing. This is achieved by executing the GGSCI INFO command with the SHOWCH option. The following example demonstrates this for a Replicat process that was started up, having been stopped for 20 days. We see the check-point move from Sequence number 3, RBA 32891 to Sequence number 4, RBA 580. The command also includes the database checkpoint information stored in the GGS_ADMIN.GGSCHKPT table.

```
GGSCI (dbserver2) 1> info REPLICAT REPLCAT1, showch

REPLICAT    REPLCAT1  Last Started 2010-11-20 15:45    Status RUNNING
Checkpoint Lag        00:00:00 (updated 00:00:01 ago)
Log Read Checkpoint   File ./dirdat/ta000004
```

```
                    2010-11-20 15:45:31.681837   RBA 580
```

Current Checkpoint Detail:

Read Checkpoint #1

  GGS Log Trail

  Startup Checkpoint (starting position in the data source):
    Sequence #: 3
    RBA: 32891
    Timestamp: 2010-11-09 13:49:05.000440
    Extract Trail: ./dirdat/ta

  Current Checkpoint (position of last record read in the data source):
    Sequence #: 4
    RBA: 580
    Timestamp: 2010-11-20 15:45:31.681837
    Extract Trail: ./dirdat/ta

Header:
  Version = 2
  Record Source = A
  Type = 1
  # Input Checkpoints = 1
  # Output Checkpoints = 0

File Information:
  Block Size = 2048
  Max Blocks = 100
  Record Length = 2048
  Current Offset = 0

Configuration:
  Data Source = 0
  Transaction Integrity = -1
  Task Type = 0

Database Checkpoint:
  Checkpoint table = GGS_ADMIN.GGSCHKPT
  Key = 528145677 (0x1f7add0d)

```
   Create Time = 2010-10-17 16:17:47

Status:
   Start Time = 2010-11-20 15:45:31
   Last Update Time = 2010-11-20 15:46:01
   Stop Status = A
   Last Result = 400
```

As discussed in *Chapter 9, Performance Tuning*, understanding GoldenGate's check-point mechanism is the key to evaluating network performance. Now let's look at troubleshooting network issues.

Investigating network issues

GoldenGate is heavily dependent on a fast and reliable network between a source and the target database—without this, data replication cannot take place. Furthermore, if your network fails, the Extract, Data Pump, and Replicat processes may not necessarily abend.

TCP/IP

By default, the GoldenGate Manager uses TCP port 7809 which starts a Collector process on port 7840. As load on the Collector increases, the Manager can dynamically spawn up to 256 additional processes running on dedicated ports, which may or may not be open and available to the operating system.

One obvious check to confirm connectivity between hosts is to use the Linux ping utility. However, ping uses the **Internet Control Message Protocol (ICMP)**, which can also be blocked by Firewalls, so to check that a TCP port is open and can pass traffic use the telnet utility as follows:

```
telnet <target hostname> <port number>
```

Despite the Telnet daemon not running by default on Linux, you should still receive the following message from the remote host confirming the requested port is open. Otherwise, the command just hangs with no response.

```
[oracle@dbserver1 ggs]$ telnet dbserver2 7840
Trying 192.168.1.66...
Connected to dbserver2 (192.168.1.66).
Escape character is '^]'.
```

The Linux `netstat` command can also be used to verify connectivity between hosts. The following example output shows the dynamic Collector processes establishing connections on ports 7847 and 7848:

```
[oracle@dbserver1 ggs]$ netstat
Active Internet connections (w/o servers)
Proto Recv-Q Send-Q Local Address        Foreign Address
State
tcp         0      0 dbserver1:ncube-lm   dbserver2:19486
ESTABLISHED
tcp         6      0 dbserver1:37296          dbserver2:7848
ESTABLISHED
tcp         0      0 dbserver1:ncube-lm   dbserver2:10099
ESTABLISHED
tcp         8      0 dbserver1:9462           dbserver2:7847
ESTABLISHED
tcp         0      0 dbserver1:7848           dbserver2:37296
ESTABLISHED
tcp         0      0 dbserver1:19486      dbserver2:ncube-lm
ESTABLISHED
tcp         0      0 dbserver1:10099      dbserver2:ncube-lm
ESTABLISHED
tcp         0      0 dbserver1:7847           dbserver2:9462
ESTABLISHED
```

SQL*Net

Although GoldenGate is decoupled from the Oracle database, it is still important that successful connections to the source and target database via **SQL*Net** can be achieved. A quick and easy test is to use the **SQL*Plus** utility using a TNS alias in the connect string to confirm connectivity. A successful TNS connection is demonstrated in the following example against the target database:

```
[oracle@dbserver2 ggs]$ sqlplus ggs_admin/ggs_admin@OLAP

SQL*Plus: Release 11.1.0.7.0 - Production on Sat Nov 20 16:26:43 2010

Copyright (c) 1982, 2008, Oracle.  All rights reserved.

Connected to:
Oracle Database 11g Enterprise Edition Release 11.1.0.7.0 - Production
With the Partitioning, OLAP, Data Mining and Real Application Testing
options
```

```
SQL>
```

We may suffer the **ORA-12541: TNS:no listener** error. In this case, check the database Listener is running and supporting services.

```
[oracle@dbserver2 ggs]$ lsnrctl status LISTENER

LSNRCTL for Linux: Version 11.1.0.7.0 - Production on 20-NOV-2010
16:30:51

Copyright (c) 1991, 2008, Oracle.  All rights reserved.

Connecting to (DESCRIPTION=(ADDRESS=(PROTOCOL=TCP)(HOST=dbserver2)
(PORT=1521)))
STATUS of the LISTENER
-----------------------
Alias                     LISTENER
Version                   TNSLSNR for Linux: Version 11.1.0.7.0 -
Production
Start Date                20-NOV-2010 15:43:32
Uptime                    0 days 0 hr. 47 min. 19 sec
Trace Level               off
Security                  ON: Local OS Authentication
SNMP                      OFF
Listener Parameter File   /opt/oracle/app/product/11.1.0/db_1/network/
admin/listener.ora
Listener Log File         /opt/oracle/diag/tnslsnr/dbserver2/listener/
alert/log.xml
Listening Endpoints Summary...
  (DESCRIPTION=(ADDRESS=(PROTOCOL=tcp)(HOST=dbserver2)(PORT=1521)))
  (DESCRIPTION=(ADDRESS=(PROTOCOL=ipc)(KEY=EXTPROC1521)))
Services Summary...
Service "OLAP" has 1 instance(s).
  Instance "OLAP", status READY, has 1 handler(s) for this service...
Service "OLAPXDB" has 1 instance(s).
  Instance "OLAP", status READY, has 1 handler(s) for this service...
Service "OLAP_XPT" has 1 instance(s).
  Instance "OLAP", status READY, has 1 handler(s) for this service...
The command completed successfully
```

That all looks fine, but we may still have a problem connecting. This may be due to the TNS admin entry in the `tnsnames.ora` file, located in the `$ORACLE_HOME/network/admin` directory. This file provides a "lookup" for **SQL*Net** connections. To verify the OLAP entry is valid and can be successfully resolved, we can use the `tnsping` utility.

```
[oracle@dbserver2 ggs]$ tnsping OLAP

TNS Ping Utility for Linux: Version 11.1.0.7.0 - Production on 20-NOV-
2010 16:43:07

Copyright (c) 1997, 2008, Oracle.  All rights reserved.

Used parameter files:

Used TNSNAMES adapter to resolve the alias

Attempting to contact (DESCRIPTION = (ADDRESS = (PROTOCOL = TCP)(HOST =
dbserver2)(PORT = 1521)) (CONNECT_DATA = (SERVER = DEDICATED) (SERVICE_
NAME = OLAP)))

OK (0 msec)
```

Of course, connectivity is one thing, but although it sounds simple, check the source and target databases are open and the `GGS_ADMIN` schema can be accessed by GoldenGate.

Investigating Oracle errors

Should an Oracle error cause the Manager, Extract, and Replicat process to abend, their corresponding report files will contain the Oracle error number and message.

The following example shows an ORA-03113 error from a failed Replicat process:

```
2010-11-21 11:10:38  GGS ERROR       182  OCI Error executing single row
select (status = 3113-ORA-03113: end-of-file on communication channel
```

This is useful in determining the root cause, but maybe it doesn't provide enough detail on how to progress the issue. Luckily help is at hand; every Oracle home contains an error lookup utility, which nine times out of ten provides additional information about the error and instruction in how to fix it. The utility is `oerr`, located in the `$ORACLE_HOME/bin` directory on Linux versions.

`oerr` accepts two arguments, the error group name and the error number. So let's execute `oerr` on the Linux command line and see what is says about ORA-03113.

```
[oracle@dbserver1 dirrpt]$ oerr ora 3113
03113, 00000, "end-of-file on communication channel"
// *Cause: The connection between Client and Server process was broken.
```

```
// *Action: There was a communication error that requires further
investigation.
//          First, check for network problems and review the SQL*Net
setup.
//          Also, look in the alert.log file for any errors. Finally,
test to
//          see whether the server process is dead and whether a trace
file
//          was generated at failure time.
```

Perfect, that is just the right approach we should adopt to resolve the communication problem in our GoldenGate environment.

Exception handling

GoldenGate does not provide a standard exceptions handler. By default, a Replicat process will abend should any operational failure occur, and will rollback the transaction to the last known checkpoint. This may not be ideal in a production environment.

The HANDLECOLLISIONS and NOHANDLECOLLISIONS parameters can be used to control whether or not a Replicat process tries to resolve duplicate record and missing record errors, but should these errors be ignored?

The way to determine what error has occurred, by which Replicat, caused by what data, is to create an Exceptions handler.

Creating an Exceptions handler

The following steps create an Exceptions handler that will trap and log the specified Oracle error(s), but allow the Replicat to continue to process data:

1. The first step is to create an Exceptions table, as shown in the example DDL:

```
create table ggs_admin.exceptions
( rep_name varchar2(8)
, table_name varchar2(61)
, errno number
, dberrmsg varchar2(4000)
, optype varchar2(20)
, errtype varchar2(20)
, logrba number
, logposition number
, committimestamp timestamp
```

```
);

ALTER TABLE ggs_admin.exceptions ADD (
  CONSTRAINT PK_CTS
 PRIMARY KEY
 (logrba, logposition, committimestamp) USING INDEX PCTFREE 0
TABLESPACE MY_INDEXES);
```

The Exceptions table must be created in the GoldenGate Admin user schema. It can log exception data for all Replicat processes.

2. Edit each Replicat process parameter file and add the exception handler Macro code block.

```
[oracle@dbserver2 ggs]$ ggsci

GGSCI (dbserver2) 1> edit params RTARGET1
-- Start of the macro
MACRO #exception_handler
BEGIN
, TARGET ggs_admin.exceptions
, COLMAP ( rep_name = "RTARGET1"
, table_name = @GETENV ("GGHEADER", "TABLENAME")
, errno = @GETENV ("LASTERR", "DBERRNUM")
, dberrmsg = @GETENV ("LASTERR", "DBERRMSG")
, optype = @GETENV ("LASTERR", "OPTYPE")
, errtype = @GETENV ("LASTERR", "ERRTYPE")
, logrba = @GETENV ("GGHEADER", "LOGRBA")
, logposition = @GETENV ("GGHEADER", "LOGPOSITION")
, committimestamp = @GETENV ("GGHEADER", "COMMITTIMESTAMP"))
, INSERTALLRECORDS
, EXCEPTIONSONLY;
END;
-- End of the macro
```

3. Remaining within the editor (**vi**), edit the MAP statements to include the call to the Macro; #exception_handler(). Also, add the REPERROR parameter to reference to the Oracle error(s) you wish to trap.

```
REPERROR (DEFAULT, EXCEPTION)
REPERROR (DEFAULT2, ABEND)
REPERROR (-1, EXCEPTION)
MAP SRC.ORDERS, TARGET TGT.ORDERS;
MAP SRC.ORDERS #exception_handler()
MAP SRC.ORDER_ITEMS, TARGET TGT.ORDER_ITEMS;
MAP SRC.ORDER_ITEMS #exception_handler()
```

```
MAP SRC.PRODUCTS, TARGET TGT.PRODUCTS;

MAP SRC.PRODUCTS #exception_handler()
```

The REPERROR parameter controls how the Replicat process responds to errors when executing the MAP statement.

The DEFAULT option sets a global response to all errors except those for which explicit REPERROR statements are specified. For example, a MAP statement to trap ORA-01403: "no data found" error would be configured as follows:

```
MAP SRC.ORDERS, TARGET TGT.ORDERS, REPERROR (-1403, EXCEPTION);
```

The DEFAULT2 option specifies a "catch all" action for any unanticipated Oracle errors that may occur. In the example in step 3, the Replicat process will abend if a unhandled exception occurs.

1. Now stop and start the Replicat process.

   ```
   GGSCI (dbserver2) 3> stop REPLICAT RTARGET1

   Sending STOP request to REPLICAT RTARGET1 ...
   Request processed.

   GGSCI (dbserver2) 4> start replicat RTARGET1

   Sending START request to MANAGER ...
   REPLICAT RTARGET1 starting
   ```

2. Check Replicat process is running.

   ```
   GGSCI (dbserver2) 5> info all

   Program      Status      Group        Lag          Time Since Chkpt

   MANAGER      RUNNING
   REPLICAT     RUNNING     RTARGET1     00:00:00     00:00:22
   ```

3. Finally start your application and begin replicating data.

Viewing Exceptions

Having trapped Exceptions, we can view them by querying our newly created GGS_ADMIN.EXCEPTIONS table. The information contained herein, is enough for the GoldenGate administrator to make decisions on whether to ignore the error, or fix and replay the failed transaction. Let's take a look at an example Exception.

The following is an example of the data collected following an ORA-00001: "unique constraint violated" error:

```
SQL> select * from ggs_admin.exceptions where rownum <= 1;


REP_NAME TABLE_NAME ERRNO DBERRMSG

-------- ---------- ----- --------

RTARGET1 SRC.ORDERS     1 OCI Error ORA-00001: unique constraint (TGT.
PK_ORD) violated (status = 1), SQL

                       <INSERT INTO "TGT"."ORDERS" ("ORDER_ID","CUST_
ID","PRODUCT_ID" ..


OPTYPE ERRTYPE LOGRBA LOGPOSITION COMMITTIMESTAMP

------ ------- ------ ----------- -------------------------

INSERT DB        988   171211460 02-APR-10 12.41.42.999468
```

> Please note that the DBERRMSG column will store the error, the error description, and the complete SQL up to 4000 bytes. So you can expect some truncation when large SQL statements fail.

The ORA-00001 error is typical of data duplication, where a primary key already exists in the target table. Be sure to synchronize your target database with your source before starting GoldenGate **Change Data Capture (CDC)**.

The ORA-01403 error is typical of a failed UPDATE or DELETE operation, where the target row's primary key cannot be found; be sure to modify the Exception handler to include the before and after images.

Before and after images

Before and after image information is valuable for exception handling as well as conflict detection. INSERT operations only have an after image, whereas DELETE operations only have a before image. UPDATE operations however, have both. Before images contain data that existed before the column was updated. This information can be captured as follows:

1. To enable the capture of Before and After images in the EXCEPTIONS table, we must add a BEFOREAFTER column.

   ```
   SQL> alter table GGS_ADMIN.EXCEPTIONS add BEFOREAFTER char(1);
   Table altered.
   ```

2. Then modify the Exceptions Handler Macro to include a call to the @GETENV function, to obtain the necessary GoldenGate environment information.

```
beforeafter= @GETENV ("GGHEADER", "BEFOREAFTERINDICATOR")
```

This will give us either a "B" for a before image, or an "A" for an after image. The actual data is visible in the SQL populated by the Macro in the DBERRMSG column of the EXCEPTIONS table.

3. To make the Before image available in the Extract Trail, add the GETUPDATEBEFORES parameter to the Extract process parameter file.

Conflict detection and resolution has previously been discussed in *Chapter 5, Configuration Options*, which allows GoldenGate to automatically make decisions when a conflict is detected.

Handling Oracle Sequences

Although GoldenGate supports the replication of Oracle Sequence values, there are a number of issues we need to be aware of. For example, GoldenGate will support replication using the following methods:

- Change Data Capture (CDC).
- Batch processing where checkpoints are not maintained. This is dependent on the SPECIALRUN parameter exiting in the Replicat parameter file.
- But the following are not supported:
  - Initial loads where the source data is derived from the source tables and not the redo logs, so the sequence values are not extracted.
  - Bi-directional environments. The database sequences must generate values on the target database independent to the source. However, in a cascade environment, GETAPPLOPS must be enabled on the Extract to capture sequence values replicated by the Replicat process.

Sequence gaps often occur in an Oracle database, depending on the associated sequence cache size and number of instances in a RAC environment. However, the target values will always be greater than those of the source (for a positive sequence), unless the NOCHECKSEQUENCEVALUE parameter is used.

Oracle recommends that the CHECKSEQUENCEVALUE parameter is enabled, (which is the default) unless you are sure there will be no gaps in the sequence. However, setting CHECKSEQUENCEVALUE does provide a performance hit, as GoldenGate has to evaluate the sequence numbers.

Using LOGDUMP

LOGDUMP is a great utility and a real bonus to the Oracle GoldenGate software bundle. Without LOGDUMP, we could not read a Trail file, which would make us blind to troubleshooting data related issues.

LOGDUMP has a command line interface that allows you to open files, format the display, and navigate through a file including filtering data. To invoke the utility, go to the GoldenGate home directory and type "logdump", as shown in the following example.

```
[oracle@dbserver1 ggs]$ ./logdump

Oracle GoldenGate Log File Dump Utility
Version 10.4.0.19 Build 002

Copyright (C) 1995, 2009, Oracle and/or its affiliates.   All rights
reserved.

Logdump 1 >ENV
Version              : Linux, x86, 32bit (optimized) on Sep 29 2009
08:53:18

Current Directory    : /u01/app/oracle/product/ggs
LogTrail             : *Not Open*
Display RecLen       : 140
Logtrail Filter      : On
Trans History        : 0 Transactions, Records 100, Bytes 100000
LargeBlock I/O       : On, Blocksize 57344
Local System         : LittleEndian
Logtrail Data        : BigEndian/ASCII
Logtrail Headers     : ASCII
Dump                 : ASCII
Timeoffset           : LOCAL
Scan Notify Interval: 10000 records, Scrolling On

Logdump 2 >
```

As with the GGSCI utility, LOGDUMP increments the number at its command prompt for each command entered. Even if you exit LOGDUMP, the number will increment when you return. This is because LOGDUMP maintains a history of commands used.

The preceding example shows the output of the ENV command, which is one of many commands required to be productive with LOGDUMP. Firstly, we must tell LOGDUMP to open a file, and then specify how much detail you require before scanning or filtering data. However, should you get stuck there is always the HELP command to get you back on track, which incidentally shows many undocumented commands.

Opening files

Let's start with the OPEN command. Before opening a file, we must choose one. Execute the following Linux command from the GoldenGate home directory to list the available files:

```
[oracle@dbserver1 ggs]$ ls -l dirdat
-rw-rw-rw- 1 oracle oinstall  3859 Jun 19 17:10 INITLOAD01.DAT
-rw-rw-rw- 1 oracle oinstall 68929 Nov  9 13:28 sa000004
-rw-rw-rw- 1 oracle oinstall 68929 Nov  9 13:32 sa000005
-rw-rw-rw- 1 oracle oinstall 68929 Nov  9 13:35 sa000006
```

Let's open local Trail file sa000004 from LOGDUMP.

```
Logdump 2 >open dirdat/sa000004
Current LogTrail is /u01/app/oracle/product/ggs/dirdat/sa000004
```

Before we can see the contents of the file, we must set up a view in LOGDUMP. The following table of commands will provide the necessary details depending on your requirements:

Command	Description
FILEHEADER [on | off | detail]	Controls whether or not the trail file header is displayed and how much detail.
GHDR [on | off]	Controls whether or not the record header is displayed with each record.
DETAIL [on | off | data]	Displays a list of columns that includes the column ID, length, plus values in hex and ASCII. DATA adds hex and ASCII data values to the column list.
USERTOKEN [detail]	Displays the actual token data.
RECLEN [<# of bytes>]	Controls how much of the record data is displayed in characters.

So, working through the list, enable the file header detail, GDHR, user token detail, and record length options.

```
Logdump 3 >fileheader detail
Logdump 4 >ghdr on
Logdump 6 >detail on
Logdump 7 >usertoken detail
Logdump 8 >reclen 128
Reclen set to 128
```

Viewing the header record

Now it's time to navigate our way through the file starting at position 0, the first record in the file. This is the beginning of the header record:

```
Logdump 9 >pos 0
Reading forward from RBA 0
```

To view the header record we must step to the next **Relative Byte Address** (**RBA**). This is easy using LOGDUMP; just type **next** or **n**.

```
2010/11/09 12:56:49.942.356 FileHeader          Len    928 RBA 0
Name: *FileHeader*
 3000 01a2 3000 0008 4747 0d0a 544c 0a0d 3100 0002 | 0...0...GG..TL..1...
 0002 3200 0004 ffff fffd 3300 0008 02f1 bad1 bae9 | ..2.......3.........
```

Included in the header record is a wealth of information, given that we have enabled a detailed view. The information is grouped by type with a list of related tokens, shown in the following example output:

```
GroupID x30 '0' TrailInfo       Info x00  Length  418
TokenID x30 '0' Signature       Info x00  Length    8
TokenID x31 '1' Compatibility   Info x00  Length    2
TokenID x32 '2' Charset         Info x00  Length    4
TokenID x33 '3' CreationTime    Info x00  Length    8
TokenID x34 '4' URI             Info x00  Length   38
TokenID x36 '6' Filename        Info x00  Length   19
TokenID x37 '7' MultiPart       Info x00  Length    1
TokenID x38 '8' Seqno           Info x00  Length    4
TokenID x39 '9' FileSize        Info xff  Length    8
TokenID x3a ':' FirstCSN        Info x00  Length  129
```

```
TokenID x3b ';' LastCSN          Info xff  Length  129
TokenID x3c '<' FirstIOTime      Info x00  Length    8
TokenID x3d '=' LastIOTime       Info xff  Length    8


GroupID x31 '1' MachineInfo      Info x00  Length  100
TokenID x30 '0' Sysname          Info x00  Length    7
TokenID x31 '1' Nodename         Info x00  Length   17
TokenID x32 '2' Release          Info x00  Length   14
TokenID x33 '3' Version          Info x00  Length   36
TokenID x34 '4' Hardware         Info x00  Length    6


GroupID x32 '2' DatabaseInfo     Info x00  Length  299
TokenID x30 '0' Vendor           Info x00  Length    2
TokenID x31 '1' Name             Info x00  Length    6
TokenID x32 '2' Instance         Info x00  Length    6
TokenID x33 '3' Charset          Info x00  Length    4
TokenID x34 '4' MajorVersion     Info x00  Length    2
TokenID x35 '5' MinorVersion     Info x00  Length    2
TokenID x36 '6' VerString        Info x00  Length  225
TokenID x37 '7' ClientCharset    Info x00  Length    4
TokenID x38 '8' ClientVerString  Info x00  Length   12


GroupID x33 '3' ProducerInfo     Info x00  Length   83
TokenID x30 '0' Name             Info x00  Length   10
TokenID x31 '1' DataSource       Info x00  Length    2
TokenID x32 '2' MajorVersion     Info x00  Length    2
TokenID x33 '3' MinorVersion     Info x00  Length    2
TokenID x34 '4' MaintLevel       Info x00  Length    2
TokenID x35 '5' BugFixLevel      Info x00  Length    2
TokenID x36 '6' BuildNumber      Info x00  Length    2
TokenID x37 '7' VerString        Info x00  Length   29


GroupID x34 '4' ContinunityInfo  Info x00  Length    8
TokenID x30 '0' RecoveryMode     Info x00  Length    4
```

Having learnt how to read the header record, we can now use LOGDUMP to view the transaction records.

Viewing the transaction record

Typing **next** or **n** again steps through each record in the file. The following example shows details of an INSERT operation against the SRC.USERS table, including the actual data and record count. You could argue that each record would always have a record count of 1. This is not true for LOBs, which are split into 2KB chunks when written to a Trail file.

```
Logdump 19 >n
```

```
Hdr-Ind      :      E   (x45)     Partition   :      .   (x04)
UndoFlag     :      .   (x00)     BeforeAfter:      A   (x41)
RecLength    :     29   (x001d)   IO Time     : 2010/11/09 13:25:14.000.000
IOType       :      5   (x05)     OrigNode    :    255   (xff)
TransInd     :      .   (x00)     FormatType  :      R   (x52)
SyskeyLen    :      0   (x00)     Incomplete  :      .   (x00)
AuditRBA     :            138     AuditPos    : 38737936
Continued    :      N   (x00)     RecCount    :      1   (x01)

2010/11/09 13:25:14.000.000 Insert            Len     29 RBA 999
Name: SRC.USERS
After  Image:                                  Partition 4   G
b
 0000 0007 0000 0003 5352 4300 0100 0500 0000 0159 | ........TEST.......Y
 0002 0005 0000 0001 4e                            | ........N
Column       0 (x0000), Len      7 (x0007)
Column       1 (x0001), Len      5 (x0005)
Column       2 (x0002), Len      5 (x0005)
```

The equivalent transaction record in the remote Trail file is identical to that found in the local Trail file, and is identifiable by the same Audit Position number.

Let's query the USERS table in the SRC schema to see the actual record that we are viewing in LOGDUMP.

```
SQL> select * from SRC.USERS
  2   where USER_ID = 'TEST';

USER_ID  REGISTERED  ASSIGNED
-------- ----------- ---------
TEST     Y           N
```

Each record in the Trail file contains the following information:

- The operation type, such as an insert, update, or delete
- The transaction indicator (TransInd): 00 beginning, 01 middle, 02 end or 03 whole of transaction
- The before or after indicator (BeforeAfter) for update operations
- The commit timestamp
- The time that the change was written to the GoldenGate file
- The type of database operation
- The length of the record
- The Relative Byte Address (RBA) within the GoldenGate file
- The schema and table name

The transaction record provides ample information to help you troubleshoot data related issues. For example, the before image of an UPDATE or DELETE operation would prove very useful in determining the reason for an **ORA-01403: no data found** error.

Miscellaneous commands

The miscellaneous commands are useful for displaying additional information, and are listed in the following table:

Command	Description
HISTORY	List previous commands
RECORD	Display audit record
SKIP [<count>]	Skip down <count> records
SFH	Scans for the file header record
ENV	Displays GoldenGate environment details
COUNT [detail]	Count the records in the file
EXIT	Exits LOGDUMP

This example highlights the power of the COUNT command:

```
Logdump 34 >count
LogTrail u01/app/oracle/product/ggs/dirdat/sa000004 has 602 records
Total Data Bytes              15703
  Avg Bytes/Record               26
```

```
Delete                        280
Insert                        320
RestartOK                       1
Others                          1
Before Images                 280
After Images                  321

Average of 17 Transactions
       Bytes/Trans .....      2623
       Records/Trans ...        35
       Files/Trans .....         1

                                            Partition 0
RestartOK                       1
After Images                    1

*FileHeader*                                Partition 0
Total Data Bytes              928
   Avg Bytes/Record           928
Others                          1

SRC.USERS                                   Partition 4
Total Data Bytes            14775
   Avg Bytes/Record            24
Delete                        280
Insert                        320
Before Images                 280
After Images                  320
```

You are now familiar with the miscellaneous LOGDUMP commands, which are commonly used for searching and counting records as well as displaying command history and environment information.

Filtering records

You can do some pretty fancy stuff with LOGDUMP filtering. A whole suite of commands are set aside for this. We can filter on just about anything that exists in the Trail file, such as process name, RBA, record length, record type, even a string!

The following example shows the required syntax to filter on DELETE operations. Note that LOGDUMP reports how many records have been excluded by the filter.

```
Logdump 52 >filter include iotype delete
Logdump 53 >n

2010/11/09 13:31:40.000.000 Delete             Len     17 RBA 5863
Name: SRC.USERS
Before Image:                                     Partition 4   G
b
 0000 000d 0000 0009 414e 4f4e 594d 4f55 53      | ........ANONYMOUS

Filtering suppressed      42 records
```

Upgrading GoldenGate

Should you be unfortunate enough to hit a bug in your GoldenGate environment, Oracle Support may suggest an upgrade to the latest release. Upgrading an Oracle database can be both complex and risky, and requires careful planning and downtime. However, GoldenGate upgrades are simple in comparison. We need to follow the following short steps to achieve a successful upgrade from Oracle GoldenGate for Linux x86-64 bit version 10.4.0.19 Build 002 to Version 11.1.1.0.0 build 78.

1. Log on to the database server as Oracle, start a GGSCI session and stop all Extract and Replicat processes.

   ```
   GGSCI (dbserver1) 1> stop *
   ```

2. Now stop the Manager process.

   ```
   GGSCI (dbserver1) 2> stop mgr
   Manager process is required by other GGS processes.
   Are you sure you want to stop it (y/n)? y
   ```

3. Exit GGSCI and copy the patch file to the GoldenGate home directory and unzip it.

   ```
   [oracle@dbserver1 ggs]$ unzip p10146318_11110_Linux-x86-64.zip
   ```

4. Now extract the archive from the resultant tar file.

```
[oracle@dbserver1 ggs]$ tar xvf ggs_Linux_x64_ora11g_64bit_
v11_1_1_0_5_003.tar
```

5. Log in to GGSCI and start the Manager process.

```
GGSCI (dbserver1) 1> start mgr
```

6. Start the Extract and Replicat processes if not already started.

```
GGSCI (dbserver1) 2> start *
```

7. Ensure all processes are running and that's it!

Summary

Whether you are a novice or an experienced DBA, you will be drawn to this chapter time and again. Troubleshooting is an everyday task for many IT professionals, but no one can master every eventuality. This chapter has captured some of the most common failure scenarios offering help and guidance to a successful resolution. From using LOGDUMP to drill into the GoldenGate Trail files, to automatic exception handling, we have learnt the importance of a methodical approach to troubleshooting.

At the time of writing, Oracle GoldenGate 11.1.1 Build 078 has been released. This chapter has shown us the ease with which to upgrade our GoldenGate environment, providing us with the ability to address the constant demand for enhanced performance and new features.

This chapter concludes the book, *Oracle GoldenGate 11g Implementer's Guide*. More than an implementation guide, it offers detailed real-life examples, encouraging additional thought and discussion by going beyond the manual. From installation to troubleshooting, it has taught you how to build, configure, and tune GoldenGate effectively in Oracle 11*g* environments.

A
GGSCI Commands

In the world of IT, writing a book takes at least a year, in which time technology has moved on and in some cases the contents can be out of date. Therefore, the objective of this appendix is two fold:

- To act as a quick reference guide to all the available GoldenGate Software Command Interface (GGSCI) commands, including the GoldenGate installed components

- To catch any subjects and terminology not addressed in the previous chapters

Some say that since the Oracle acquisition of GoldenGate, the product has changed its name. This is indeed true; GoldenGate Software (GGS) is now known as Oracle GoldenGate (OGG). No surprise there. However this is not true for the GoldenGate Command Interpreter; it is still called GGSCI and not OGGCI, even in the latest version of GoldenGate!

The following table lists and describes the available GGSCI commands, arranged by command group:

Command Group	Command	Description

MANAGER	INFO MANAGER	Displays the Manager process status information.
		
		For example:
		
		`INFO MGR`
		
		Or
		
		`INFO MANAGER`

MANAGER	REFRESH MANAGER	Updates the Manager process configuration without stopping and starting. Valid for all configuration parameters except `PORT`.
		
		For example:
		
		`REFRESH MGR`
		
		Or
		
		`REFRESH MANAGER`

MANAGER	SEND MANAGER	Obtains addition status information when used with the following options:
		
		`CHILDSTATUS [DEBUG]`
		
		`GETPORTINFO [DETAIL]`
		
		`GETPURGEOLDEXTRACTS`
		
		For example:
		
		`SEND MANAGER CHILDSTATUS DEBUG`
		
		`SEND MANAGER GETPORTINFO DETAIL`
		
		`SEND MANAGER GETPURGEOLDEXTRACTS`

MANAGER	START MANAGER	Starts the Manager process. The command supports wildcards. For example: • `START MGR` Or • `START MANAGER`
MANAGER	STATUS MANAGER	Same as `INFO` command.

Command Group	Command	Description
MANAGER	STOP MANAGER	Stops the Manager process. The command supports wildcards. For example: • `STOP MGR` Or • `STOP MANAGER`
EXTRACT	ADD EXTRACT	Creates a new Extract group. For example: `ADD EXTRACT EOLTP01, TRANLOG, BEGIN NOW, THREADS 1`
EXTRACT	ALTER EXTRACT	Alters an existing Extract group. For example: `ALTER EXTRACT EOLTP01, EXTSEQNO 556, EXTRBA 775531`
EXTRACT	CLEANUP EXTRACT	Deletes the run history for the specified Extract group. The Extract process must first be stopped. When used with the `SAVE` option, the command will delete all except the last specified number of records. The command supports wildcards. For example: `CLEANUP EXTRACT *, SAVE 3`
EXTRACT	DELETE EXTRACT	Deletes an Extract group. The Extract process must first be stopped. When used with an exclamation mark, the command will delete all Extract groups associated with a wildcard without prompting for confirmation. For example: `DELETE EXTRACT E* !`
EXTRACT	INFO EXTRACT	Displays status summary for an Extract process. The `DETAIL` option provides more information. The command supports wildcards. For example: `INFO E*, DETAIL`

Command Group	Command	Description
EXTRACT	KILL EXTRACT	Kills an Extract process. Use when the process cannot be stopped gracefully. For example: `KILL EXTRACT EOLTP01`
EXTRACT	LAG EXTRACT	Displays the lag time between the Extract process and the data source. The command supports wildcards. For example: `LAG EXTRACT *`

EXTRACT	SEND EXTRACT	Sends requests to the Extract process, such as; ad-hoc report generation and statistics. The command can also be used to force the Extract process to be rolled over to next trail file.
		
		For example:
		
		`SEND EXTRACT EOLTP01, REPORT`
		`SEND EXTRACT EOLTP01, ROLLOVER`

EXTRACT	VIEW REPORT	Allows process reports generated by the SEND command to be viewed. For example: `VIEW REPORT EOLTP01`
EXTRACT	START EXTRACT	Starts the Extract process. The command supports wildcards. For example: `START EXTRACT *`
EXTRACT	STATS EXTRACT	Displays Extract process statistics. For example: `STATS EXTRACT EOLTP01, TOTALSONLY SRC.ORDERS`
EXTRACT	STATUS EXTRACT	Provides basic Extract process state. The command supports wildcards. For example: `STATUS EXTRACT E*`
EXTRACT	STOP EXTRACT	Stops the Extract process. The command supports wildcards. For example: `STOP EXTRACT *`

Command Group	Command	Description
REPLICAT	ADD REPLICAT	Creates a new Replicat group.
		For example:
		`ADD REPLICAT ROLAP01, EXTTRAIL ./ dirdat/ta`
REPLICAT	ALTER REPLICAT	Alters an existing Replicat group.
		For example:
		`ALTER REPLICAT ROLAP01, BEGIN 2010-09-07 10:00:00`
REPLICAT	CLEANUP REPLICAT	Deletes the run history for the specified Extract group. The Replicat process must first be stopped. When used with the SAVE option, the command will delete all except the last specified number of records. The command supports wildcards.
		For example:
		`CLEANUP REPLICAT *, SAVE 3`
REPLICAT	DELETE REPLICAT	Deletes an Extract group. The Replicat process must first be stopped. When used with an exclamation mark, the command will delete all Replicat groups associated with a wildcard without prompting for confirmation.
		For example:
		`DELETE REPLICAT R* !`
REPLICAT	INFO REPLICAT	Displays status summary for a Replicat process. The DETAIL option provides more information. The command supports wildcards.
		For example:
		`INFO R*, DETAIL`
REPLICAT	KILL REPLICAT	Kills a Replicat process. Use when the process cannot be stopped gracefully.
		For example:
		`KILL REPLICAT ROLAP01`
REPLICAT	LAG REPLICAT	Displays the lag time between the Replicat process and the data source. The command supports wildcards.
		For example:
		`LAG REPLICAT *`

Command Group	Command	Description
REPLICAT	SEND REPLICAT	Sends requests to the Replicat process, such as adhoc report generation and statistics.
		For example:
		`SEND REPLICAT ROLAP01, REPORT`
REPLICAT	VIEW REPORT	Allows process reports generated by the SEND command to be viewed.
		For example:
		`VIEW REPORT ROLAP01`
REPLICAT	START REPLICAT	Starts the Replicat process. The command supports wildcards.
		For example:
		`START REPLICAT *`
REPLICAT	STATS REPLICAT	Displays Replicat process statistics.
		For example:
		`STATS REPLICAT  ROLAP01, TOTALSONLY *, REPORTRATE SEC`
REPLICAT	STATUS REPLICAT	Provides basic Replicat process state. The command supports wildcards.
		For example:
		`STATUS REPLICAT R*`
REPLICAT	STOP REPLICAT	Stops the Replicat process. The command supports wildcards.
		For example:
		`STOP REPLICAT *`
TRAIL	ADD EXTTRAIL	Creates a local trail for an Extract group.
		For example:
		`ADD EXTTRAIL ./dirdat/sa, EXTRACT EOLTP01, MEGABYTES 50`
TRAIL	ADD RMTTRAIL	Creates a remote trail for an Extract or Data pump group.
		For example:
		`ADD RMTTRAIL ./dirdat/ta, EXTRACT EPMP01, MEGABYTES 50`

Command Group	Command	Description
TRAIL	ALTER EXTTRAIL	Allows the trail file size to be altered. The Extract process must be restarted for the changes to take effect.
		For example:
		`ALTER EXTTRAIL ./dirdat/sa, EXTRACT EOLTP01, MEGABYTES 500`
TRAIL	ALTER RMTTRAIL	Allows the trail file size to be altered. The Extract process must be restarted for the changes to take effect.
		For example:
		`ALTER RMTTRAIL ./dirdat/ta, EXTRACT EPMP01, MEGABYTES 100`
TRAIL	DELETE EXTTRAIL	Deletes the local trail.
		For example:
		`DELETE EXTTRAIL ./dirdat/sa`
TRAIL	DELETE RMTTRAIL	Deletes the remote trail.
		For example:
		`DELETE RMTTRAIL ./dirdat/ta`
TRAIL	INFO EXTTRAIL	Provides information on the local trail status. The command supports wildcards.
		For example:
		`INFO EXTTRAIL *`
TRAIL	INFO RMTTRAIL	Provides information on the remote trail status. The command supports wildcards.
		For example:
		`INFO RMTTRAIL *`
PARAMS	EDIT PARAMS	Allows a process' parameter file to be edited. The command invokes the default editor, such as **vi**.
		For example:
		`EDIT PARAMS EOLTP01`
PARAMS	SET EDITOR	Changes the default editor.
		For example:
		`SET EDITOR VI`

Command Group	Command	Description
PARAMS	VIEW PARAMS	Allows a process' parameter file to be viewed.
		For example:
		`VIEW PARAMS EOLTP01`
DATABASE	DBLOGIN	Provides access to the database with username and password.
		For example:
		`DBLOGIN USERID ggs_admin@OLTP,` `PASSWORD Password01`
DATABASE	ENCRYPT PASSWORD	Allows the database password to be encrypted in the parameter file. Since Oracle 11*g*, the password is case sensitive.
		For example:
		`ENCRYPT PASSWORD Password01`
DATABASE	LIST TABLES	Lists tables in a database schema. The command supports wildcards. The command must follow a successful `DBLOGIN`.
		For example:
		`LIST TABLES SRC.*`
TRANDATA	ADD TRANDATA	Adds supplemental logging to a database table, necessary for transactional changes to be written to the redo logs. The command must follow a successful `DBLOGIN`.
		For example:
		`ADD TRANDATA SRC.ORDERS`
TRANDATA	DELETE TRANDATA	Stops the supplemental logging on a database table. The command supports wildcards and must follow a successful `DBLOGIN`.
		For example:
		`DELETE TRANDATA SRC.*`
TRANDATA	INFO TRANDATA	Provides supplemental logging status on a database table. The command supports wildcards and must follow a successful `DBLOGIN`.
		For example:
		`INFO TRANDATA SRC.*`

Command Group	Command	Description

CHECKPOINT	ADD CHECKPOINTTABLE	Adds a Checkpoint table on the target database. The command must follow a successful `DBLOGIN`.
		
		For example:
		
		`ADD CHECKPOINT TABLE GGS_ADMIN.`
		`GGSCHKPT`

CHECKPOINT	CLEANUP CHECKPOINTTABLE	Removes obsolete checkpoint records from the Checkpoint table. Use when Replicat groups are deleted or Trail files are removed. The command must follow a successful `DBLOGIN`.
		
		For example:
		
		`CLEANUP CHECKPOINTTABLE GGS_ADMIN.`
		`GGSCHKPT`

CHECKPOINT	DELETE CHECKPOINTTABLE	Deletes the Checkpoint table from the database. The command must follow a successful `DBLOGIN`.
		
		For example:
		
		`DELETE CHECKPOINTTABLE GGS_ADMIN.`
		`GGSCHKPT`

CHECKPOINT	INFO CHECKPOINTTABLE	Displays the existence and creation date of the Checkpoint table. The command must follow a successful `DBLOGIN`.
		
		For example:
		
		`INFO CHECKPOINTTABLE GGS_ADMIN.`
		`GGSCHKPT`

MISC	!	Runs the last executed command. For example: `!`
MISC	CREATE SUBDIRS	Creates the GoldenGate subdirectories. For example: `CREATE SUBDIRS`
MISC	FC	Display, edit, and execute the last command. For example: `FC`

Command Group	Command	Description
MISC	HELP	Provides help on command syntax.
		For example:
		`HELP`
MISC	HISTORY	Lists a history of GGSCI commands used.
		For example:
		`HISTORY`
MISC	INFO ALL	Displays a summary of the configured processes.
		For example:
		`INFO ALL`
MISC	OBEY	Invokes a GGSCI command script.
		For example:
		`OBEY dirprm/config.oby`
MISC	SHELL	Allows OS commands to be executed from GGSCI
		For example:
		`SHELL ls -l dirdat`
MISC	SHOW	Shows environment information.
		For example:
		`SHOW`
MISC	VERSIONS	Displays version of OS and database.
		For example:
		`VERSIONS`
MISC	VIEW GGSEVT	Displays the contents of the GoldenGate event log
		For example:
		`VIEW GGSEVT`

B
GoldenGate Installed Components

GoldenGate is architecturally a simple product with relatively few installed components. This is one of the main reasons for its performance and flexibility. Let's take a look at the software bundle that is installed on both the source and target database servers.

The following table of files and directories make up the "GoldenGate Home":

Sub-directories	Description
dirchk	Stores GoldenGate checkpoint files
dirdat	Stores GoldenGate trail files
dirdef	Stores GoldenGate definition mapping files
dirout	Stores GoldenGate output files
dirpcs	Stores GoldenGate process files
dirprm	Stores GoldenGate process parameter files
dirrpt	Stores GoldenGate process report files
dirsql	Stores GoldenGate user defined SQL files
dirtmp	Stores GoldenGate temporary files
dirver	Stores GoldenGate Veridata files
UserExitExamples	Stores GoldenGate User Exit example files

SQL Filename	Description
chkpt_ora_create.sql	Creates the Goldengate checkpoint table
ddl_cleartrace.sql	Clears GoldenGate DDL Replication Trace file
ddl_ddl2file.sql	Saves DDL from marker table to a file
ddl_disable.sql	Disables GoldenGate DDL Replication trigger
ddl_enable.sql	Enables GoldenGate DDL Replication trigger
ddl_nopurgeRecyclebin.sql	Allows the use of the Oracle database recyclebin functionality
ddl_ora10.sql	Support script for version specific Oracle10g logic
ddl_ora10upCommon.sql	Support script for version specific Oracle10g and 11g common logic
ddl_ora11.sql	Support script for version specific Oracle11g logic
ddl_ora9.sql	Support script for version specific Oracle9i logic
ddl_pin.sql	Pins GoldenGate DDL Replication packages in memory (Shared Pool)
ddl_purgeRecyclebin.sql	Purges the Oracle database recyclebin
ddl_remove.sql	Removes GoldenGate DDL Replication trigger and package
ddl_session1.sql	Support script for proceeding with DDL installation in case of other sessions active
ddl_session.sql	Support script for proceeding with DDL installation in case of other sessions active
ddl_setup.sql	Installation script for GoldenGate DDL Replication trigger and package
ddl_status.sql	Obtain status of GoldenGate DDL Replication Installation
ddl_staymetadata_off.sql	Turns OFF STAYMETADATA
ddl_staymetadata_on.sql	Turn ON STAYMETADATA
ddl_tracelevel.sql	Sets Tracing Level for GoldenGate DDL Replication trigger
ddl_trace_off.sql	Turns OFF Trace DDL execution
ddl_trace_on.sql	Turns ON Trace DDL execution for use with TKPROF
demo_more_ora_create.sql	Demonstration SQL
demo_more_ora_insert.sql	Demonstration SQL
demo_ora_create.sql	Demonstration SQL
demo_ora_insert.sql	Demonstration SQL
demo_ora_lob_create.sql	Demonstration SQL
demo_ora_misc.sql	Demonstration SQL

SQL Filename	Description
demo_ora_pk_befores_create.sql	Demonstration SQL
demo_ora_pk_befores_insert.sql	Demonstration SQL
demo_ora_pk_befores_updates.sql	Demonstration SQL
marker_remove.sql	Removal script for GoldenGate Marker table
marker_setup.sql	Installation script for GoldenGate Marker table
marker_status.sql	Obtains status GoldenGate Marker Installation
params.sql	Customizable parameters for GoldenGate
role_setup.sql	Installation script for GoldenGate Security Role

TPL Filename	Description
bcpfmt.tpl	Template file used specify the BCP version
db2cntl.tpl	DB2 Control File Template
ddl_access.tpl	Template file used by DEFGEN to determine how Tandem types are defined in MS Access
ddl_db2_os390.tpl	Template file used by DEFGEN to determine how Tandem types are defined in MS Access
ddl_db2.tpl	Template file used by DEFGEN to determine how Tandem types are defined in DB2
ddl_informix.tpl	Template file used by DEFGEN to determine how Tandem types are defined in Informix
ddl_mss.tpl	Template file used by DEFGEN to determine how Tandem types are defined in MS SQL Server
ddl_mysql.tpl	Template file used by DEFGEN to determine how Tandem types are defined in MySQL
ddl_nssql.tpl	Template file used by DEFGEN to determine how to convert Tandem Enscribe DDL to NS SQL DDL
ddl_oracle.tpl	Template file used by DEFGEN to determine how Tandem types are defined in Oracle
ddl_sqlmx.tpl	Template file used by DEFGEN to determine how to convert Tandem Enscribe DDL to NS SQL/MX DDL
ddl_sybase.tpl	Template file used by DEFGEN to determine how Tandem types are defined in Sybase
ddl_tandem.tpl	Template file used by DEFGEN to determine how to convert Tandem Enscribe DDL to NS SQL DDL
sqlldr.tpl	SQLLDR Control File Template

Text Filename	Description
bcrypt.txt	Copyright/License agreement file
freeBSD.txt	Copyright file/License agreement
help.txt	GoldenGate help file for GGSCI
libxml2.txt	Copyright/License agreement file
notices.txt	Notices
zlib.txt	Copyright/License agreement file

Executable Filename	Description
cobgen	Source definition generator utility for Cobol
convchk	Oracle GoldenGate checkpoint conversion utility for newer versions
ddlcob	DDL generator for Cobol
ddlgen	DDL generator utility
defgen	Source table definitions generator utility
emsclnt	Program to send messages to an Event Management System
extract	GoldenGate Extract process program
ggsci	GoldenGate Command Line Interpreter
keygen	Encryption key generator utility
logdump	Log Dump utility
mgr	GoldenGate Manager process program
replicat	GoldenGate Replicat process program
reverse	A utility that reverses the order of transactional operations
server	GoldenGate Collector process program

User Created Filename	Description
ENCKEYS	Stores encryption keys generated by the keygen utility
GLOBALS	Stores global parameters for the GoldenGate instance

C
The Future of Oracle GoldenGate

At the time of writing, a new version of Oracle GoldenGate was released; version 11.1.1. This is being marketed by Oracle as 11*g* to bring the product in line with their 11*g* product suite. The new version is mentioned in *Chapter 9*, *Performance Tuning* due to its performance enhancing new features. However, another mention allows other benefits to be realized.

Oracle GoldenGate 11*g* now falls into the Oracle Data Integration product line along with Oracle Data Integrator (ODI), Oracle Veridata, and Oracle Management Pack for GoldenGate. When coupled with GoldenGate 11*g*, ODI provides fast, efficient, loading, and transformation of data into a data warehouse through its Extract Load and Transform (ELT) technology.

In addition, Oracle GoldenGate 11*g* includes the following enhancements:

- Certified for operational reporting solutions on Oracle Applications such as Oracle E-Business Suite, Oracle PeopleSoft, and Oracle JD Edwards
- Certified with the Oracle Exadata 2 Database Machine

 The Oracle GoldenGate certification matrix can be found on the Oracle website at the following address:
`http://www.oracle.com/technetwork/middleware/`
`goldengate/downloads/index.html`.

- When coupled with ODI, it provides integration with Oracle JDeveloper and Oracle Enterprise Manager
- Support for Oracle TimesTen in-memory databases

Although not a new product, Veridata is a new member of the Oracle Data Integration product suite. It is a high-speed data comparison solution that identifies and reports on data discrepancies between heterogeneous databases. The product's operation is transparent to the live business processes, allowing comparisons to be run during peak times whilst incurring minimal overhead.

Oracle Management Pack for GoldenGate is another product under the Oracle Data Integration umbrella. Already mentioned in *Chapter 8, Managing Oracle GoldenGate,* it is essentially GoldenGate Director, a web-based client application for centrally managing GoldenGate instances. It provides real-time monitoring including automatic alert notifications, as well as managing deployments in GoldenGate environments. Like Oracle Veridata, Oracle Management Pack for GoldenGate runs transparently, with little to no impact to live systems.

Oracle GoldenGate documentation and the Data Replication forum can be found on the Oracle Website at the following respective addresses:

- `http://www.oracle.com/technetwork/middleware/goldengate/documentation/index.html`
- `http://forums.oracle.com/forums/forum.jspa?forumID=69`

As the need to store and report on data increases, the demand for data integration and replication tools will continue to increase. Oracle's continued development of GoldenGate will prove very interesting over the next few years, as they strive to maintain high performance against high data volumes and transaction rates.

Index

Symbols

@CASE function 164
@COLTEST function 163
@EVAL function
  using 164
@GETENV function 223
@IF function 163
@RANGE function 29
  about 189
  Replicats, adding 190-194
@STRCAT function 152
@SUBEXT function 152

A

ACFS 128
ADD CHECKPOINTTABLE command 241
ADD EXTRACT command 235
ADD EXTTRAIL command 238
ADD REPLICAT command 237
ADD RMTTRAIL command 238
ADD TRANDATA command 240
ALO 59
ALTER EXTRACT command 235
ALTER EXTTRAIL command 239
ALTER REPLICATcommand 237
ALTER RMTTRAIL command 239
architecture, GoldenGate
  about 16
  Bi-directional (active-active), benefits 21
  Bi-directional (active-passive) 22
  Bi-directional (active-passive), benefits 22
  cascading 20
  Many-to-One 19
  One-to-Many 18, 19

One-to-One, benefits 17, 18
Archive Log Only. *See* ALO
ASSUMETARGETDEFS, GoldenGate parameters 73
ASSUMETARGETDEFS parameter 85
Automatic Storage Management Cluster File System. *See* ACFS
AUTORESTART, GoldenGate parameters 72
AUTOSTART, GoldenGate parameters 72

B

BATCHESPERQUEUE parameter 100
BATCHSQL
  exceptions 101
  SQL cache 100
  using 99, 100
  using, situations 101
BEFOREFILTER parameter 114
BEFORE option 164
BEGIN NOW command 212
bi-directional configuration, options
  conflict detection 113
  conflict resolution 114
  loop detection 113
  Oracle sequences 114
  Oracle triggers 115
BULKLOAD, GoldenGate parameters 73
Business Intelligence (BI) 17
BYTESPERQUEUE parameter 100

C

CDC
  about 24, 75
  configuring 87, 88

MAP, GoldenGate parameters 73
MGRPORT, GoldenGate parameters 73
multiple parallel process groups configuration
about 194
Source system configuration 195
target system configuration 198

N

netstat command 216
networking
about 60
network outages, surviving 60
NIC teaming 60-62
redundant networks 60
Network Interface Card. *See* NIC
network tuning
about 203
Bequeath connection, configuring 205, 206
Linux TCP tuning 204, 205
NFRs
about 62
availability 63
backup 63
example architecture 64
latency 62
recovery 63
NIC 60
NOCHECKSEQUENCEVALUE parameter 223
Non-functional requirements. *See* NRFs
non-Oracle databases, list 24

O

OBEY command 242
OCR 128
OGG 233
OPEN command 225
OPS 66
OPSPERBATCH parameter 100
OPSPERQUEUE parameter 100
ORA-01403
no data found error 229
Oracle Certification Matrix
obtaining 22
Oracle Cluster Registry. *See* OCR

Oracle Database 11g
supported platforms 23
Oracle GoldenGate. *See* OGG
Oracle GoldenGate 10.4. *See* GoldenGate
Oracle GoldenGate 11g
enhancements 247
Oracle GoldenGate certification matrix
URL 247
Oracle GoldenGate documentation
URL 248
Oracle Large Objects. *See* LOBs
Oracle Parallel Server. *See* OPS
Oracle Sequences
handling 223
LOGDUMP, using 224, 225
OUT parameter 156

P

parallel process groups
load, balancing 188
using, considerations 189
parameters, GoldenGate
about 72
ASSUMETARGETDEFS 73
AUTORESTART 72
AUTOSTART 72
BULKLOAD 73
DISCARDFILE 73
EXTFILE 73
EXTRACT 72
HANDLECOLLISIONS 73
MAP 73
MGRPORT 73
PASSWORD 73
PORT 72
PURGEOLDEXTRACTS 72
REPLICAT 73
RMTFILE 72
RMTHOST 72
RMTTASK 72
RMTTRAIL 72
RUNTIME 73
SETENV 73
SOURCEISTABLE 72
SPECIALRUN 73
TABLE 73
USERID 73

Thank you for buying
Oracle GoldenGate 11g Implementer's guide

About Packt Publishing

Packt, pronounced 'packed', published its first book "Mastering phpMyAdmin for Effective MySQL Management" in April 2004 and subsequently continued to specialize in publishing highly focused books on specific technologies and solutions.

Our books and publications share the experiences of your fellow IT professionals in adapting and customizing today's systems, applications, and frameworks. Our solution based books give you the knowledge and power to customize the software and technologies you're using to get the job done. Packt books are more specific and less general than the IT books you have seen in the past. Our unique business model allows us to bring you more focused information, giving you more of what you need to know, and less of what you don't.

Packt is a modern, yet unique publishing company, which focuses on producing quality, cutting-edge books for communities of developers, administrators, and newbies alike. For more information, please visit our website: www.packtpub.com.

About Packt Enterprise

In 2010, Packt launched two new brands, Packt Enterprise and Packt Open Source, in order to continue its focus on specialization. This book is part of the Packt Enterprise brand, home to books published on enterprise software – software created by major vendors, including (but not limited to) IBM, Microsoft and Oracle, often for use in other corporations. Its titles will offer information relevant to a range of users of this software, including administrators, developers, architects, and end users.

Writing for Packt

We welcome all inquiries from people who are interested in authoring. Book proposals should be sent to author@packtpub.com. If your book idea is still at an early stage and you would like to discuss it first before writing a formal book proposal, contact us; one of our commissioning editors will get in touch with you.

We're not just looking for published authors; if you have strong technical skills but no writing experience, our experienced editors can help you develop a writing career, or simply get some additional reward for your expertise.

Oracle 11g Streams Implementer's Guide

ISBN: 978-1-847199-70-6   Paperback: 352 pages

Design, implement, and maintain a distributed environment with Oracle Streams

1. Implement Oracle Streams to manage and coordinate the resources, information, and functions of a distributed system

2. Get to grips with in-depth explanations of the components that make up Oracle Streams, and how they work together

3. Learn design considerations that help identify and avoid Oracle Streams obstacles – before you get caught in them

Oracle Database 11g – Underground Advice for Database Administrators

ISBN: 978-1-849680-00-4   Paperback: 348 pages

A real-world DBA survival guide for Oracle 11g database implementations

1. A comprehensive handbook aimed at reducing the day-to-day struggle of Oracle 11g Database newcomers

2. Real-world reflections from an experienced DBA—what novice DBAs should really know

3. Implement Oracle's Maximum Availability Architecture with expert guidance

4. Extensive information on providing high availability for Grid Control

Please check **www.PacktPub.com** for information on our titles

Made in the USA
Lexington, KY
17 July 2011